THE WINEGROWERS OF FRANCE
AND THE GOVERNMENT SINCE 1875

THE *Winegrowers of France*
AND THE GOVERNMENT SINCE 1875

By Charles K. Warner

COLUMBIA UNIVERSITY PRESS

NEW YORK 1960

DRAWINGS ON TITLE PAGE AND FOREWORD BY ANGELA CONNER

COPYRIGHT © 1960 COLUMBIA UNIVERSITY PRESS, NEW YORK

PUBLISHED IN GREAT BRITAIN, INDIA, AND PAKISTAN

BY THE OXFORD UNIVERSITY PRESS

LONDON, BOMBAY, AND KARACHI

LIBRARY OF CONGRESS CATALOG CARD NUMBER: 60-7130

MANUFACTURED IN THE UNITED STATES OF AMERICA

Par./6.00/4.50/7/15/68

FOR

R. L. F. IV

C. C. S. W.

AND

N. F. W.

Comment la viticulture n'aurait-elle pas à la sollicitude du gouvernement des droits particuliers, imprescriptibles et, je dirai volontiers, privilégiés?

Poincaré as premier of France, speaking during the *Semaine Nationale du Vin,* Paris, March, 1922.

FOREWORD

Winegrowing has always enjoyed an important position in France's economy. Before 1875 this position rested on the fact that wine was one of France's leading exports and her most valuable cash crop. After 1875, when the destructive phylloxera epidemic first hit the French vineyards in force, the relative value of wine to the economy began to decline. The succeeding crises that accompanied this decline and the role the government played in trying to check them form the subject of this study. The main issues that emerge are, first, the pampering of the winegrowers with increasingly numerous laws so that winegrowing came to be described as the "spoiled child" of French agricultural legislation and, second the increasing cost to the national economy occasioned by this solicitude.

The phylloxera epidemic is more than just a convenient starting point for such a study. It destroyed virtually the entire French vineyard. The replanting was an extraordinary epic of courage and perseverance, but it had its bad side. Eager to get as quick a return as possible on the heavy investment involved in replanting, the larger part of the winegrowers abandoned their traditional methods of viticulture and concentrated on quantity production of low-grade wines for a market inflated by years of deprivation. This development led during the period from 1900 through 1907 to an enormous slump in wine prices, especially in the Midi, which was the leader in the new orientation of the vineyard.

Overabundant harvests, the replacement of wine alcohol by beet alcohol, the growth of the Algerian vineyard, and a decline in exports all contributed to this first great wine crisis following the phylloxera, as they have to succeeding ones. But a consensus held a vast quantity of adulterated or otherwise fraudulently manufactured wine chiefly responsible for the depressed state of the market. Although there were forms of direct aid to winegrowers, the greatest part of government legislation during this period dealt with the problem of fraud—a problem that was not important when every winegrower was an artisan and the taste of the public had not been debased by the bad wines of the phylloxera period.

Thus by increasingly complicated legislation which is still being added to, the government began to protect the winegrower from himself by protecting his product. It is interesting that at this point legislation which would seem so limited in its purpose affected other sectors of the agricultural economy as well, and that along with such measures as reductions in wine taxes it first gave rise to charges that winegrowing enjoyed the special solicitude of the government.

It has been felt useful to include a chapter on the relations between government and winegrowers during World War I because the war shows some unusual aspects of this solicitude. Also a system of military wine requisitions may be said to have served as a laboratory for economic controls that would affect the wine industry in the future. But the chief significance of the war period is that with the vineyard reduced in area through neglect and wine prices spiraling (uncontrolled), the postwar years saw a frenzy of replanting similar to that inspired by the phylloxera.

The result was that after a sharply alternating cycle of boom and bust, winegrowing settled into its second great price slump, which lasted from 1930 through 1935. Excepting fraud, the causes were the same as those of the 1900–1907 crisis, with overproduction now playing the leading role. What was new during the second crisis was the intensity of the relations between the government and the winegrowers. In 1907 the winegrowers limited themselves to asking for government aid. After World War I, organized and articulate, they pushed to success and near success demands to which the government was opposed. And with government policies that were proposed to control overproduction, they effected compromises which were at least partially crippling.

In spite of this the scale of government control over the wine-grower's activities became immense after 1930. Regulations concerning the making of his product were tightened. He was told how much wine he could sell and when. He was told how many hectares of new vines he could plant, and what proportion of them could be reserved for tax-free family consumption. There were penalties too. Growers whose production was considered excessive had to have their wine distilled into alcohol, which was paid for at a price less than cost. And growers whose yield per hectare passed a certain point were subject to a progressive tax.

But vast as the scale of government intervention was, it did not penetrate deeply enough. The big growers, who were a minority, bore the brunt of the penalties. In deference to a parliamentary bias, supported by the winegrowing associations, the small growers, representing the great majority and accounting for about half of total production, were permitted to escape free of most controls and penalties. Also, if the government penalized overproduction with one hand, it may be said, in a sense, to have supported it with another.

At the height of the crisis, the government several times had to resort to extraordinary purchases of wine alcohol at prices that were profitable to the winegrower. This alcohol was in turn sold at a loss to industrial users through the state industrial alcohol monopoly. In 1935 wine alcohol purchases by the monopoly were made permanent. Thus, in effect, an important part of the winegrower's excessive production was permanently subsidized. This was not done without great cost to the state, its citizens, and the national economy. Still it may be said that the government, for the most part, did not question what it considered practical measures to cope with an exceptional situation from 1930 to 1935. This attitude was to change after World War II.

During this war and for some time after it, the government, through rationing and price fixing, took over the supplying of wine. This led the government, in spite of some wise advice to the contrary, to suspend the prewar limitations on new plantings and other legislation that curbed production in order to satisfy the demands of a market that was at times in very short supply. With fabulous profits to be made on the black market, this suspension of controls led to a repetition of the frenzied replanting that had occurred after the phylloxera epidemic and after World War I. In 1950 the wine-grower once again found himself drowned in a series of over abundant harvests which have only recently terminated.

The government's answer to these was a new *Code du Vin,* promulgated in 1953. Part of this legislation is an attempt to bring more winegrowers under more or less the same overproduction controls as existed before the war, but the most significant part of it looks to a long-term reduction of the vineyard area through the pulling up of vines. This part stems from the realization that overproduction has become chronic and is not just the exceptional problem which the legislation of the 1930's tried to solve.

But the change in attitude goes deeper than that. One may generalize that before World War II very few people questioned the economic or social value of protecting winegrowing. Now increasing statistical research and advances in the new discipline of demography have revealed hitherto unsuspected costs, both economic and social, of excessive wine and alcohol production. With the economic and financial difficulties which France faces today, it seems improbable that these costs can be successfully endured for long. In even the most superficial catalogues of France's present troubles the problem of excessive wine production occupies a prominent place. For these reasons a final chapter has been added to carry our study to the harvest of 1958 and analyze the new attitudes towards winegrowing and alcoholism that have become especially prominent since 1953. An attempt has also been made to relate the problem of winegrowing and the alcohol monopoly which helps to subsidize it to the larger problem of France's economic recovery.

Such, in brief, is the story to be told in the pages that follow. In general we have concentrated on a chronological account emphasizing the interplay of government, viticultural, and other related interests during succeeding wine crises. The Algerian vineyard, the problem of wine exports and imports, the complicated question of the state alcohol monopoly, and the problems treated in the last chapter have, however, involved some departures from a strict chronological approach. The scope of this study has also presented some problems.

Obviously government is not a thing all of one piece. It is composed of many individuals; it speaks with many voices and is a compound of many interests. By the same standards winegrowing is an exceedingly atomistic activity with one million and a half producers supplying probably less than thirty million consumers. Moreover the *vin de cru* of Burgundy and the *ordinaire* from the Midi are really two different products, and the interests of all winegrowing regions do not exactly coincide.

Although these factors have not been entirely overlooked in this study, it has been felt that too great a concentration on them would result in the first instance in a chronicle of personalities, organizations, lobbies, and backroom *pourparlers* and in the second instance in a series of regional monographs. Our story has therefore been told chiefly in terms of aggregates and what W. H. B. Court has called "the set of general relationships in which a whole economy [or in our case a part of it] turns." It is hoped that this approach is valuable and that this study, although primarily concerned with one form of agricultural enterprise, will in some way add to the history of French economic policy.

I wish to express a lasting debt of gratitude to Professor Shepard B. Clough, of Columbia University, under whose direction this study was first prepared and in whose seminar I was first confronted with high standards of historical scholarship. If this book does not in every way meet such standards, the teachers, colleagues, and friends who have helped me with it are in no way responsible for its shortcomings.

I wish to thank Professor J. R. T. Hughes of Purdue University for many helpful suggestions and criticisms, especially of my presentation of economic data. And I am grateful to Professors Walter L. Dorn and Garrett Mattingly of Columbia University for a careful reading of my manuscript, for trenchant criticism, and valuable counsel. Elizabeth Evanson of Columbia University Press has offered editorial suggestions and saved me from errors of omission and fact.

I owe a particular debt to William P. Davisson of the Société

d'Histoire Moderne for his own competence and interest in my subject and for the valuable bibliographic and other assistance he has
given me from France. To Elizabeth Fuller I am also indebted for
collecting materials in France. Thomas H. Thomas helped me by
reading and criticizing the earlier portions of my manuscript and
supplying his first-hand recollections of the events of 1907 in the
Midi. My record of thanks would not be complete without mention
of the hosts who patiently acquainted me with the problems of winegrowing during many pleasant hours in the vineyards along the
"Route du Vin" and in the Midi.

Acknowledgment is due Presses Universitaires de France for
permission to quote from *Alcool, alcoolisme, alcoolisation,* by Sully
Ledermann, and from *L'Alcoolisme,* by Georges Malignac and Robert Colin.

My wife, Patricia Cutler Warner, in spite of other more pressing
responsibilities has conscientiously helped me at every stage in the
preparation of the study. Her assistance has been invaluable.

Middlebury, Vermont   CHARLES K. WARNER
January, 1960

CONTENTS

TABLES

1. THE PHYLLOXERA EPIDEMIC

The coming of what Sir John Clapham has called the "railway age" brought a number of significant changes to France's wine industry. Improved communications meant increased domestic consumption. They also meant concentration of the vine in the Midi where higher yields were to be had, and they brought a new stimulus to exports. The latter movement coincided with the negotiation of commercial agreements like the Cobden Treaty of 1860 which favored French wine on foreign markets.

As a result the period from 1860 to 1875 saw the vineyard area of France grow by about 10 percent, while the average yield per hectare (a hectare equals 2.5 acres) nearly doubled, and production figures increased by 75 percent over the average for the preceding ten years.[1] Prices were good and relatively steady, and prosperity in the expanding winegrowing regions became almost legendary.[2]

The year 1875 topped this "golden age" for the industry with a bumper wine harvest of 83,000,000 hectolitres—a record never since equaled.[3] The same year, wine and the brandy distilled from it paid the nation some 380,000,000 francs in taxes. This was the largest single item of revenue and represented over 15 percent of the total budget.[4] At the same time exports, which had been breaking records for four years out of the previous five, reached an all-time high of 3,700,000 hectolitres. They were exceeded in value only by the exports of the textile industry.[5]

The year 1875, then, was a memorable one for the winegrowers. But it was to be remarkable for still another reason. For several years the existence of what was presumed to be a new vine disease had been noted with anxious concern in several parts of France. Unlike other illnesses of the vine, the new "disease," or phylloxera, as it came to be called when recognized as a pest, defied treatment and eventually killed the entire vine. The various infected regions had been small and widely scattered, however, and there was even talk of a cure. Then in 1875 the phylloxera struck with unsuspected fury in the vineyards of the department of Gard. Within four years it became epidemic in the Midi, and before it ran its course there caused a loss to the national economy equal in amount to the Prussian war debt which had just been paid.

TABLE 1. VINEYARD AREA OF THE DEPARTMENTS OF GARD AND HÉRAULT DURING THE PHYLLOXERA EPIDEMIC (*In hectares*)

Year	Gard	Hérault
1870–75, yearly average	83,173	217,330
1876	35,635	199,711
1877	23,742	167,145
1878	17,487	142,125
1879	14,190	118,655
1880	18,120	106,189
1881	16,695	87,715
1882	17,409	87,290
1883	20,422	91,898
1884	19,702	87,219
1885	23,347	95,658
1886	28,822	103,903
1887	31,913	86,615
1888	38,245	111,471
1889	42,284	131,442

Source: Ministère du commerce, Statistique générale de la France, *Annuaire statistique.*

After the first savage attacks in the Midi, the phylloxera settled down to conquer the rest of the country in slow and irregular fashion. It moved without any discernible pattern; a region next to an infected area would be spared while another a hundred miles away would be attacked. But by 1887, when the Ministry of Agriculture felt confident enough to announce that the phylloxera was under control, it had infected nearly every winegrowing region of France.

TABLE 2. VINEYARD AREA OF FRANCE DURING THE PHYLLOXERA EPIDEMIC
(*In thousands of hectares*)

Year	Area	Year	Area
1870–75, yearly average	2,383	1882	2,180
1876	2,394	1883	2,175
1877	2,343	1884	2,195
1878	2,305	1885	1,971
1879	2,299	1886	1,908
1880	2,259	1887	1,920
1881	2,245	1888	1,838

Source: *Annuaire statistique.*

THE PHYLLOXERA AND THE SCIENTISTS

The phylloxera epidemic in France was caused by *phylloxera vastatrix,* a minute plant louse that attacked the roots of the vine.[6] The pest was believed to be imported into Europe some time between 1858 and 1863 when grafting experiments with American grape varieties were being tried in several countries.[7] Its effects were first noted on grapes raised in hothouses near London, by an English botanist, in 1863. The same year it was believed to have been observed in the vineyards of the Gard.

What may well have been the first public notice of the phylloxera took place at a meeting of the Société Centrale d'Agriculture at Paris in June of 1867, when a winegrower from the Gard spoke of a "mysterious malady" which had been attacking the vineyards of that department and Vaucluse for the last three years.[8] Samples of infected vines were shown and a communiqué addressed to the society's natural history section. The following year a group of scientists from the University of Montpellier first observed the phylloxera insects on the roots of vines, and associated them with the "mysterious malady." Their findings were submitted in a report to the Ministry of Agriculture, where the disease was properly defined as a pest and referred to as phylloxera.

In 1870, for the first time, phylloxera became a subject of discussion in the Chamber of Deputies, and on July 14 of that year the government announced a prize of 20,000 francs for an "efficacious and practical method of fighting the new disease of the vine." [9]   At the same time the winegrowers of Hérault, on their own initiative, opened a public subscription for a study of the new pest and predicted that the pest might annihilate the national vineyard.[10]

These and several other similar projects produced no results, and in 1872 the problem of checking the phylloxera was turned over to the learned heads of the Academy of Sciences along with a 10,000 franc grant from the Ministry of Agriculture.   Evidently the Academy's deliberations were neither as swift nor as spectacular as hoped for.   Two years later a note of impatience was sounded in an editorial by the *Journal d'agriculture pratique,* which suggested that the scientists spend less time studying the natural history of the pest and concentrate on "curative and preventive measures." [11]   The same year, 1874, the Société des Agriculteurs de France offered a prize simply for the "best method of *destroying* the phylloxera." [12]

Again in 1874, a High Commission on Phylloxera was set up, with the Minister of Agriculture as chairman, and scientists from the Academy making up the membership.   The principal task of the new group was to look over the suggestions for the prize-winning method of fighting the phylloxera.   These were now running to over two hundred a year and included such diverse remedies as burying a toad near the roots of the vines, placing snow, volcanic ashes, or tobacco at their base, or urinating on the soil around them.

The reward, which had been raised to 300,000 francs in 1874, was never claimed, however.   The Academy of Sciences likewise never produced a cure-all of its own, and the High Commission was never able to decide which of the available methods for fighting the phylloxera was best.   The economist Leroy-Beaulieu has called the episode the "defeat of official science," [13] and this judgment is perhaps justified if it is clear what information the Academy and the Commission possessed.

Actually the true nature of the phylloxera was outlined as early as 1870 in an important paper read to the Academy by J. E. Planchon, one of the scientists who had first observed the pest in the Gard.[14]   Also all the means that were to be used subsequently in combating the phylloxera were known to both the Commission and the Academy by 1875. These consisted of treating the vine with chemicals, flooding the base and the roots of the vine with water, or grafting French grape varieties on to phylloxera-resistant American vine or root stocks. The first method was only a delaying measure at best; the second, although effective, could only be used in areas favorable to irrigation. The third was the most successful and turned out to be the universally adopted remedy.

In the beginning, however, the greatest hopes were placed in chemicals. Leroy-Beaulieu has pointed out that this was because the High Commission was composed chiefly of chemists,[15] but in view of the widespread interest in chemical fertilizers and insecticides during the period, it should not seem remarkable that chemicals were the first thought. At all events, early experiments, chiefly with sulfocarbonates and other sulfur and carbon compounds, were promising if inconclusive. Also people were ready to grasp at straws— it was even rumored that President MacMahon was ready to announce that the phylloxera had been vanquished by these experiments—and so sulfur-carbon sprays were much used. These were able to keep sick plants producing for awhile, but it is, of course, arguable that the money spent on such treatments might better have been used by the winegrowers in buying American root stocks.

The use of American vine cuttings and root stocks was first suggested by a commission under the leadership of M. Planchon, which was sent to the United States in 1873 to study the phylloxera there. All native American vines were found to be in some degree resistant to attacks of the insect. If French grape varieties were grafted on to the most resistant, the French vineyard might be reconstituted in all its original variety.[16] Again, however, hasty experimentation distorted the picture. There were many failures; not enough thought had gone into selecting the American vines appropriate to the different types of French soil, and some growers, impatient of grafting, imported *producteurs directs,* American grape varieties like the Isabella, Catawba, or Delaware, which gave a low-grade wine.[17]

Further mistrust was inspired by the initial high cost of the American vine cuttings and root stocks and the fact that a lively speculators' market developed in their sale. For its part the gov-

ernment passed laws, as will be seen in more detail later on, which
hampered the free circulation of American vines, while the Academy of Sciences declared that the American vines were "costly and
doubtful," even before the commission that visited America had a
chance to publish its findings.[18]

Under such conditions an atmosphere of indecision was formed
which did not help in the fight against the phylloxera. In the long
run, however, it was neither the scientists nor the government which
decided the issue. As early as 1878, the growers of Hérault, who
had had a more disastrous experience with the phylloxera than most,
pronounced against chemicals and in favor of the American vines.[19]
And as Table 3 suggests, the method used by the growers of Hérault
was widely adopted in the years that followed.

TABLE 3.   COMPARATIVE RATES OF DIFFERENT METHODS USED IN RELATION TO
       ALL VINES TREATED FOR PHYLLOXERA (*In percentages*)

Method	*1882*	*1889*
Grafting on American vines	25	74
Spraying with sulfocarbonates	8	2
Spraying with sulfur of carbon	45	15
Flooding the roots	22	9

Source: Ministère de l'agriculture, *Bulletin,* II (1883), 457; IX (1890), 41-42.

THE PHYLLOXERA AND THE GOVERNMENT

While the debate and indecision described above were taking
place it became obvious that until a method for stamping out the
phylloxera could be arrived at, the immediate problem was containing the spread of the epidemic. To the Ministry of Agriculture the
most effective solution appeared to be the uprooting and destruction
of sick vines. The High Commission, however, in its initial report
to the Minister of Agriculture in 1874, took a timid stand on this
matter, claiming that indemnities would have to be paid and special
laws be passed before the government could require such rigorous
measures.

The same year, however, a prefect of the Rhône department ordered the destruction of healthy as well as diseased vines within a

radius of five metres of infected areas in his department. No indemnities were paid, and opposition to the orders was so strong both locally and at Paris that they were finally declared illegal. The government then proceeded to fill the vacuum left by the prefect's vigorous action with a multiplication of committees—departmental committees with vague powers and no appropriations, and parliamentary commissions from both the Senate and the Chamber.

It was not until 1878, in fact, that the first concrete legislation, aimed at controlling the spread of the phylloxera, appeared on the books. This was the famous law of July 15, 1878, which gave the introduction of American vines such a setback, forbidding as it did "the entry of foreign plants, roots, and leaves into the nation, or certain parts of it." [20] Actually the door was not closed tight against the American vines, but France was divided into departments that were either infected or clear of the phylloxera, and elaborate *cordons sanitaires* surrounded the healthy departments so that no vines or fruits could be brought into them. Meanwhile, the disease did not progress along strictly departmental lines, and so there were many growers who either needed, or through foresight wanted, American vines and who were unable to get them. The law was frequently criticized, but it was not modified until 1891 when a new law permitted the free circulation of vine stocks and, almost as an afterthought, provided aid to those departments and communes which had voted subsidies for the replanting of vineyards with "resistant [American] roots." [21]

The law of July 15, 1878, also provided for governmental aid to a commune or department that voted to treat its sick vines, but money for the purpose (125,000 francs) was not appropriated until the following January. By the end of 1879 only two departments had taken advantage of this aid. The law, according to its critics, had generated apathy and fear—growers and departmental authorities alike were afraid of spending money on doubtful treatments even if the alternative meant destruction of the vines, and departments and communes already in debt because of the phylloxera had no desire to go further, with or without government aid.

In the debates that followed over these aid provisions it was pointed out that some leadership should come from the government, which did not even have the power to compel a peasant to treat his vines at the government's expense.[22]   As a result a new law was passed which gave the government the right to order the treatment of sick vines in certain localities, if necessary.[23]   The new law also provided that the government could match any subsidies given to the growers by a department, commune, or syndicate.   Arranging for the latter remained a voluntary affair, however, with the initiative mainly left to the growers.[24]

One obvious disadvantage of local initiative was that a few unmanageable growers could hold up the entire aid program in their area.   To get around this obstacle the so-called "obligatory syndicate" law was passed in 1887.[25]   It provided for competent and self-sustaining syndicates which could not be impeded by the "ill will of a few individuals." [26]   The new law was encumbered with weighty machinery, however, that demanded the intervention of the prefect and departmental councils, and it still left the initiative of forming the syndicates up to the growers.   The syndicates nevertheless multiplied rapidly and after 1887 they were especially successful in enrolling the small growers.[27]

In general, then, the initiative in the fight against the phylloxera fell to the winegrowers themselves.   Charles Gide has praised the spirit and effectiveness of their efforts, calling the struggle "great and almost heroic," while dismissing the government's role as obstructionist.[28]   Admitting that the government showed neither judgment nor courage in the matter of the American vines, it might still be worth asking if more aggressive government leadership would not have eased the effects of the phylloxera and brought about a more rapid recovery than would have otherwise been possible.   As distinguished a political economist as Paul Cauwès was led to point out how in other countries much more severe measures were taken against the phylloxera than in France, criticizing by implication a timid government policy.[29]   But these were judgments without benefit of historical perspective.   A marked policy of government intervention was born during the phylloxera; meanwhile the phylloxera was creating conditions that would make this policy less and less timid.

REPLANTING OF THE VINEYARD

The year 1887 represents a turning point in the fight against the phylloxera. That year the Minister of Agriculture was able to report for the first time that the area of infected vines was less than the area currently being replanted.[30] At the same time the government passed a law exempting all new vine plantings from land taxes (*impôts foncières*) for a period of four years—in other words, the time necessary before they could start producing.[31]

This legislation seemed to have an immediate effect. Significant increases in vineyard areas were registered the next year in the Midi, and in the years that followed area and production figures both showed that replanting of the national vineyard had begun.

This replanting must be described mainly, however, as the development of an intensive monoculture in the four chief wine-producing departments of the Midi—traditionally devoted to the production of *vin ordinaire*. A shift in planting to this area has already been noted. In 1850 the four departments—Gard, Aude, Hérault and Pyrénées-Orientales—accounted for 10 percent of the total vineyard area. In 1887, at the height of the phylloxera, they were able to account for 16 percent. By 1897 this figure had grown to 25 percent.[32]

The speed of the above development can be gauged better if it is realized that the phylloxera had reduced the vineyard area of the four departments to an all-time low of 258,375 hectares in 1887. By 1900 this figure had increased to 462,502 hectares. In 1903 a total planting of 467,944 hectares passed the pre-phylloxera high of 465,359 hectares registered in 1874.[33] During the same period there were similar if less spectacular gains in a few other regions, but the national vineyard area as a whole was never again to recover its pre-phylloxera extent.

Unfortunately the replanting of the Midi vineyards did not represent an attempt to get back to the *status quo ante* of pre-phylloxera days. Thus, although the pre-phylloxera Midi vineyard area was surpassed in 1903, as early as 1894 production for the four departments topped their share of the bumper harvest of 1875 with an output of 17,752,850 hectolitres. This figure was surpassed in

1897 and again in 1899 and 1900 by record-breaking harvests. And from 1890 to 1900 the four departments accounted for 42 percent of the nation's total production.[34]

These figures reflected a change in the winegrower's attitude toward his product. Formerly an artisan even though his product was almost all *vin ordinaire,* the Midi grower now became a "manufacturer" turning out increasing quantities of a lower-grade wine that for some time brought prices out of all proportion to its worth.

The beginnings of this change can be traced directly to the phylloxera. The replanting of his vineyard involved the grower in heavy expenses which, because of the feeble support of the Crédit Foncier, had to be paid for the greatest part out of capital.[35] At the same time caught in a price boom caused by phylloxera-induced shortages, the grower was naturally avid for the quickest return on his considerable investment. Thus he was led to favor methods of viticulture which insured a maximum yield per hectare with a minimum cost. By the nature of winegrowing, such methods mean a lowering of quality. This policy, as will be seen, was short-sighted but, in the words of Professor Fromont, "it revealed itself as entirely lucrative at the time." [36]

One of the chief agents in the transformation described above was the Aramon grape, a variety that was planted nearly everywhere in the Midi during and after the phylloxera. Whereas older varieties, such as the Oeillade or Terret Noir, which were all but replaced by the Aramon, even enjoyed a small measure of distinction among connoisseurs, the only remarkable thing about the Aramon was its high-yield quality. According to Charles Gide a vine of the older varieties would average 1 to 1.25 kilograms of grapes, which meant a yield of 35 to 40 hectolitres of wine per hectare, whereas the Aramon averaged 10 to 12 kilograms per vine with a yield of from 200 to 300 hectolitres the hectare.[37]

These yields were further improved by new methods of dressing the vine,[38] increased use of chemical fertilizers, and by irrigation. The last two methods received particular development during the phylloxera, when the second was much used to keep sick vines in partial production, while—as has been noted—the third was an effective means of warding off the disease. In fact, the relative suc-

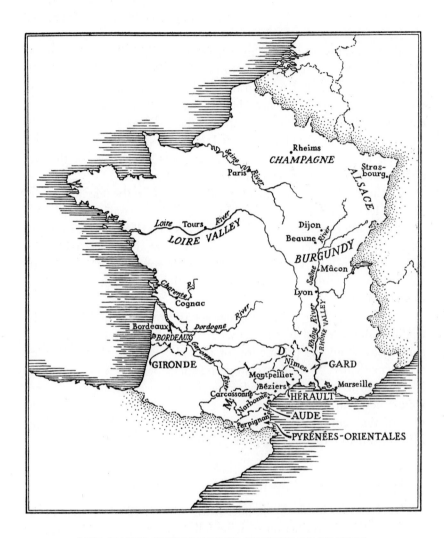

THE MAJOR WINEGROWING REGIONS OF FRANCE

cess of the low-land growers in riding out the phylloxera by watering their roots inspired another trend that contributed to increased yields.

This was the so-called "march from the hills," which saw the old vineyards deserted for new ones which sprang up in the fertile fields formerly planted with grains and other crops.[39] In addition, valuable woods and mulberry bushes were cut down, and the vine was even planted in the dried-up marshes and sands of the Mediterranean. Such developments led observers of this frenzied replanting to claim that each new hectare was worth two of the old, and production figures seemed to confirm this view.

In the rest of France wine production after the phylloxera increased less rapidly. For one thing the alternative of quantity production at the expense of quality was not so feasible in other regions as in the Midi. The Aramon grape does not do well outside of a Mediterranean-type climate. Moreover, beyond the Midi, climate and other growing factors made reconstitution of the vineyard a slower process.

On the other hand, in such regions as Bordeaux and Burgundy, traditionally devoted to the growing of quality wines, there was a shift away from the production of *vins de cru* [40] to the production of *vin ordinaire*.[41] If this change meant a deterioration in quality it speeded the recovery of production volume. Also, there were advances in scientific viticulture to be taken advantage of so that by the turn of the century the greater part of the vineyard outside of the Midi began to experience higher yields from a reduced area.

FRAUD

During the 1880–89 decade, when the phylloxera was at its height, national production of wine fell 46 percent from the average for the previous decade. With wine in such short supply and prices at scarcity levels, the winegrowers were increasingly led to augment the volume of their production by methods which, if not entirely prohibited by law, were not widely practiced when good cheap wine was abundant.

This development was reflected in the increased use of sugar in winemaking. Normally sugar is used during fermentation to increase the alcoholic strength of weak wines. The process is called *chaptalisation,* and properly carried out does not increase the quantity of wine. Sugar can be used with "second wines," however, and this process is real adulteration.

Second wines, or *piquettes,* as they are familiarly called, are made by adding sugar and a certain quantity of hot water to the fermenting residue left in the vats after the first wine is drawn off. Also, by adding increasing amounts of sugar each time, hot water can be drawn through this residue several times, making "third," "fourth," and even "fifth" wines whose alcoholic strength, if nothing else, can be as great as the first wine.

This last practice was limited in theory by law and in fact by the abundance of good cheap wine and the relatively high price of sugar. Second wines were legal, but were commonly distributed as a supplement to the vineyard worker's wage or consumed by the family of the small grower. Wine assigned for these purposes was exempt from taxation. As a result it was profitable to sell *piquettes* and even "third" or 'fourth" wines illegally when, after a short harvest, wine prices rose high enough to cover the cost of the additional amounts of sugar used. Such wine circulated locally in the wine-growing regions. But with the high prices of the phylloxera period it began to be profitable to sell *piquettes* through regular channels.

The latter development was helped by a law of July 29, 1884, which lowered the tax on sugar used in winemaking from 50 francs, the ordinary rate, to 20 francs the 100 kilograms. In 1885, further regulations interpreting the law permitted the use of sugar after the second fermentation. The latter regulations, especially, opened the way for making unlimited quantities of what was really "sugar wine." However, the law was enthusiastically approved by the Midi and widely hailed as a "relief measure for the winegrowers—victims of the phylloxera." [42]

In 1885, the year the law went into effect, 8 million kilograms of sugar were used in winemaking. The following year this figure rose to 26 million.[43] These were, of course, years when the harvest had been cruelly weakened by the phylloxera—28,500,000 hectolitres of wine were produced in 1885 and 25,100,000 hectolitres in

1886. But in 1899, the year of a relatively abundant harvest (47,-900,000 hectolitres), and two years after a law had been passed to prohibit the sale of sugar wine, 39 million kilograms of sugar were used by the winegrowers.[44]   Thus the use of sugar, which had been facilitated to bolster phylloxera-weakened harvests, was first abused and then fraudulently practiced.

Of course some of the sugar was used legally.   The foregoing figures indicate an increase in fraud but do not measure its volume. According to one authority, however, it was still possible in 1900 under remaining provisions of the law of 1884 "to have the output of sugar-produced wine double that of natural wine."[45]   And in 1903, a year in which the price of sugar fell following the Brussels Sugar Agreement of 1902,[46] the Midi indulged in what may fairly be called an orgy of fraud.   That year, thirty-five winegrowing communities in the department of Hérault declared an official harvest of 1,004,915 hectolitres, but it was noted that 2,284,848 hectolitres of wine left the same communities for markets to the north.[47]   On the national level, it was estimated that 15,490,000 hectolitres of fraudulent wines, an amount equal to more than 40 percent of the officially declared harvest, had been dumped on the national market.[48]   The harvest of 1903 was light, but, as will be seen in a subsequent chapter, fraud was to continue in similar proportions during years of great abundance.

IMPORTS, EXPORTS, AND FALLING PRICES

During the decade of 1880–89, when the phylloxera epidemic was at its height, national production of wine fell 46 percent from the average for the previous decade.   Over the same two periods the average for imports increased from 824,383 hectolitres to 9,372,-400 hectolitres.   Thus in 1887, when production reached its lowest point (24,333,000 hectolitres), a record 12,282,000 hectolitres of low-grade wines—chiefly from Italy and Spain—were imported into France.   As Table 4 shows, imports continued in nearly this same proportion to production until 1892 when they were abruptly cut back by the protectionist Méline Tariff of that year, which raised the duty on foreign wines 55 to 60 percent.

TABLE 4. WINE PRODUCTION, EXPORTS, IMPORTS, AND PRICES AT THE PRODUCTION LEVEL IN FRANCE, 1890–99

Year	Production	Exports	Imports	Average Price per Hectolitre
	(in thousands of hectolitres)			(in francs)
1870–79, yearly average	54,671	3,283	824	29
1880–89, yearly average	29,675	2,469	9,372	38
1890	27,416	2,162	10,830	36
1891	30,140	2,049	12,278	34
1892	29,082	1,845	9,400	31
1893	50,070	1,569	5,895	25
1894	39,053	1,721	4,492	24
1895	26,688	1,697	6,337	31
1896	44,656	1,784	8,814	26
1897	32,351	1,775	7,531	25
1898	32,282	1,636	8,603	30
1899	47,908	1,717	8,466	26

Source: *Annuaire statistique.*

Such advantage as was gained by the winegrowers from the Méline Tariff was lost, in part, by increasing shipments of wines from Algeria. The development of Algeria's vineyard had received a tremendous impetus from the effects of the phylloxera in France.[49] Moreover, Algerian wines, similar in quality to those of the Midi, enjoyed a longer growing season and lower labor costs which, combined with favorable freight rates in France,[50] permitted them to compete on even terms with the Midi wines. Thus Algeria, which in 1878 exported 320,000 hectolitres to France out of a total production of approximately 1,000,000 hectolitres, in 1900 sent 2,443,-000 hectolitres out of a production of 5,217,000.[51] During the same period Algeria's share of total French wine imports increased from 20 percent to nearly one half.

The advantages of the Méline Tariff for the winegrowers were further lessened by retaliatory attacks on French wines, some countries all but closing their markets to them. As will be seen in a subsequent chapter, exports eventually recovered somewhat, but in the decade immediately following the enactment of the Méline Tariff they decreased by about 25 percent from what they had averaged during the previous decade, and the long-term trend has been downward. Thus during 1890 to 1899, the so-called "decade of reconstitution," the problems of shrinking exports, Algerian competition, and an emphasis on the quantity production of low-grade wines were born.   These problems would last and cause recurring price crises which would involve the government in more and more intervention in the affairs of the winegrowers and in a policy which, as it turned out, subsidized a large part of their excess production.   The latter policy, it is one of the aims of this study to prove, has been in the long run detrimental to the French economy.

As Table 4 suggests, the conjunction of the problems described in the preceding paragraph, along with that of fraud, was already causing a decline in prices from 1890 to 1899.   In 1893 a relatively abundant although not extraordinary harvest had produced a price slump which lasted for two years.   But if this was a danger signal nobody cared to notice it.   The price level was still comparable to that of the pre-phylloxera era, returns from the high-yielding vineyards brought greater profits to the growers, and new plantings continued throughout the decade.   The prevalent mood in the vineyards was one of optimism.   An amusing contemporary account described the Midi as "a Pactolian basin which drained towards the Mediterranean shore the merchandise of the North and Center paid for at double and triple prices," while the city of Béziers became a center where "each vineyard owner on market days would come to buy his piano and jewels for his wife and daughters." [52]

2. THE CRISIS OF 1900–1907

With the turn of the century, the fortunate situation of
the winegrowers described in the preceding chapter came to an ab-
rupt end.[1] In 1900, after a particularly abundant harvest, wine
production for the whole of France reached the figure of 67,352,661
hectolitres, a quantity surpassed only in 1869 and in the record year
of 1875.[2] Production in the four departments of Gard, Aude,
Hérault, and Pyrénées-Orientales accounted for 24,493,503 hectolitres of this total, an all-time record for the region. At the same
time the Bordeaux vineyard topped its 1875 record with a bumper
harvest of 5,738,000 hectolitres, while records were also broken
in Burgundy and the Loire Valley vineyards.[3] Significant increases
were registered in other winegrowing regions, and Algeria sent a
record shipment of 2,443,000 hectolitres to the metropolitan market.

Under any circumstances, these figures promised lowered returns
for the growers, especially in the Midi. How low, though, no one
could have predicted on the basis of market activity in previous
bumper-crop years. Starting after the 1900 harvest at 15 to 10
francs the hectolitre, the price of wine at the production level[4] in
the Midi dropped rapidly, until late in the year the case was recorded
of a grower in the Pyrénées-Orientales who could find no takers for
35,000 hectolitres at 1.75 francs the hectolitre.[5] The average price
per hectolitre for the four departments in 1900 has been estimated
at seven francs.[6] For all but the highest-yielding vineyards this
price level meant losses.[7]

But in 1901 even ruder shocks were in store for growers and
dealers. With an abundant harvest predicted, wine was commonly
selling by July and August of that year at three francs the hectolitre in the market cities of Narbonne and Béziers.[8] However, the
harvest, though abundant, showed a production drop of about 15
percent from the year before. Still, after the harvest prices started
at from two to three francs the hectolitre lower than in 1900, and
the average for 1901 has been estimated at around five francs the
hectolitre. In some instances prices of less than one franc were recorded.[9]

In 1902, however, Midi prices rose to an average of ten francs
the hectolitre. And in 1903, after a harvest partially destroyed by
frost, they climbed to a twenty-five-franc average. But such encouragement as was offered by this break in the market was quickly
dissipated in the years that followed.

In 1904, 1905, and 1906, the average price of wine in the four
departments stayed around six francs the hectolitre. During the
same three years, national production, although it remained high,
dropped from 66,000,000 to 52,100,000 hectolitres and production
in the four departments from 26,780,000 to 16,175,000 hectolitres—
but prices were not appreciably affected. By 1907, a type of dis-
couragement unknown during the phylloxera had set in. For five
years out of seven most Midi growers had had to sell their wine at
cost or below. Here, it must have appeared to them, was no enemy
like the phylloxera, which could be seen and fought.

Nowhere else in France did prices fall as low as they did in the
Midi, but they dropped proportionately. Contemporary observers
were not slow to point out the dominating weight of Midi production on the market. In the words of one of them:

Since the replanting that followed the phylloxera, first the *vins ordinaires*
of Gironde and later the *grands ordinaires* have been more directly subject to price fluctuations which are most often dictated by the situation
in the winegrowing Midi.

As a result the slightest anomaly in the harvests, especially where the
four departments of the Midi are concerned, accentuates and aggravates
the crisis [in the Gironde].[10]

Moreover production costs were proportionately higher outside
the Midi. In the Bordeaux vineyard, for example, price drops of

from 20 to 40 percent meant losses for growers of some *vins de cru* as well as of *vins ordinaires*.[11]   Even in Burgundy, where one half the value of an annual harvest represented *vins de cru,* there were complaints of the *contre-coup* from Midi production and prices.[12]

As noted above, however, there was a definite trend toward quantity production at the expense of quality taking place in the vineyards of Bordeaux and Burgundy as well as in the Midi.[13]   On the other hand, in some of the "vassal" vineyards adjoining the major regions, and in other scattered winegrowing areas, production and the vineyard area had stayed well below the pre-phylloxera level. Yet during 1900–1907, even these regions experienced price drops which saw the national average tumble to as low as 50 percent of what it had been in 1890–99.   Clearly the price slump, whatever its cause, was a national phenomenon.

THE CRISIS AND THE REGIONAL ECONOMIES

Generally, one of the most noticeable effects of the continuing crisis was a rapid decline in the value of vineyard properties.   There was a long-term trend in this direction, but the greatest drops were registered during the crisis years.[14]   Caziot, in his study of land values, referred to the depreciation as being "in some instances unbelievable." [15]   Writing of the Bordeaux vineyard he noted that

la grande propriété, which had lost between two thirds and four fifths of its value, was almost unsaleable, and only those [owners] who possessed a fortune independent of their vineyards were able to hold their own against the crisis.[16]

Typical examples quoted by Caziot include a twenty-nine hectare property in the commune of Roaillon (Gironde department) appraised at 80,000 francs in 1882 and sold at 31,000 francs in 1905, and a *domaine* of one hundred hectares in the commune of Lesparre (Gironde) valued for tax purposes at 180,000 francs in 1895 and sold for 55,775 francs in 1900.[17]

In Burgundy the situation was more stable, especially in the areas that produced the *grands crus*.[18]   Caziot, however, quotes for the commune of Savigny-lès-Beaune (Côte-d'Or) a price of 5,500 francs the hectare for vines producing quality wines in 1907, whereas

TABLE 5. WINE PRODUCTION AND PRICES IN VARIOUS AREAS AT THE
PRODUCTION LEVEL DURING THE CRISIS OF 1900–1907
(*In thousands of hectolitres and in francs*)

Year	Production in France	Average Price per Hecto- litre	Production in the Midi Depart- ments [a]	Average Price per Hecto- litre	Production in the De- partment of Gironde	Average Price per Hecto- litre [b]
1890–99, yearly average	35,980	29	12,509	16	2,575	35
1900	67,353	19	24,494	7	5,738	20
1901	57,964	16	20,235	5	4,308	15
1902	39,884	21	15,305	10	2,867	23
1903	35,402	27	13,340	25	2,097	38
1904	66,017	19	26,782	6	4,521	22
1905	56,066	15	21,708	7	4,300	16
1906	52,079	18	16,175	6	3,507	22
1907	66,070	17	30,547	9	5,439	20

[a] Departments of Aude, Gard, Hérault, and Pyrénées-Orientales.
[b] *Vin ordinaire.*

Source: *Annuaire statistique;* Meyrueis, *De la défense des intérêts de la viticulture méridionale,* p. 123.

the same type of vineyard brought 11,300 francs the hectare in 1894.[19] On a particularly good property in Villefranche (Rhône) he notes a decline in value from 15,000 francs to 11,600 francs the hectare during 1901–07.[20] And in the Loire vineyard, property depreciation of up to 50 percent was also observed.[21]

In the Midi, however, depreciation was even more spectacular and because of the intensive monoculture practiced there, distress was more general than in the other winegrowing regions.[22] In the closely knit economy of the departments of Aude, Gard, Hérault, and Pyrénées-Orientales, for example, the price depression produced effects that went far beyond a decline in property values.

In 1904, for the first time since the end of the phylloxera epidemic, the vineyard area of the four departments began to diminish. This started a trend that continued beyond the price crisis, but the greatest decreases were registered between 1905 and 1907.[23] At the same time, land values which had soared during the decade of prosperity now dropped just as far from their true worth. In the Aude before 1900 a hectare of vineland brought from 10,000 to 22,500 francs, and even at times 25,000 francs.[24] But from 1900 on, land values fell until they reached 1000 francs a hectare for hill-side vineyards and 5000 francs for the richest lowland properties.[25]

It would be an exaggeration, however, to say that there was a normal market for properties at the time. When vineyards were put up for sale, they often found no takers: when sold by the courts, which were carrying a heavy schedule of liquidations and bankrupt-cies, they retained only a fraction of their former value. Thus the tribunal at Narbonne in 1909 sold for 3,500 francs a property in the rich plain of Coursan, which had been purchased for 100,000 francs as late as 1904.[26] In the Commune de Salleles (Aude), the *domaine de Treilhas,* which had brought 1,000,000 francs several years previously, was bought by the Crédit Foncier for 100,000.[27] Again in the Aude, at Fitou, a *domaine* on which a 100,000 franc loan had been made was sold by the court for 20,000 francs.[28]

Those vineyard owners who did not sell or go into bankruptcy carried on under an increasing debt load and with virtually no capi-tal reserves. Their difficulties are reflected in the transactions of the local banks. For example, from 1900 to 1906 loans made by the Caisse Régionale de Crédit Agricole du Midi at Narbonne rose from 542,000 francs to 9,137,000 francs.[29] At the same time de-posit accounts in this bank "practically vanished," while demand ac-counts became a "rare curiosity." [30] In some cantons every vine-yard carried a heavy mortgage, while at the height of the crisis it has been estimated that two thirds of all vineyard properties in the Midi were in the hands of the Crédit Foncier.[31] The government, facing the inevitable, was forced to delay collection of taxes. Any wholesale and stringent application of foreclosure and tax laws might have meant bankruptcy for the entire region. The winegrowing Midi was truly, as one observer put it, "a vast factory running at a loss, but which could not afford to shut down." [32]

The commerce and industry of the region were also seriously af-fected. The Union Commercielle et Industrielle of Montpellier noted a 50 percent decline in sales by commercial establishments of all categories during the crisis years.[33] Department stores, in a des-perate bid to improve their situation, sent out *bazaars ambulants* to serve growers who, it seems, no longer came to town.[34] At Béziers the number of unoccupied stalls in the public market increased from 20 in 1904 to 68 in 1907.[35] The latter year the Office du Travail reported 50 percent unemployment in the industrial establishments of Montpellier and Béziers[36] In 1907 for the first time on record, no building materials entered the last-named city, and *octroi* receipts diminished accordingly.[37] A description of Béziers by its inhabitants mirrored the gloom that had descended on the urban areas of the Midi: the market center of the free-spending winegrowers had become "the city where nobody laughs." [38]

In the countryside wage cuts, unemployment, and strikes among the vineyard workers produced additional misery. In the first years of the crisis, the owners for the most part did not consider reducing the field workers' basic wage of three francs a day. But from the beginning they cut down as much as possible on the amount of labor employed. These measures provoked resistance: as early as 1900 at Aimargues in the Gard a number of workers forced themselves on several proprietors and went to work in spite of being forbidden to do so.[39]

However, the most spirited resistance took place in 1903 when the proprietors finally threatened, and, in most cases, carried out, wage cuts The same year, it will be remembered, the price of wine had climbed to 25 francs the hectolitre after a severe frost destroyed part of the harvest. The workers, either feeling they had been taken advantage of, or mistaking the price rise for a break in the market, protested, so that between November, 1903, and July, 1904, 150 strikes involving 50,000 strikers took place in the vineyards of the four departments.[40]

These strikes resulted in temporary wage increases, but after 1904 reductions were again carried out. This time there was little protest. The year 1905 saw only small and scattered strikes. In 1906 there were two; in 1907, none. At the same time unemployment increased. The monthly bulletins of the Office du Travail list unemployment figures running as high as 90 percent in some wine-producing communes during each of the three years just mentioned. For 1905 the average for these same communes would be about 25 percent. A conservative estimate for 1907 would be 50 percent. The *syndicats,* probably representing the least skilled elements of the agricultural workers, reported even higher percentages among their membership.[41]

This decrease in the number of strikes coincident with the rise of unemployment suggests that the workers came to realize the true dimensions of the wave of misery that engulfed them.   At all events, 1907 saw vineyard owner and laborer alike, as well as others, joined in popular and often violent protest.

That year an unusual leader, Marcellin Albert, popularly known as the "Messiah" or "Redeemer," began attracting huge crowds wherever he appeared in the Midi.   At a much-advertised meeting in Montpellier on June 9, he collected, according to newspaper estimates, the almost incredible total of one-half million demonstrators, to whom he and his lieutenants read a proclamation calling for a ban on the payment of all taxes.[42]   The next day, as part of a plan to support the proclamation, the mayors and municipal councilors of over three hundred communities in the region, including all the principal cities, resigned their offices.

This was revolt, and the government under Clemenceau moved swiftly.   A whole army corps was dispatched to the Midi, and several bloody clashes occurred between troops and the local population at Narbonne and Montpellier.   In the countryside troop trains were halted and attacked, and at Perpignan the prefecture was burned, the prefect narrowly escaping with his life.   Within two weeks, however, active resistance was crushed.

Albert's revolt was a picturesque and pathetic episode in French history.[43]   It has some importance, however, in the direct insight it gives as to how the winegrowers felt about their industry and the government in 1907.   The attitude was one of complete if grudging surrender by the former to the latter.   The following are typical:

We want . . . wine sold above cost.   The means to do it?   Let Parliament find out.   That's its business.[44]

Let them [the government] take the measures they want to, but to live we need to have wine selling for at least 1.50 to 2 francs the degree. For the rest we can practically say we don't care.[45]

Albert, himself, with characteristic naïveté, spoke of the winegrowing Midi as a patient and the government as a doctor.   Was it up to the patient to tell the doctor what to do?[46]   Before discussing the government's reaction to this challenge, however, it is necessary to look at the causes of the crisis of 1900–1907.

3. CAUSES OF THE CRISIS OF 1900–1907

Among economists, political observers, and other interested parties, the onset of the crisis was the signal for a flurry of opinions as to its causes and the problems of the wine industry in general. This opinion may be said to have assumed the form of an argument among three schools of thought, at least two of which included some of the foremost economists of the time .

One group believed that the crisis was caused by overproduction, and so advocated measures that would have the effect of limiting production—if only indirectly. Another group believed that actually there was no real overproduction, but that instead the existence of a large surplus caused by widespread fraud in the manufacture or sale of wine was having a depressing effect on prices. Fraud included such practices as adding water directly to wine, or as has already been described, raising its alcoholic content with sugar and adulterating it, as well as subtler forms of misrepresentation. A third group saw the crisis as a result of the government's high-tariff and protectionist policies. From the latter's point of view, lowered tariffs would increase outlets abroad for the wines of France, and thus presumably solve the whole problem.

Generally speaking, support for the first point of view was intellectual; for the second, popular; while the third stand was more or less automatically taken by groups and individuals opposed to government tariff policy, as expressed in the protectionist Méline Tariff of 1892 and subsequent increases in import duties.

The opening blow of the main argument may be said to have been struck by the economist Charles Gide. At a conference held on May 20, 1900, by the Musée Sociale at Paris, and presided over by the Minister of Agriculture, he read a paper in which he concluded that rising production in the face of diminishing consumption was responsible for the low prices being offered for wine.[1] In regard to production, he expressed alarm at the increased yields made possible by advances in scientific viticulture and the new plantings in high-yielding grape varieties.

As regards consumption, Gide pointed out that the population of France was to all intents stationary and could not be expected to keep pace with the promised increases in production But he placed more emphasis on the fact that a major revolution in French drinking habits was taking place "Wine was formerly the national drink of France," lamented M. Gide, "but now our distinguished people are drinking tea." [2]

More specifically, he deplored the rise in consumption of cheap spirits among the lower classes and a very marked prejudice against wine developing among the upper classes in favor of tea and mineral waters. These contentions Gide buttressed with figures, the most startling of which claimed that one fifth of all the men in France and three quarters of all the women drank no wine at all.[3] As a result of this and further population analysis, Gide concluded that France could not drink more than 60 million hectolitres of wine a year, and that this amount was likely to decrease rather than increase.

To remedy such a situation Gide proposed legislation that would discourage further planting His proposals included repeal of the five-year tax exemption on new vine plantations—a post-phylloxera emergency measure—and the abandonment of high import duties on foreign wines which he claimed encouraged domestic overplanting. But Gide's greatest emphasis was on producers' associations and consumer cooperatives as aids in reducing production. Formation of such groups, he felt, would improve the quality of wine produced and elevate the public's taste, thus placing more of a premium on quality wine. These developments, in turn, would limit production "naturally" by driving inferior or "quantity" wines off the market. This was the road to be followed if the wine industry wished to avert a crisis that would see prices drop lower each year.

If one considers that 1900 marks the first year of the threatened crisis, the reply of the Minister of Agriculture, M. Jean Dupuy, to Gide's paper makes interesting reading. It concludes as follows:

The Minister of Agriculture praises what the speaker has said about the benefits of cooperation in the wine industry, but he has his reservations about the gravity of the crisis which might menace this industry. M. Charles Gide has perhaps painted too somber a picture of this crisis. . . .

The vine can continue to develop in our country without major inconvenience, and perhaps one should not become overly alarmed at the drop in wine prices. *Falling prices for luxury articles are a current phenomenon and wine is a luxury article.*[4]

Actually, in the first three or four years of the crisis, many who spoke with authority agreed with Gide. Méline's influential journal, *Le Travail national,* flatly asserted in 1901 that "in reality practically the sole cause of the wine crisis is the excess in wine production." [5] The free-trade organ, *Journal des économistes,* seconded this conclusion two years later,[6] and *Le Temps,* although it acknowledged fraud as a factor in the crisis, likewise placed major blame on overproduction.[7] Even M. Dupuy, about a year and a half after his reply to Gide, was forced to admit that there was a crisis and that "it might appear that overproduction was the cause, due to overabundant harvests." [8]

Around 1905, however, a decided shift in opinion can be detected. Although as far back as 1893 a prescient deputy had declared that "fraud was a second phylloxera for the wine growers," [9] in 1901, after the Chamber's first interpellation on the wine crisis, only one of thirteen resolutions adopted dealt with fraud, and that only indirectly.[10] However, by 1905, during the long debate on the same subject, fraud figured almost exclusively as the villain of the piece,[11] and by 1906, the then Minister of Agriculture, M. Ruau, reporting on a proposed bill against fraud, stated that suppression of fraud was "the correct remedy for the present crisis." [12]

Support for the fraud argument was largely popular. It was sparked by the Midi deputies, the southern newspapers, and, once the issue had been joined, by an overwhelming majority of the wine-growers themselves. *"Morte aux fraudeurs"* was the slogan most frequently seen on the banners and placards carried in the giant demonstrations of 1907, and so clamorous was agitation on this subject that it undoubtedly produced a certain amount of consumer resistance to cheap wine—a move that could not fail to harm the Midi.[13]

Nevertheless the Midi deputies continued to agitate, seeing the ineffectiveness of anti-fraud legislation as a "northern" conspiracy, and, although the fraud argument was well presented in some quarters, certainly the hue and cry raised in the Chamber did not appear to indicate a sober consideration of the facts. Perhaps this partisan and popular support caused intellectuals like Gide to shy away from the fraud viewpoint. At all events, as indignation over fraud mounted and Albert's protest meetings grew, there were economists who took up the fraud argument. The most prominent of them was Paul Leroy-Beaulieu.

In an article in his weekly, *L'Économiste français,* Leroy-Beaulieu first belittled those who sought to limit wine production in the Midi.[14] Provoked by a prefect of the Pyrénées-Orientales who, early in 1907, had advised diversified agriculture for his winegrowing department, Leroy-Beaulieu pointed out that if the Pyrénées-Orientales planted pine and almond trees as its prefect suggested, one half to three quarters of the population would have to emigrate. "Also," he added, "how can you expect the winegrower to tear up his vines, even though they are not producing profits now, when reconstituting them after the phylloxera cost from 3,000 to 4,000 francs the hectare?"[15]

In the course of the same article, Leroy-Beaulieu claimed that wine production was not surpassing consumption, but on the contrary a careful examination of production and consumption figures would show that production was falling a little short of demand. The current state of the market he attributed to a surplus caused by fraud. He did not estimate its extent but concluded that it must be considerable to have such an unbalancing effect on the market. The way out of the crisis, he felt, consisted in first of all combating fraud and then finding new outlets for wine in the beer- and cider-drinking regions.   To this end he proposed a trade association that would occupy itself with these objectives.

As might have been expected, Leroy-Beaulieu's stand on fraud did not silence the overproduction camp.   Gide reentered the lists with a long and detailed analysis of the crisis in the July, 1907, issue of the *Revue d'économie politique*.[16]   In it he again took up the position he had adopted in 1900, pointing out how developments since then had justified his stand.   The abundant harvests and falling prices that he had predicted in 1900 were now a bitter reality, and worse, the whole Midi was up in arms in blind revolt against a situation resulting from its own folly.

By 1907, Gide of course had to recognize the fraud problem. But he had little use for the Midi's special argument that it was the victim of fraud practiced elsewhere—in the cities and other parts of the country.   Gide rightly pointed out that the Midi had sinned in this respect as much as, if not more than, any region, and did not do so now only because the price of wine had fallen so low that fraud was no longer profitable.[17]   However, this seems rather flimsy ground on which to minimize the whole fraud situation, especially after having acknowledged its extent in at least one part of the country.   But this in a sense is what Gide did, taking the attitude that fraud was a minor if inescapable nuisance born of the consuming public's lack of discrimination.   True, he advocated educating public taste, but towards stamping out fraud by legislation he maintained a defeatist attitude, claiming that the anti-fraud bills then pending before Parliament would not work any more than had previous legislation on the same subject.[18]

Opposition to the pending legislation was also expressed in the *Journal des économistes* [19] and the *Journal des débats,* both publications seeing a dangerous *étatisme* in it.   More, the *Journal des débats* found fraud was "an enemy which, for our part, we believe to be imaginary." [20]   However, Parliament, on its part, thought otherwise, and in the wake of the uprisings the much-debated anti-fraud legislation became the law of June 29, 1907.[21]

Possibly because of this the editors of the *Journal des économistes* felt they had to have a new reason for the crisis.   At all events they dragged out a very familiar whipping-boy—and so by July of 1907, although overproduction was not forgotten, it was protectionism "that has aggravated *if not created* the crisis in viticulture by encouraging production at the same time as it has closed off production's outlets." [22] In a later issue the symptoms which a sick Midi was exhibiting were none other than the symptoms of

the serious illness of protectionism with which all Frenchmen are more or less afflicted.

They will not all die of it, but all are stricken.

The "Mélinistic" microbe is everywhere. It has simply produced more rapid and abnormal effects in the Midi than elsewhere.[23]

EXPORTS AND IMPORTS

The arguments of the anti-protectionists expressed in the preceding paragraphs were founded on the tariff wars that followed the adoption of the Méline Tariff in 1892 and on a resulting decline in wine exports. By 1900, however, the main difficulties occasioned by these wars had been overcome,[24] and wine exports along with French exports in general were increasing.

For example, French wine exports to Switzerland, which had averaged 262,000 hectolitres a year during the ten-year period prior to 1892, fell to an average of 48,000 hectolitres for 1893–95. With new agreements arrived at in 1895, 131,000 hectolitres were shipped to the Swiss market the following year. By 1901 this figure had increased to 228,500, and the average for the 1900–1907 period was 330,000 hectolitres.[25] Drops in wine exports to other countries directly attributable to the Méline Tariff were less drastic than the

TABLE 6. EXPORT OF WINE FROM FRANCE, 1900–1907
(*In hectolitres*)

Year	Exports
1890–1899, yearly average	1,795,500
1900	1,905,000
1901	2,022,000
1902	2,052,000
1903	1,726,000
1904	1,643,000
1905	2,606,000
1906	2,110,000
1907	2,788,000

Source: *Annuaire statistique.*

TABLE 7. COMPARATIVE PRODUCTION, EXPORT, AND IMPORT OF WINE IN
FRANCE, 1870–1907 (*Periodic yearly averages, in hectolitres*)

Period	Production	Exports	Imports
1870–79	54,670,800	3,283,500	824,383
1880–89	29,675,000	2,468,900	9,372,400
1890–99	35,964,600	1,795,500	8,264,600
1900–07	55,179,200	2,053,750	5,299,750

Source: *Annuaire statistique.*

above, and many tended to work themselves out by 1900. Exports of fine wines were affected less than other varieties, champagne exports actually increasing in the decade following 1892.[26]

Thus, although there was a long-term decrease in wine exports, it is difficult to establish a direct relationship between the problem of wine exports under a high tariff and the crisis of 1900–1907. It is nevertheless true that an increase in the exportation of low-grade wine would have helped the growers, but they would have had to develop such exportation to a much greater degree than was true at any time, prosperous or otherwise. However, the opportunity, if it existed, had been well lost before 1892. The French phylloxera epidemic was a great incentive for other countries to plant vineyards. With France's demands for imports soaring, the vineyard area in Italy grew from 1,926,000 hectares in 1872 to more than 3,000,000 in 1882. In 1892 it stood at 3,466,000. By 1900 it had dropped a little to 3,446,000, although production gained in the same period.[27] The fact that in the process Italy had captured some of France's export trade would seem, then, more directly attributable to phylloxera than high tariffs.

Spain experienced an increase in vineyard area comparable to Italy's, although Spanish production actually fell considerably during the 1900–1907 period while Spain's imports from France increased.[28] The period before 1892 also marked the growth of important vineyards in California, Chile, Australia, and South Africa. Finally, one must ask if an average drop in exports of approximately 1,130,-000 hectolitres from the last "normal" decade,[29] 1870–79, was enough in itself to depress prices to the levels they reached in the four departments of the Midi or the nation at large from 1900 through 1907.

As Table 7 suggests, imports would seem to have been a much more serious problem, although they had naturally declined from what they had been during the phylloxera and post-phylloxera decades. Moreover, the growing share of Algeria in the import market continued under the competitive conditions described in an earlier chapter. Ironically Algeria was supplying just that competition some anti-protectionists felt would be so helpful in limiting domestic production. Rightly or wrongly such competition angered the Midi, and in the minds of the southern growers it came to be one of the chief causes of their troubles.

Although by 1912 it may have been said that the wines of the two regions were "coexisting" peacefully in a favorable market, the problem did not end there. In the long run there has been less and less relation betwen Algerian production and metropolitan requirements. The whole question of Algerian competition is still an open one as far as French winegrowers are concerned, and it was undoubtedly a contributing factor to the crisis of 1900–1907.

TARLE 8. ALGERIAN WINE PRODUCTION AND EXPORTS TO FRANCE, 1900–1907
(In hectolitres)

Year	Wine Produced	Wine Exported to France	Total Wine Imported by France from All Sources
1900	5,634,000	2,443,000	5,217,000
1901	5,738,000	2,786,000	3,708,000
1902	4,353,000	3,900,000	4,447,000
1903	6,589,000	4,772,000	6,189,000
1904	7,630,000	5,224,000	6,686,000
1905	7,051,000	4,818,000	5,175,000
1906	7,347,000	5,407,000	5,764,000
1907	7,853,000	5,689,000	5,923,000

Sources: *Annuaire statistique;* Ministère de l'agriculture, *Statistique agricole annuelle,* 1909, p. 271.

MARKET ABUSES

During the crisis years new attention was also directed towards abuses and grievances of long standing in the wine industry, some of which came to be identified with the decline in prices itself.

Thus at the beginning of the crisis much was said of the inequitable tax penalties to which wine was subject—so much, that in 1900 the legislature passed a new *Loi des Boissons*,[30] which lowered taxes on wine, cider, and beer, and another in 1901 which removed all *octroi* duties on these beverages.   The former law saved the wine industry and trade an estimated 100 million francs in taxes, while the latter took off an additional 67 million.[31]   Both measures more than halved the tax revenues from wine.   The loss to the state was compensated by surtaxes on alcohol.   These measures, however, though well intentioned, did little to ease the crisis.   Their most immediate effect was to increase the number of middlemen.   The *octroi* law in particular brought with it an increase in the number of small local dealers, "emancipated from the traditions of the wine industry," and out for a quick profit.[32]

As the crisis wore on there was naturally less and less incentive for the big dealers to carry large stocks for any length of time.   And if we are to believe the Midi deputies, the large dealers were increasingly replaced by speculators and other middlemen,[33] who had always been part of a complicated marketing system but who played a more odious role during the crisis.   For example, there were the *indicateurs* who arranged sales between growers and dealers.   These people, while charging the grower a commission, were in effect agents of the dealers.   They prospered only by getting the dealers a lower price than would have been possible unaided.   And they accomplished this by an intimate knowledge of the financial position of the growers in their neighborhood—a position in which they were sometimes involved as lenders or futures buyers.

There were also *courtiers,* who worked as agents for dealer or grower and were described in the Midi as "men without any real talents, moral or financial responsibility, spreaders of false and misleading news aiming at and provoking the lowest price for the product."[34]   So entrenched were some of these people that during the crisis years they were often able to force repurchase agreements on the growers in case the buyers could not dispose of their stocks—a type of bargain which had not been seen in the Midi since the beginning of the eighteenth century.[35]

These conditions created an opportunity for cooperation.   In spite of a traditional dislike of such undertakings some growers, chiefly small ones, organized themselves into cooperatives.[36]   These ventures were more noteworthy for the interest they aroused than any effect they had on the market. Much was made of the example of one cooperative, the Vignerons Libres de Maurassan, which was able to survive the bad years by selling direct to workers' societies in Paris, the growers receiving five to six francs more the hectolitre than they would have on the regular market.[37]

Another attempt at self-help which also received wide publicity was the organizing of a popular cartel. In 1907 a certain M. Palazy, a proprietor of importance, obtained the signatures of some twenty thousand growers in the four departments of Aude, Garde, Hérault, Pyrénées-Orientales, representing a combined production of about twelve million hectolitres, pledging them to sell all their wine to the cartel for a down payment of four francs the hectolitre. The cartel would then regulate the sale of their product so as not to glut the market, even to the point of not selling some wine—an unheard-of idea in the Midi up to then.

Another novel idea was the plan to divide the profits of the organization among the members on a basis that put a premium on quality wine and minimized to a certain extent the quantity produced. However, in spite of its broad support, the cartel failed to raise the capital that would have permitted it to start operations.

In general it can be said that the crisis of 1900–1907 emphasized the need for some sort of cooperation between the growers, and the unique Confédération Generale des Vignerons, which will be discussed in a later chapter, was the result of that need. However, the crisis did not produce any appreciable growth in the number of marketing cooperatives.[38] Of market abuses it can be said that they had existed in good days as well as bad and so cannot be held responsible in anything but a small way for the problems of 1900 to 1907. Rather, as the very organization of the Palazy Cartel suggests, by 1907 sober minds believed that the most effective way of tidying up the market was to improve the quality of the product and to limit its quantity.

THE DISTILLATION OF WINE: A REMEDY FOR OVERPRODUCTION?

During the 1865–75 period an average of approximately 500,000 hectolitres of brandy and other alcohols were distilled from wine each year.[39]   For winegrowers this figure represented the not inconsiderable total of four to five million hectolitres of wine profitably disposed of in the still [40]—a practice that had a beneficial effect on the market, acting as a sort of safety valve in years of overabundant harvests.

With the high prices of the phylloxera era (1880–89), little wine was used up in this manner.   The production of wine alcohol dropped 90 percent from the average of the previous decade, and an all-time low of only 19,513 hectolitres was reached in 1886.[41]   However, with the return of normal conditions, the practice of distilling was resumed to a certain extent.   But when abundant harvests became commonplace in 1900–1907, it was noted that less than half as much wine was being distilled as during the 1870–79 period.

The suppression in 1900 of the ancient *privilège des bouilleurs de cru,* and other laws passed in 1903 to increase the government's control over the production of alcohol, concentrated attention on this problem.[42]   It was argued that the *privilège* had encouraged the small proprietor to "burn off" his excess or bad wine in the still.   With the revocation of the *privilège* the winegrowers who were only incidentally distillers came under the same laws and tax rates as the commercial distillers (*bouilleurs de profession*).   These laws included a complicated system of inspection by government agents which, along with taxes, worked a disproportionate hardship on the small proprietor.   Thus it was pointed out that the suspension of the *privilège* made it hard for the winegrower to distill just when such a brake on wine production was badly needed.   Although this argument did not resolve the "alcohol question," it finally carried the day, and in 1906 the *privilège* was restored as a relief measure for the winegrowers.[43]

A look at alcohol statistics will show, however, that the argument over the *privilège* was peripheral to the main problem, the competition of beet alcohol.[44]   The latter product had gained the field during the phylloxera, and its production increased in the years that followed.   Moreover, the development of a commercial distilling industry in the North during the same period, combined with the abandonment of small distilling equipment and practices among the winegrowers, tended to cut further into the production of wine alcohol.[45]

By the period 1900–1907, there was no longer any question of wine alcohol competing on even terms with the technology and cheaper raw materials (grain and beets) used in the North. Production of wine alcohol had so fallen that it accounted for only 7.5 percent of all alcohol produced during the latter period, whereas it had represented 26.6 percent of total alcohol production from 1870 through 1879. This drop unquestionably aggravated the problem of overproduction. It meant that 3,000,000 hectolitres of wine which in 1870–79 would have been shunted to countryside stills were being placed on the market each year. If this figure is added to the excess of imports over exports during 1900–1907, the dimensions of the overproduction problem begin to appear formidable.

TABLE 9. ALCOHOL PRODUCTION IN FRANCE, 1870–1907
(Periodic yearly averages, in hectolitres)

Period	Alcohol Distilled from Wine	Alcohol Distilled from Beets	Taxed Consumption of Alcoholic Beverages	Total Alcohol Produced
1870–79	399,916	309,531	1,073,000	1,535,930
1880–89	30,874	664,900	1,446,800	1,944,524
1890–99	74,861	816,808	1,657,700	2,289,896
1900–1907	180,237	904,910	1,415,000	2,389,807

Source: Ministère des finances, *Bulletin de statistique et de législation comparée*, July, 1913, pp. 34–35.

THE WAR OF THE BEET AND THE GRAPE

The winegrowers did not accept the northern invasion of the alcohol market passively. Indeed, the period from 1900 to 1907 was referred to in the Chamber of Deputies as the "war of the beet and the grape." Thus the Midi deputies were especially eager to see in the suppression of the *privilège des bouilleurs de cru* in 1900 a maneuver directed against the southern winegrowers by the beet alcohol interests of the North.[46] Those interests for their part complained that alcohol alone carried the burden of the tax reductions accorded wine. And representatives of both groups engaged in lively exchanges as to who enjoyed the most government protection.[47]

The North was right about the burden carried by alcohol, but it should be pointed out that this burden was also shared by wine alcohol. This was not lost on the Midi. In 1902 a bill was proposed to tax "natural" alcohols (i.e., wine and fruit alcohols) at a lower rate than "industrial" alcohols (i.e., beet, grain, and other vegetable alcohols) on the basis that the former were more "hygienic" than the latter.[48] The government stood firm against losing any more revenue for the sake of the winegrowers, but the proposal resulted in a law which required industrial-alcohol transactions to be accompanied with a yellow voucher while those of natural alcohol were to carry a white one.[49]

More important were efforts, again inspired by the Midi, to develop alcohol as a motor fuel with the intention of diverting beet alcohol to purely industrial uses, leaving wine alcohol in a dominant position on the beverage market. From 1900 on, numerous experiments with alcohol motor fuels were carried out, and in 1907 an extra-parliamentary commission reported on them in a hopeful vein. But with the end of the wine crisis the question of an alcohol motor fuel was abruptly dropped.[50] The best that was accomplished in the way of diverting northern alcohol to industrial uses was a reduction in the special tax levied when alcohol was denatured (3 francs the hectolitre to 35 centimes the hectolitre).[51] The "war" did nothing to alleviate the wine crisis, and the beet alcohol distillers continued to dispose of a large part of their production in the form of beverage alcohol, especially to the lower-paid urban industrial workers.[52] As will be seen in a later chapter, however, the ideas and regional antagonisms developed during this period were subsequently to play an important part in the relations of the government with the winegrowers.

OVERPRODUCTION AND FRAUD

During the crisis of 1900–1907 it was frequently recalled that the record harvest in 1875 of over 83 million hectolitres of wine had brought respectable prices. This in spite of the fact that it had been preceded the year before by an abundant harvest which had totaled more than 60 million hectolitres. Such a statement, of course, ignored the changes in volume of the export, import, and distilling of wines that had occurred since then. If, as in Table 10, we make adjustments for exports, imports, and distilling, it will be seen that while from 1870–79 to 1900–1907 production had increased by less than one percent, the total of wine available for the market (in face of a population growth of only 5 percent) had increased by approximately 20 percent.

TABLE 10. COMPARISON OF TOTAL WINE AVAILABLE IN FRANCE
AFTER EXPORTS, IMPORTS, AND DISTILLATION, 1870–1907
(*Periodic yearly averages, in hectolitres*)

Period	Production	Exports	Imports	Distillation	Total Wine Available for Domestic Market
1870–79	54,670,800	3,283,500	824,383	4,998,300	47,212,783
1900–1907	55,179,200	2,053,750	5,299,750	2,252,900	56,172,300

Sources: *Annuaire statistique; Bulletin de statistique et de législation comparée,* July, 1913, pp. 34–35.

The above comparison, however, overlooks the amount of fraudulently produced wine. In an earlier chapter we saw the beginnings of fraud and the dimensions it had already assumed by 1903. Under the continuing pressure of the crisis further revelations of its extent were brought to light. Thus, in 1905, Gaston Doumergue was able to say in the Chamber of Deputies that 20 million hectolitres of wine made with sugar and water were circulating in France.[53] And in a report delivered by the Commission des Boissons to the Chamber the same year, it was estimated that ten to twelve million hectolitres of 10° sugar wine were actually on the market.[54] Also in 1905, the municipal laboratory of Paris found that out of 617 samples of wine tested at random in various warehouses, only 117 had neither been doctored nor adulterated.[55] In 1907, the year of a very abundant harvest when there should have been less excuse for fraud, the Ministry of Finance estimated the production of fraudulent wine to be in excess of 6,500,000 hectolitres —and this may be considered a conservative estimate.[56]

But not all fraud was carried out on the production level. Parisians, for example, were amazed to learn that in 1903 they had each consumed only 185 litres of wine, while the suburbs, with fewer restaurants and wine shops and a much smaller working-class population, had consumed an average of 354 litres per inhabitant.[57]

Since the comparison was based on *octroi* receipts,[58] it was suggested that the difference was more than made up by fraudulent wine manufactured in the city proper.

An earlier estimate made in 1900 would seem to bear out this suggestion. Then, according to the *Revue de viticulture,* two million hectolitres of fraudulent wine were manufactured right in Paris, depriving the city and state of some forty million francs revenue.[59] These figures may have been exceptional due to the needs of the Exposition of 1900—and estimates for other cities are not available. But if it is realized that there were over 450,000 wine shops in France during this period, and that if each proprietor added only five litres of water a day to his stock, it meant that at the end of a year an additional eight million hectolitres of wine had been dumped on the market at the retail level only.[60]

If this figure seems large, it may be pointed out that watering was an easy course for the retailer to follow. Most wine sold on the retail level was drawn off from bulk containers by the customer; and by a law of December 29, 1900, the wine shops were specifically exempted from inspection by government agents.

Fraud then, in its dimensions, although they could not be definitely established, would seem to have greatly exceeded the amount of extra wine made available for the market by increases in imports and decreases in exports and distilling. Thus a consensus held it chiefly responsible for the depressed prices of the 1900–1907 period, and it was towards stamping it out that the first large-scale intervention by the government in the affairs of the winegrowers was directed.

4. *THE GOVERNMENT AND THE CRISIS OF 1900–1907*

The lowering of the sugar tax for the winegrowers in 1884 and the regulations of 1885 gave a dizzy boost to the manufacture of sugar wine. It is not an exaggeration to say that they were the seed from which the fraud problem grew. It would be unfair, however, to imply total government responsibility for this development. Actually, legislators were not long in recognizing the problem the lowered sugar tax had created. As early as 1889 the famous *Loi Griffe* was passed, which superseded existing legislation affecting the manufacture of wine.[1]

This law went to considerable lengths to define "wine" as the product of the natural fermentation of unpreserved grapes, and it required all other wine products to be labeled accordingly. Thus, presumably sugar wine and other artificial wines would no longer be sold as real wine; and to avoid confusion on this point, the law forbade the mixing of these products with naturally fermented wine.

Obviously these regulations did not prevent the manufacture of sugar wine itself; such a measure was not even desired at the time. But the *Loi Griffe* was the first official recognition of the fraud problem, and it was the first of many steps by which the government tried to keep one jump ahead of the *fraudeurs,* while pleasing the entire wine industry with its sometimes contradictory requirements. This was not an easy task, nor was it always a successful one.

THE DEVELOPMENT OF ANTI-FRAUD LEGISLATION

Some of the difficulties of the policy described above became apparent with the first legislation to follow the *Loi Griffe*. A law passed in 1894 forbidding the sale of watered wine aroused unexpected opposition.[2] It meant that the wine shops would have to be inspected by government agents, and, according to Gide, these were the "sacred temples" of Parisian and other urban deputies.[3] As a result, in 1900 a special law exempted these numerous outlets from inspection for fraud, although the law of 1894 presumably remained in force.[4]

Attempts to control sugar wine met with the same type of difficulty. In 1891, at the insistence of the Midi deputies, the Chamber had passed a law which made all sugar requisitions under the winegrowers' reduced tax rate a matter of public record, "in order to facilitate researches by interested parties."[5]

This sort of control proved ephemeral, however, and a new type of regulation was tried in 1897. Again at the insistence of the Midi, a law was passed which forbade the sale of sugar wine, but said nothing about its manufacture.[6] This seeming anomaly was a concession to the small growers. They too had their "sacred temple" and would have bitterly opposed any tampering with their right to make tax-free "second wines" for family consumption.

In 1900 the ineffectiveness of all the foregoing legislation was admitted. And now the Midi deputies proposed that the lower tax be abandoned in October to check the use of sugar, since "existing regulations were not being carried out."[7] The result was the law of December 29, 1900, which kept the reduced rate of 24 francs per 100 kilograms on sugar earmarked for use in wine made by the growers for their own consumption, but applied the higher rate to all other sugars.[8]

Whatever effect the new law might have had was prevented by domestic legislation complementing the Brussels Sugar Agreement of 1902. Under this agreement the internal tax on all sugar was lowered from 60 to 25 francs the 100 kilograms.[9] The effect of the agreement on the fraud situation has already been noted. It was from this time on that the sugar question and the problem of fraud aroused national interest and received their fair share of attention in the Chamber.

Parliamentary committees were formed and laws and regulations followed rapidly,[10] while in August, 1905, and June, 1907, comprehensive laws were passed which treated the whole question of fraud in terms of the wine industry's situation.[11]

The trend with these last two laws was towards tighter control of sugar, increasing limitation on the amount of family wine that could be made, and closer surveillance of the quantity of wine produced.   A comparison of the main provisions of the laws shows this trend and indicates how far the government was willing to go in controlling sugar and helping the winegrower.   Some of the regulations, notably those affecting the circulation of sugar, were considered excessive in non-wine-producing areas.

Law of August 6, 1905

1. Use of sugar limited to the harvest period.

2. Sugar for use in making wine for family consumption only limited to 40 kilograms per member of the family and servant attached to the household.   (Law of December 29, 1900.)

3. Second wines permitted to be made but not sold.

4. Sugar for use in winemaking not subject to any detax or surtax.

5. All sales or shipments of sugar over 50 kilograms to someone not in the sugar business or in an industry that uses it must be accompanied by a permit.

Law of June 29, 1907

1. Provisions of the law of 1905 in force.

2. Sugar for use in making family wine limited to 20 kilograms per member of the family and servant attached to the household, or 20 kilograms for every 3 hectolitres produced—not to exceed a total of 200 kilograms per property.

3. Second wines limited to 40 hectolitres per property.

4. Sugar for use in winemaking subject to a surtax of 40 francs per 100 kilograms.

5. All sales or shipments of sugar over 25 kilograms . . . must

be accompanied by a permit. Any sugar transaction involving more than 25 kilograms must be recorded by the seller. Anyone having in his possession wine for sale or possessing dried grapes, rapes, musts, or lees and having more than 25 kilograms of sugar in his possession must have a permit.

6. Winegrowers and shippers after each harvest must declare to the mayor of their community: (a) the area of their producing vineyards; (b) total wine produced plus stocks from preceding years in their cellars; (c) volume or weight of harvested grapes shipped or received; (d) quantity of musts (unfermented wine) shipped or received.

These regulations evidently did not go far enough; June, 1907, was a time of desperate measures, and the Midi deputies clamored for stricter controls. After the law of June 29, 1907, had been drafted, they proposed the following amendments: [12]

(1) The use of sugar in wine-making to be forbidden, except for strictly controlled quantities in making champagne; (2) All manufacture of sugar wine to be forbidden; (3) The sale, shipping, or placing on sale of any adulterated wine or wine other than natural wine to be forbidden; (4) All sales or shipments of sugar over 15 kilograms to be accompanied by a permit.

Some of these propositions were all but impossible to enforce. For example, other wine-producing areas, notably Burgundy, although they had supported previous anti-sugar legislation, needed certain amounts of sugar in their wines.[13] And the sugar industry was bound to object to a further extension of controls that would have applied equally to non-wine-producing areas.

It would be a mistake, however, to dismiss these amendments as a selfish promoting of Midi interests. After all, they implied an ending of the peasant grower's traditional right to make second wines—a move that would have had more repercussions in the Midi than elsewhere. Rather, the proposed legislation, which was ultimately defeated, reflected a feeling of hopelessness about controlling fraud, short of forbidding every practice that encouraged it, no matter how indirectly.

THE ENFORCEMENT OF ANTI-FRAUD LEGISLATION

The problems mentioned in the preceding paragraphs were aggravated by the enforcement of anti-fraud legislation. As already noted, early legislation, particularly in the matter of sugar, was concerned almost entirely with taxes. According to legal opinion, the first truly penal and preventive law dealing with fraud was the law of August 6, 1905.[14] Earlier laws sought to effect control through separating the artificial products from real wine and submitting them to higher duties, as in the law of April 6, 1897, which placed all artificial wines under the heavy alcohol-tax rate.

Thus the enforcement of anti-fraud legislation became, for the most part, the responsibility of the Ministry of Finance and its Administration des Contributions Indirectes. With them the first emphasis was on the collection of revenue; if incidentally they discovered fraud, then they could take samples and proceed by complicated steps to bring the criminal to justice. This arrangement had some unusual results.

For example, the Court of Nancy, trying a case in November of 1903 in which watered wine had been sold, declared that watered wine was not wine (*Loi Griffe*), but an alcoholic dilution and therefore taxable as alcohol.[15] Thus a tax instead of a fine was imposed as a penalty for a practice presumably forbidden by the law of July 24, 1894. The opinion of the court, however, is not too difficult to understand. Responsibility for watering was hard to prove when a bottle or cask passed through the hands of one or more middlemen; and so if the Treasury was the plaintiff, why not let it benefit directly from the sentence imposed?

At all events, incidents like the above contributed to the attitude that as long as taxes were paid, everything was permissible. And later in 1905 and 1907, when shipping permits and declarations supplemented taxes as a method of control, the same attitude prevailed: "As long as your papers are in order, the *agents du fisc* won't bother you too much." [16]

Further difficulties came from the noncooperation, as well as the indifference, of local officials. In 1900 the Commission sur la

Reforme des Boissons, reporting to the Chamber, spoke of the difficulty of enforcing the laws "when they clash with local interests." [17] And in 1905, the municipal laboratory of Paris offered a classic example of noncooperation when called in on a fraud case.[18]

But attitudes and lack of cooperation notwithstanding, the difficulties described in the preceding paragraphs might not have existed had there been agencies powerful enough to carry through enforcement from beginning to end. A law of August 1, 1905, seemed to offer hope along these lines.[19] It made possible the appointment of special agents to investigate fraud, thus taking the load off the Ministry of Finance and removing the problem of fraud from its tax-biased jurisdiction.

Unfortunately the regulations interpreting the law transferred the new powers to police commissioners, commissioners of the various special police, agents of other bureaus, and local officials. To all of these, their new duties were of secondary importance and in most cases were a burden. However, the law permitted the designation of special agents by the departments and communes subject to approval by the local prefects. But these agents were limited to action within their department or commune, and operated under all the disadvantages of local attachments.

It can be believed that this last feature was proposed less as a solution than as an attempt to transfer initiative and responsibility for fighting fraud to the departments and communes. The government may have become weary in the fight, and among other things it had always been harassed by a lack of funds for the purpose. At all events, the departments and communes did not accept the challenge, and when M. Ruau, the Minister of Agriculture, asked for a budget of 1,000,000 francs to implement the new anti-fraud law of June 29, 1907, he was voted only 275,000 francs.[20]

Meanwhile, winegrowers continued to make fraudulent wine even while denouncing the practice most strongly. It may have been a question of morality; but if one's neighbor was making more money by dumping sugar in his wine, who wanted to be taken for a fool? Clearly, radical solutions were needed in 1907, and they were not to be found in laws and regulations.

THE C. G. V.

It was the spirit of collective action, inspired by the uprisings of 1907 in the Midi, that supplied the answer. "If no one will promote the winegrowers' interests—then let them defend themselves," the *Journal d'agriculture pratique* had written.[21] And the Midi growers accepted this challenge—for all their traditionally fractious and anti-collective ways.

As early as June 20, 1907, when violence was still raging, the Committee of Argelliers the first of many rebel "committees" which sprang up in the winegrowing centers to direct the revolt, declared that "the first and immediate aim of all its efforts was to establish a Confédération Générale des Vignerons du Midi on solid, legal, and durable bases." [22] And in September, 1907, the new organization came into being, grouping in its membership the local *syndicats* which had in many instances provided the cadres of the committees.

But the new organization, starting its existence so soon after the uprisings, reflected none of the aimlessness of the fighting or the earlier demonstrations. The statutes of the member syndicates left no doubt as to the principal aims of the Confédération. They were stated as follows:

1. *General objectives:* Everything connected with the repression of fraud in wine-making in France, Algeria, and the colonies, and with the study and defense of the viticultural, agricultural, economic, and social interests of its members.

2. *Special objectives:* (a) To seek out frauds and to initiate or provoke any judicial proceedings they may give rise to; (b) to examine and propose all legislative or other reforms, and all economic measures relative thereto, to support them before the public authorities, and to follow up their application.[23]

In spite of these announced aims, there was some understandable suspicion that the C.G.V., as it came to be called, was really organized to continue resistance against the government.[24] Also there were some incidents involving forcible coercion of nonmembers during the early days.[25] But these inauspicious beginnings belonged to the times and uprisings just past. The new organization went to work honestly, swiftly, and with high motivation.

Taking advantage of the provisions of the law of August 1, 1905, the Syndicate of Béziers-St. Pons sent special agents into the field to seek out fraud almost immediately after calm was restored in 1907. And already in the second issue of the C.G.V. weekly, *Vendémiaire,* published on December 1 of that year, there was the following relevant description of their activities:

In view of the urgency of the situation these agents left without being sworn in or approved by the Ministries of Finance or Agriculture. . . .

These agents simply carried a letter from the President of the Syndicate accrediting them to the agents of the government. It was the first time that an agricultural organization had tried such an experiment, and it was necessary in the interests of the work undertaken by the Confederation that it be carried out with prudence, in order to prove to the government, to reliable commerce, to viticulture, and to public opinion that our legitimate action could defend winegrowing interests without disturbing the countryside.[26]

The agents were handicapped by limitations imposed on the projected special departmental and commercial agents by the law of August 1, 1905.[27] And if they wished to operate outside these limits they were subject to irksome, or at the least cumbersome, control by local prefects. So from the beginning the C.G.V. agitated to have its agents commissioned directly by the Ministry of Agriculture. This precedent-making request involved legal and organizational complications as well as some grudging suspicion on the part of the government.[28] However, the good faith or persistence of the C.G.V. carried the day, and in 1912 its agents received their commissions directly from Paris.[29] From that time on, their numbers have grown, as has the importance of their work.

Until 1912, although their scope of activity was more limited, they still achieved impressive results, as Table 11 shows.

However, a mere record of investigations and condemnations will not explain the importance of the C.G.V. in the years following the crisis. The example it set, the demands it made on its members, and most of all, the broad base of its membership all contributed to its effectiveness. From this point of view its organization is worth a closer look.

Whereas the Palazy Cartel, the only noteworthy attempt at

TABLE 11. ACTIVITY OF C.G.V. AGENTS, 1907–12

Year	Agents	Investigations of Fraud	Trials	Convictions
1907–8	12	867	142	67
1908–9	14	1225	190	120
1909–10	21	1659	337	263
1910–11	27	2047	446	358
1911–12	30	3042	777	601

Source: Rapport de M. Marius Cathala au Congrès viticole de Narbonne, *Vigneron de Sud-Est,* January, 1913; Rapport de M. Schmitt Donnadieu au Congrès viticole de Béziers, *C.G.V.,* November, 1913. Quoted in Meyrueis, *De la défense des intérêts de la viticulture méridionale,* pp. 92–93.

cooperation before the C.G.V., looked to the proprietors for its membership, the C.G.V. went beyond these limits and united proprietors, tenants, laborers, and the different types of dealers in a unique and strong organization. Also, it derived important financial strength from a sliding assessment which depended on a member's production or sales. This system proved much more effective than the dues and periodic assessments of the syndicates, and if it brought plural voting with it, the new arrangement did not smother the small producer or laborer.[30]

The C.G.V. also gained strength by moral pressure on its members. Each new member had to swear to sell only natural wine, and producers could, if they wished, submit to extra requirements and severe inspections. The latter entitled them to use the organization's "label" on their bottles—a practice that has since spread in one form or another to most French wine-producing areas.

Through these and other measures the C.G.V. grew rapidly: in 1912, only five years after its founding, it had a membership of 20,000, representing 425 winegrowing communes.[31] A measure of its strength may be guessed from the fact that in the same year it spent 412,000 francs in carrying out its campaign against fraud,[32] while the government budget for the repression of frauds of all kinds in 1912 was 1,143,000 francs.[33]

Another measure of the C.G.V.'s effectiveness may be gauged from the number of similar organizations that sprang up in other wine-producing areas. In 1909 the Confédération des Vignerons du Sud-Est was formed to include the remaining departments of Provence. Then in rapid order came the Confédération des Associations Viticoles de Bourgogne, the Fédération des Syndicats de la Champagne Viticole, the Ligue des Viticulteurs de la Gironde, and finally, with the leadership of the C.G.V., the Fédération des Associations Viticoles Régionales de France was founded on February 18, 1913.

END OF THE CRISIS: SUMMARY AND CONCLUSIONS

Increasing enforcement of anti-fraud laws and the healthy influence of the new winegrowers' associations were undoubtedly major forces behind the price rise that took place after 1907. It is difficult to explain the suddenly improved position of Midi wine prices in relation to the national average in any other terms. It is also true that the rise was helped in 1910 by a very light nationwide harvest of only 28,530,000 hectolitres. But even allowing for an extended shortage in the years following, there still appears to

TABLE 12.   WINE PRODUCTION AND PRICES AT THE PRODUCTION
LEVEL, 1900–1913

Year	Production (in hundreds of hectolitres)	Average Price per Hectolitre in France (in francs)	Average Price per Hectolitre in the Midi Departments [a] (in francs)
1900	67,353	19	7
1901	57,964	16	5
1902	39,884	21	10
1903	35,402	27	24
1904	66,017	19	6
1905	56,666	15	6
1906	52,079	18	6
1907	66,070	17	9
1908	60,545	16	12
1909	54,446	18	15
1910	28,530	39	37
1911	44,886	30	26
1912	59,384	30	25
1913	44,172	34	28

[a] Departments of Aude, Gard, Hérault, and Pyrénées-Orientales.

Source: *Annuaire statistique.*

be a healthier relationship between production and prices after 1910 than existed during the crisis years.

In 1914 a bumper harvest of 59,850,000 hectolitres should have provided an excellent test for this hypothesis, but an almost total lack of transportation to move the crop drove the average price of wine down to 16 francs the hectolitre. During the rest of the war years manpower shortages, requisitions for the army, controls and other measures so distorted the price and production picture that it is useless to carry price comparisons any further than 1913.

At all events, it is possible to say that on the eve of World War I, the wine industry appeared to be enjoying another period of prosperity.[34] There is dramatic significance in the fact that when the four departments of Aude, Gard, Hérault, and Pyrénées-Orientales produced a record harvest of 26,506,000 hectolitres in 1912 (out of a large national total of 59,400,000 hectolitres), the average price they received was a generous 25 francs the hectolitre. As Caziot wrote, "It was no longer only a river of wine that flowed in the Midi, but a river of gold." [35]

For such a fortunate state of affairs the growers felt themselves largely responsible. To the extent that fraud had been the cause of their immediate troubles, this view was probably correct. But it tended to obscure other problems such as the continuing possibility of overproduction. Important as the victory over fraud was, it did not of itself insure a healthy wine industry.

Indeed, the very suddenness of the new prosperity only emphasized the patternless course of "boom and bust" that had characterized the industry's previous fifty years. The only consistent development during this period was the government's increasing preoccupation with the demands of the growers. This turn of events led an authority like Augé-Laribé to describe the wine industry as "the spoiled child" of French agricultural legislation, and the description remains valid.[36]

True, in the actual fight against the phylloxera the initiative was almost entirely up to the growers. But as we have seen, the government was no less willing to assist them with legislation. Timidity and inexperience counteracted much of what was proposed, but there were positive measures like subsidies and tax abatements for the growers and lowered duties on foreign wine for the trade. Also for both there was the famous reduced tax rate on sugar used for winemaking in 1884.

Then as production returned to normal, the government obligingly changed its legislation. New tariffs were raised against foreign wines,[37] and new laws and taxes sought to limit the use of sugar in the wine vats. Meanwhile production climbed to the levels of 1900–1907. But agriculture had just achieved "equality" with industry under a protection that was to bring both new yields and prosperity.[38] It is not likely there was much talk about overproduction of wine at the Ministry of Agriculture.

Instead, when the price crisis suddenly broke out in 1900, the government was quick to respond with emergency legislation like the abolition of the *octroi* duties and other measures. Later, as we have seen, laws of increasing scope and cumbersomeness attempted to legislate fraud out of existence. If, as one critic puts it, these laws were "incoherent and inefficient," [39] the government can take only the smallest part of the blame. From the phylloxera years on, legislation was tailored to the requirements of the growers, even if it did not completely satisfy them.

There were limits beyond which the government could not go, however. Colonial assimilation was part of the same system of national economics [40] that watched over the wine industry, and the Algerian vineyards were a *fait accompli*. Beet sugar was the object of special treatment both before and after the question of using sugar in wine became prominent. And no matter how it affected the wine industry, there was not much the government could do after the Brussels Conference of 1902 except to find domestic outlets for the sugar production it had encouraged for so long with export bounties. Alcohol too, as we have seen, was linked with the beet and also with the question of distilling. Its problem was one of taxation—after 1900 one of the heaviest excise taxes on the books. But before this tax could be considered just, the winegrowers' right to tax-free distilling had to go.

These clashes of interests brought on quarrels; the North and the South fought like children over "the beet and the grape." And the analogy is a good one. During this period the government can be compared to a father trying to please two difficult and selfish children without slighting either of them.

The method collapsed, however, before the impact of the continuing wine crisis. Sugar saw itself penalized by excessive regulations, and when in 1906 the controversial *privilège des bouilleurs de cru* was restored, when its effectiveness was little more than a gesture to the winegrowers, alcohol taxes were not lowered. At this point it may be said that the wine industry was *the* spoiled child.

In the years that followed it remained a spoiled child, but the parent became somewhat less indulgent. The reason was overproduction. Whereas in the face of widespread fraud overabundant harvests may be said to have only partly contributed to the troubles of 1900–1907, overproduction emerged as an all-important and chronic condition after World War I. This, as will be seen in later chapters, caused an increase in the relations between the government and the winegrowers. First, however, it should be useful to note the unusual aspects of this relationship brought on by World War I.

5. THE GOVERNMENT AND THE WINE INDUSTRY DURING WORLD WAR I

When World War I broke out French agriculture, as Augé-Laribé has put it, was "as ill prepared as possible for the shock and test of war."

The French idea of war, a purely defensive one where the whole nation would answer the call to arms to resist the invader, did not even allow for the maintenance of regular agricultural production. Not a single plan for agricultural mobilization, for maintaining or increasing cultivation, had been studied.[1]

As a consequence the winegrowers, along with the rest of the agricultural economy, found their production seriously disorganized by the requirements of military mobilization. Transportation became unavailable to them, vineyard laborers were called to the colors, and during the first years of the war army wine requisitions were often summary and drastic. The government worked hard to ease these difficulties but was often credited by the growers with creating new ones in their place. It was perhaps too much to hope that the growers could be happy with the many and various authorities with which they had to deal. On the other hand wine, in spite of its position in the French diet, escaped some of the controls imposed on other basic foodstuffs. It also enjoyed not a little distinction as a national morale builder.

EFFECTS OF MOBILIZATION: TRANSPORTATION

On August 2, 1914, by order of the Ministry of War, the entire French railway system was requisitioned and placed under military control. Article 2 of the order "suspended until further notice all commercial transportation whether of passengers or goods." [2] This provision worked a particular hardship on the winegrowers. Within the month they had begun the harvest of what turned out to be an exceedingly abundant crop (59,856,779 hectolitres). With scant prospect of this large quantity being moved to the market, prices at the production level took an immediate plunge, reaching an average of 6 francs the hectolitre for August.[3]

The situation was possibly eased by the resumption of commercial carrying on a very limited scale later in the fall of 1914.[4] And life was certainly restored to the wine market by military requisitions in the spring of 1915.[5] The latter, however, involved the requisition of most of the tank cars belonging to the wholesale wine trade, thus complicating the transportation problem for the industry as a whole.[6] Meanwhile, although an interministerial order of March 31, 1915, allowed for the nearly complete return of commercial carrying on railways in the zone of the interior, winegrowers found the scramble for shipping space difficult enough to ask the government for help.

It came in the form of "special recommendations" to the railway authorities that shipments of wine be given a month of priority during the 1916 harvest period.[7] Measures such as this were made unnecessary, however, by an order of February 9, 1917, signed by the Ministers of War and Public Works, which fixed a schedule of priorities for the conveyance of nonmilitary goods by rail. The order established three categories of goods according to the urgency of their shipment. Essential foodstuffs were included in the first category, but wine was ranked last in the second category after such products as farm animals, oils, soaps, preserves, and canned goods. Since the third category enjoyed no priorities and was made up of all products not included in the other two, wine was literally at the bottom of the list as far as shipping priorities were concerned.

Although there was no sign that the new plan might not prove more advantageous to the winegrowers than the lack of any planning at all, there were immediate protests. The C.G.V., in the forefront as usual, called wine an essential foodstuff "as necessary for the civilian population as the army," and demanded that it be placed in the first category ahead of goods of "lesser utility." [8] The government, however, stood firm. Meanwhile it was taking other steps to assure the transporation of the civilian wine supply.

On January 17, 1917, a reserve depot of civilian tank cars was set up at Montpellier in the shadow of the larger one requisitioned by the army at the beginning of the war. Ineffectual at first because it depended on the voluntary cooperation of the car owners, the new depot rapidly grew in importance with the sweeping changes in the Food Supply Service that were carried out by the Clemenceau ministry.

This development was helped by a decree of December 5, 1917, which ordered the registry of all tank cars not requisitioned by the army and provided for their requisition by the government as needed for purposes of civilian supply. Another decree (March 26, 1918) organized a Tank-Car Service under the Food Ministry to carry out and coordinate the latter activities. And finally a decree of December 6, 1918, provided for an enlarged depot of 600 tank cars under control of the Ministry but managed by a committee of car owners.

Pierre Pinot, in his study of civilian food supply during the war, claims the depot rendered "without a doubt the most useful service in assuring the regular transport of wine to the chief consumption centers." [9] But almost at the same time as the steps described above were being taken, the Midi deputies were complaining about the "seriousness of the wine transportation crisis," and demanding an accounting from the government. [10] None was forthcoming, and periodic complaints about transportation difficulties continued until the end of the war and after. Meanwhile, in 1918 the army continued to requisition tank cars to carry increasing quantities of wine to the troops, thus aggravating the situation. And plans to join representatives of the growers and the trade with the military in the direction of the army's tank-car operations did little to satisfy the growers. [11]

The peak of government intervention in the matter of civilian wine transport was reached in 1919. Then Vilgrain, Minister of Food Supply, obtained five hundred freight cars which were assembled in special trains carrying wine exclusively. The Vilgrain trains, as they were called, offered lower freight rates and were dispatched with rapidity and efficiency.[12] But they were available only to those shippers who cooperated in the ministry's drive to reduce food prices. Shipments were made mostly to cooperatives and other organizations of a public nature including the famous Vilgrain shops. This probably accounts for the contradiction between the winegrowers' complaints and the vigorous transportation measures the government took in 1918 and 1919. The measures were primarily for the benefit of the consumer; to the grower they must have seemed in some degree to limit his chance of getting the most profitable price for his product.[13]

Without any detailed figures, however, it is difficult to assess the effects of the government's transportation policies on the wine industry in anything but a very general way. Marcel Peschaud in his study of the French railway system during the war gives the tonnage of commercial shipments by freight train as follows: [14]

| 1913 | 193,300,000 metric tons | 1916 | 116,000,000 metric tons |
| 1915 | 105,200,000 metric tons | 1917 | 122,200,000 metric tons |

Lacking a breakdown of the above into type of goods carried, Augé-Laribé goes on to suggest that shipments of agricultural products (which would include wine) suffered a proportionately greater decrease.[15] Still, considering the demands of military transportation which in some areas accounted for 70 percent of the total traffic, the record of commercial shipments is not a bad one. And it may be that the winegrowers received no more or less than fair treatment in the matter of transportation.

EFFECTS OF MOBILIZATION: PRODUCTION AND LABOR

In the vineyards as elsewhere mobilization made serious inroads on the labor supply. But the harvest of 1914 was everywhere gathered in what has been described as an explosion of patriotic

energy.[16]   Such an extraordinary effort, however, could not be
sustained on the day-to-day basis required for proper care of the
vines.   In 1915 wine production dropped to 20,400,893 hectolitres
—a figure lower than that of the worst phylloxera year and little
more than a third of the 1914 figure.   In the remaining war years
the lack of manpower, insecticides, and fertilizers took their toll,
and production remained considerably below prewar levels.

TABLE 13.   FRENCH WINE PRODUCTION AND YIELD DURING WORLD WAR I
(In hectolitres)

Year	Production	Yield per Hectare
1910–14, yearly average	47,366,000	30.4
1915	20,401,000	13.3
1916	36,017,000	32.7
1917	38,227,000	25.0
1918	44,985,000	29.9

Source: *Annuaire statistique.*

The first step taken by the government to relieve the agricultural labor shortage was the establishment of the Office de la Main-
d'oeuvre Agricole on March 15, 1915.   At first this organization
devoted most of its energies to directing workers from the shut-
down factories and refugees from the North to the different agricultural communities that asked for them.   At the same time immigration bureaus were set up at various points on the Italian and
Spanish frontiers to encourage agricultural labor from these countries to come to France.

The Office was really only a semi-official clearing house, however, and labor was voluntary.   Whereas over a million peasants
were mobilized in 1914, only 13,000 workers were placed on farms
in the month and a half after the Office opened.   During the first
ten months of 1916, the figure dropped to 4,726 and after that it
became negligible.[17]   By the end of 1916 surplus labor was all but
absorbed in the war factories and these in turn had begun to draw
some labor from the farms.[18]

In general, then, the program does not appear to have been a
success.   The unemployed workers did not make good peasants,
and the refugees from the North, although there were many agri-

culturists among them, were too miserable to be effective.[19]   The winegrowing regions in particular complained that this labor was inept and that the vineyards, because of the hard work involved, were the least favored by both groups.[20]   By 1916 the proportion of women and children working in the vineyards appears to have been higher than in other forms of agriculture.[21]   And in the same year the labor shortage in the Midi vineyards was critical enough so that the southern deputies asked for what would have been a separate agricultural labor bureau for the benefit of the winegrowers.[22]

In the matter of imported labor, chiefly from Spain, the winegrowing Midi also had special problems.   Although the recruitment of this labor was perhaps the most successful part of the program of the Office de la Main-d'oeuvre Agricole,[23] it appeared as something less than that to the winegrowers.   Whereas before the war Spanish laborers came freely and in large numbers to the vineyards, wartime regulations apparently made it more difficult to obtain them in spite of immigration bureaus, suspension of the passport requirement, and half-fares on the trains.[24]   After 1916 these measures tended to cause the Spaniards to by-pass the Midi in favor of the industrial regions of Grenoble, Saint-Étienne, Orléans, and Paris, where there were fairly large numbers of them at the end of the war.[25]

In 1917, this displacement assumed such proportions as to cause the Midi growers to fear for their crops.   As a result the southern deputies proposed a bill which demanded a better distribution of foreign labor and a "special effort" on the part of the government to save the harvest.[26]   But the government was not willing to control the foreign workers to this extent.   While assuring the winegrowers of its concern, it simply rested its case by pointing out the efforts that had been made to encourage Spanish labor to come to France.[27]

Long before 1917, however, the government had been concentrating its chief efforts in relieving the agricultural labor shortage by a system of military leaves, delays in induction, and the assignment of troops to agricultural work.   As early as October 24, 1914, fifteen-day agricultural leaves were given to men in the reserve depots. And on May 5, 1915, this privilege was extended to other classes of soldiers as well.

The program was hampered, however, by the reluctance of commanders to part with their troops. Moreover, the winegrowers appear to have been at a particular disadvantage for there were complaints that officers were interpreting the regulations which limited the leaves to "agriculturists" so as to exclude "viticulturists." [28] On the other hand, between September 5, 1915, and October 15, 1915, special leaves were granted to winegrowers stationed in the reserve depots or serving with the army in the zone of the interior. Detachments of troops were also promised to those departments where winegrowing was of "particular importance." [29]

Promise and performance turned out to be two different things, however. Only six thousand troops were regularly assigned to agricultural work in 1915. And the plan to detach troops for a day or a half day to lend a hand in the fields near their cantons was such a failure that in December of 1915 General Gallieni was led to remind commanders that "the interests of the country should be defended in the name of good sense and not fought in the name of military regulations." [30] The same year the famous *domaine* of Haut Brion in the Bordeaux region complained that all offers of military labor made by the prefecture of Gironde and accepted by the *domaine* did not produce a single soldier.[31]

In 1915 a system of delays in calling certain types of agriculturists to the colors was begun. But this time the winegrowers were specifically excluded, the privilege not being granted to them until March 6, 1917. Meanwhile, although special leaves for the wine harvest continued, there were complaints that the military authorities were not making allowance for the different harvest times in the various winegrowing regions. Soldiers had actually arrived in the Midi well after the harvest was finished.[32]

Again, however, as in the case of transportation, the disabilities under which the winegrowers labored were general to the wartime economy. Any program that attempted to bridge the gap left by the mobilization of over three million peasants was doomed to at least partial failure.[33] The relatively greater decrease in wine production compared to that of some other crops, and the complaints described above might suggest that the winegrowers could have enjoyed more favors from the government. But there were the special wine-harvest leaves which, it should be remembered, were independent of agricultural leaves. In theory, at least, the mobilized winegrowers were eligible for both. Any further favors might have raised the question of production priorities.

REQUISITIONS AND PRICES

In spite of a large measure of intervention in matters of transport and labor, the greatest area in which the government dealt directly with the winegrowers was in the matter of military requisitions of wine for the troops. As in so many other cases of supply, there was no advance planning. In the field and in barracks, unit commanders had bought or requisitioned wine locally, paying out of special mess funds as the occasion warranted, there being no regular ration. With the large-scale mobilization of 1914, this system broke down.

In autumn of that year the government appealed to the generosity of the growers to obtain wine for the armed forces. The Midi growers had already anticipated this appeal by gifts of wine to the military hospitals in their region—"even paying the taxes on this wine," it was patriotically observed.[34] Now that the appeal to generosity was official, the *Revue de viticulture* predicted, the response would be "great and widespread in the entire French vineyard." [35] The four large producing departments of the Midi quickly gave 200,-000 hectolitres, 100,000 being supplied by the department of Hérault alone.[36] And other regions followed the example of the Midi, giving smaller but important amounts.[37]

Without questioning the generosity of the growers, Augé-Laribé has noted they could not have served their interests better than by these actions.[38] The enthusiasm aroused by the *vin aux soldats* campaign, as it was described in the press, undoubtedly influenced Millerand, Minister of War, to adopt a daily wine ration for the troops early in 1915. Meanwhile, it should be remembered, the suspension of commercial transportation had virtually cut off the civilian market, and the price of wine received by the growers had tumbled to disastrous levels at the end of 1914. Table 14 shows the growing importance of the government's military requisitions; Table 15 reflects their influence on prices in 1914–15.

TABLE 14. MILITARY REQUISITIONS OF WINE IN FRANCE
DURING WORLD WAR I

Year	Departments of Hérault, Aude, Gard, Pyrénées-Orientales, and Gironde (in hectolitres)	Other Departments (in hectolitres)	Total (in hectolitres)	Approximate Percentage of Total Harvest
1914	1,771,000	367,000	2,138,000	3
1915	2,311,000	631,000	2,942,000	14
1916	3,211,000	898,000	4,109,000	11
1917	6,836,000	739,000	7,575,000	20
1918	4,600,000	——	4,600,000	10

Sources: *Annuaire statistique;* Augé-Laribé, *L'Agriculture pendant la guerre,* p. 126.

TABLE 15. MONTHLY VARIATION IN PRICES OF VIN ORDINAIRE AT THE
PRODUCTION LEVEL, 1914–15 (*In francs*)

Month	Price	Month	Price
Aug., 1914	6	May, 1915	12.50
Sept.	9	June	13
Oct.	10	July	26
Nov.	10	Aug.	35
Dec.	8	Sept.	40
Jan., 1915	7	Oct.	41
Feb.	8	Nov.	42.50
March	10	Dec.	51
April	13.50		

Source: *Commission centrale d'études relatives au coût de la vie,* quoted in March, *Mouvement des prix,* p. 52.

During the first half of 1915 the government's wine purchases were made both on the open market and through public bidding and private contracts.[39] With a large stock left over from 1914's bumper harvest, and prices as low as they had been during the worst years of the crisis earlier in the century, these methods worked to the government's advantage, at least from the point of view of economy. As prices started to climb under the influence of government buying, however, satisfactory contracts became more difficult to make. Speculation added its share to this rise, especially when in the spring, blights, caused by lack of care for the vines, promised a very short harvest. From May on, according to an official report, offers to sell to the government became "rare and insufficient" in spite of appeals to patriotism.[40]

Faced with these conditions, the government adopted more drastic methods. Wines were requisitioned while in transport. Whole cellars were requisitioned with a view to buying part of the stock later on at the price determined at the moment of requisition.[41] Meanwhile the grower was burdened with the cost of carrying the stock, for which he received no indemnity, not to mention the losses he suffered from the rapid rise in prices.[42]

In August, 1915, military supply services were reorganized and some changes in procedure were carried out. Wine could no longer be requisitioned in transport nor could whole cellars be tied up for eventual purchase. On the other hand, the supply services arranged for a general requisition. Each grower was to consider one sixth to one third of his crop under requisition, the eventual percentage to depend on the size of the national harvest. At the same time the price paid for requisitioned wine was to be fixed by decree on a schedule arranged by departments, taking into account quality, alcoholic strength, and production costs.

These last two measures appeared to rob the growers of whatever consolation they might have received from the first two. In December, 1915, with wine selling at 51 francs the hectolitre, an all-time high, the requisition price fixed in August averaged 35 francs. As a result there were many pleas for a return to regular purchases, and the complaints continued [43] while the price of wine on the commercial market rose in a dizzy spiral, reaching averages of 56 francs the hectolitre in 1916, 98 francs in 1917, and 102 francs in 1918.[44] Rightly or wrongly the spirit of 1914 seemed quite dead.

Actually the method of fixing requisition prices was not unrealistic. They were based on prices quoted in the commercial market, and the government was advised on them by a special commission on which sat representatives of the growers and the wine trade.[45] Moreover, the government appears to have been generous. Thus in 1916 the commission recommended a requisition price of

43.50 francs the hectolitre for Midi wines while the government, evidently under some pressure from the deputies of that region, settled on 45 francs. Better yet, in 1917, when the commission proposed a price of 55 francs, the government fixed it at 72.[46]

Other complaints of the wine growers were inspired by the inevitable red tape involved in dealing with the services of supply. Even after 1915 payments continued to be notoriously slow.[47] The storing of requisitioned wine still presented problems. The services of supply still had to learn many of the techniques required by their new role as one of the nation's largest distributors of wine.[48] And finally, procedures in the matter of adjudicating price disputes had to be worked out.

In keeping with a cardinal principle of human behavior, some of the loudest complaints were heard over the unequal burden of requisition carried by the chief wine-producing departments. In 1915 the government, moved by an uneconomical sense of fair play, tried to make the requisition general on every producer in every wine-growing department. But as a glance back at Table 14 will show, purchases came to be concentrated more and more in the Bordeaux vineyard and the four chief wine-producing departments of the Midi.

This trend was made official in 1918 when the requisition was lifted in all other departments but the latter four and Gironde. Producers of more than one hundred hectolitres were requisitioned the maximum one third. Producers of less than sixty hectolitres were exempted; in between, what was described as a "bizarre schedule" [49] fixed the remaining proportions to be requisitioned.

The heavier burden of requisition placed on the producers of more than one hundred hectolitres and other aspects of the military requisition system were most significant from the point of view of the history of the future relations between the government and the winegrowers. As will be seen in a subsequent chapter, when, in the 1930's, the government enacted production penalties through taxes on yields and compulsory distilling of part of the wine harvest, these penalties fell on the big producers to a degree disproportionate to their share of total production. Although requisitions in 1918 affected many more winegrowers than the production penalties of the 1930's, it might be said they saw the beginnings, at least, of a government bias in favor of small growers, especially if it is realized that in 1918 as in the later period approximately 90 percent of all growers accounting for one half of total production produced less than one hundred hectolitres each. Also, the mechanisms of the general requisition in 1915 suggest those which kept part of the harvest from the market as practiced after 1930. And the method of fixing prices for requisitioned wine was very similar to that used for controlling wine prices after World War II. Thus, to a certain extent, the system of military wine requisitions during World War I served as a laboratory for economic controls that would affect the wine industry in the future.

The concentration of requisitions in the four departments of the Midi and the Gironde was of course prompted by urgent economic and strategic considerations. But it can be imagined that the latter affected the grower of sixty hectolitres very little when his neighbor in the next department who produced one thousand hectolitres escaped all levies. For such a situation the government obviously had no remedy, but for the earlier complaints there was some relief.

Payment for requisitioned wine was to be made on delivery, and at the same time in 1916 it was decided that where delivery could not take place immediately, 5 percent of the payment price was to be advanced for storage and cellarage charges. As the cost of wine climbed, the government changed the basis of this charge and fixed it at 10 centimes the hectolitre. But this figure had to be twice raised and stood at 30 centimes in 1918.[50] In addition to advancing these charges the government, in imitation of commercial practice, began to advance up to 10 percent of the value of a future crop—a much appreciated measure.[51] An extraordinary concession was the advancing of two thirds of the government's offering price to growers who had found this price too low and were carrying their fight to the courts.

The latter cases created some special problems and were the cause of much interest and not a little excitement in the winegrowing regions. But it should first be pointed out that in comparison with the large numbers of growers the government traded with, the number of these cases was relatively low. Moreover, in the majority of cases the plaintiffs were small growers.[52] Still, in certain regions where price schedules failed properly to take into account local cost factors, there was often much litigation. In the Ardèche, for example, for 50,750 hectolitres of wine furnished there were 700 lawsuits.[53]

The special problems created by these and cases involving the requisition of other goods turned on the definition of the word "value" as mentioned in Article 2 of the law of July 3, 1877, which governed military requisitions. Was "value" represented by the current market price of goods or their cost to the producer? On February 3, 1915, in a case where Article 2 was brought to bear, the Court of Rennes decided in favor of the former interpretation.[54] But the government, moved by the inflated price of wine and other goods, carried its case to the Court of Cassation which, on March 6, 1917, adopted the second interpretation.[55]

The reaction of the winegrowers was one of dismay bordering on outrage. The question, however, cannot be separated from a consideration of the profits the growers were making on the commercial market. As one undersecretary of supply who had the boldness to lecture the growers pointed out, with the high prices received for the three quarters more or less of a harvest not requisitioned, they could recover whatever losses requisitioning imposed.[56] Discussion of losses, however, appears to be academic. As has already been pointed out, the government was generous in the matter of requisition prices. An official Senate investigation found it "too generous" and estimated the profit of the winegrowers on requisitioned wine alone at 200 to 300 million francs.[57] The investigation summarized its findings as follows.

In this way, as a result of wartime conditions, wine prices experienced a rise unknown until then, and the magnitude of which, as we have pointed out, is altogether out of proportion with the undeniable increase in cost of production. In inquiring into the real value of the wines requisitioned by the army from the harvests of 1914 and those of the following years and in comparing this value with commercial prices quoted for each of these harvests, we have been led to glimpse by approximation a figure of nearly 4 billion [francs] as representing the *super-profits* realized by viticulture, that is, profits originating from the state of war and superior in their magnitude to normal profits realized by this industry before the war.[58]

The above estimate may not be without a trace of polemic, but even such a stanch defender of agriculture against charges of wartime profiteering as Augé-Laribé estimates the winegrowers' profits as "very appreciable." [59] For further reference there are the various lists of price indexes which show the price of wine increasing between 300 to 400 percent during the war while the cost of labor approximately doubled and that of heavy farm tools and fertilizers increased three and five times respectively.[60] The use of the last two items, however, was very greatly reduced from what it had been before the war.

PRICE CONTROL AND TAXES

The rise in wine prices described in the preceding paragraphs was paralleled and even surpassed in a few cases by rises in the prices of other foodstuffs and food products. These developments naturally led the government to consider the problem of price controls. The only legislation affecting controls was an obsolete but unrepealed law of July 19–22, 1791, which allowed the mayors of communes to fix the prices of bread and meat. Consequently, late in 1915 the government presented a bill "for fixing the prices of commodities and substances necessary for alimentation, heating, and lighting." [61]

This bill was passed by the Chamber of Deputies with only a few amendments of an administrative nature. In the Senate, however, the whole principle of the general powers asked for by the government was opposed. As a result the government offered a compromise bill calling for the right to fix the prices of a specified list of commodities only. This bill became the law of April 20, 1916. The articles whose prices could be regulated were sugar, mineral oil and petroleum, potatoes, milk, margarine, food fats and oils, dried vegetables, fertilizers, copper sulfate, and sulfur—wine being conspicuously absent from the list.

Evidently wine figured in the compromise bill and the text adopted by the Chamber, but it was removed in the Senate and remained absent in the definitive text adopted by both houses.[62] The circumstances of this removal are not clear, but it was apparently effected without debate. At all events, almost immediately after the

passage of the law of April 20, a large group of deputies offered a
bill to bring wine under the controls of the new law.[63]   This was
followed later in the year by a resolution that called wine "almost as
necessary to the French as bread" and invited the government to fix
maximum prices for its sale.[64]   Neither measure was ever acted on.

Meanwhile, a law of October 30, 1916, extended price controls
to butter, cheese, and some types of cattle feed.   And in August of
1917 a press campaign to fix the price of wine got underway with
strong parliamentary support.   It was also suggested in the press
and parliament that the wine harvest be subject to a general requisition as was done for wheat.   Happily for the growers nothing came
of either of these two projects.

Under pressure, however, of increasing public dissatisfaction
with the high prices of wine, a special committee was set up on September 2, 1917, in the Ministry of Food Supply.   Its purpose was
"to study the situation" and "to see to the execution of all measures
suitable in facilitating civilian consumption during the next harvest
season and to protect it from the eventual excesses of speculation." [65]

Public opinion pinned its hopes for price controls of one sort or
another on this committee.   And controls seemed certain when on
February 10, 1918, an omnibus law gave the government the right
"to regulate or suspend by decree the production, manufacture, distribution, sale or offering for sale, storing or consumption of commodities used as food for man or animals." [66]   By the end of 1918 this
law had led to the decreeing of maximum prices (in preference to
the fixed prices of the 1916 legislation) for all essential foodstuffs
and a great many food products.   But not wine—almost miracu-
lously it seems, it escaped the wide embrace of the new law.   And
on May 7, 1918, a final attempt to bring wine under price controls
was as unsuccessful as the previous ones.[67]

In the matter of taxes the wine industry also seems to have with-
stood some of the pressure brought to bear against it.   In 1916, in
line with a general increase in indirect taxes, the government proposed that the *droits de circulation* on wine be increased from 1.50
francs to 5 francs the hectolitre.   To the winegrowing associations
the new rate appeared to "surpass somewhat fiscal and financial
possibilities," and they proposed a figure of 3 francs, which became

the new tax on January 1, 1917.[68] In February of 1918, however, this figure was raised to 5 francs. The winegrowers complained, but the measure was part of an increase in all *droits de circulation* to offset the suppression of *octroi* taxes in the towns.[69]

Of course, from the above it may be said that wine's tax position was not necessarily a privileged one. It would be harder, however, to say the same thing in respect to price controls. True, it may be argued that the prices of a few controlled items experienced proportionately greater rises than wine.[70] Also, wine was never in critically short supply. On the other hand wine did remain the great exemption in a far-reaching system of controls, and, in view of its price, this did affect public opinion and morale. Perhaps the best summary of the tax and price-control question as well as the requisition problem is found in the Senate investigation quoted earlier. "Taken as a whole," it concluded, "viticulture's interests were far from being impaired by the war." [71]

THE ANTI-ALCOHOL CAMPAIGN AND PROPAGANDA FOR WINE

One of the most immediate social consequences of the outbreak of war was the launching of an intensive drive against the consumption of alcoholic beverages.[72] As early as July 23, 1914, the Chamber of Deputies proposed the suppression of the license tax for liquor stores that sold only wine, beer, and cider. At the same time and during the whole mobilization period, local commanders on their own initiative took steps to cut down or prevent the use of strong drink by the troops.[73] In 1915 the campaign reached a crescendo of sorts with no less than seven laws passing through the Chamber to regulate "public drunkenness, consumption of alcohol, and policing of liquor-selling establishments." Complementing the legislative program, public citizens and groups passed high-sounding resolutions against alcohol, alcoholism, and related problems.

The Confédération Générale du Travail, for example, "urgently appealed . . . for the total suppression of alcoholic drinks." [74] The Ligue Nationale Contre l'Alcoolisme, in a more moderate vein, asked for the "definitive suppression" of the *privilège des bouilleurs de cru*.[75] This last demand, it is interesting to note, was signed by

Bergson, Clemenceau, Herriot, Lavisse, and the Marquis de Vogüé, who was the head of the Société des Agriculteurs de France.

Parallel to the anti-alcohol campaign—and it may be presumed not unrelated to it—was a campaign in favor of wine. "Wine is an antidote for alcoholism," *Le Temps* editorialized.[76] And the *Revue de viticulture* came up with the happy slogan, "Wine chases and replaces alcohol." [77] Much was made of the "energy-giving" and "anti-microbic" qualities of wine.[78] And as has been noted, furnishing wine to the troops became a prime concern of the press and the public.

The wine ration for the troops established at half a litre in 1915 was increased three times until it stood at a litre at the end of the war. A whole folklore sprung up about the soldier's wine. It was the subject of one of the most popular war songs, and in anecdote and cartoon it became impossible to picture the *poilu* without his *pinard*.[79] To a deputy back from the front wine was "the ray of sunshine" in the trenches, a source of "hope and strength" for the soldiers.[80]

Caught up, perhaps, in a mood of patriotic enthusiasm, the wine-growers did not at first notice any threat to their interests in the anti-alcohol campaign.[81] Its dangers became manifest, however, with the passage of the famous *Loi Ribot* in 1916 (law of June 30, 1916). In the book-length report that preceded the bill there was included a detailed study of alcoholism in France, which did not entirely spare wine, and a confession that the alcohol tax laws did not contribute to the "battle against alcoholism," but even favored "the extension of that terrible scourge." [82]

The new law set up a state monopoly of industrial alcohols which gave the alcoholic beverage market entirely to fruit alcohols. This measure, as will be shown later, was not against the interests of the winegrowers. But at the same time the new law raised the tax on beverage alcohols from 220 francs to 400 francs the hectolitre and suppressed the *privilège des bouilleurs de cru*.[83]

The government was prepared to go even further than this, however. On December 14, 1916, Briand, then premier, mounted the tribune of the Chamber of Deputies to ask for decree powers to bring about "the total suppression of the consumption of alcohol." [84] The powers were not given, and the request was only important as marking the high water mark of the anti-alcohol campaign.[85]   The success of the latter, moreover, was always extremely doubtful, but under its pressure the wine industry became almost hysterical about defending its interests.

Withholding the wine ration from sick soldiers, for example, became a matter of parliamentary concern at the instigation of deputies from the Midi.[86]   An even greater stir was occasioned when a general forbade wine to native colonial troops while permitting them beer.[87]   The C.G.V., in commenting on the incident, charged that the anti-alcohol campaign was deviating from its original goal by "incessantly attacking wine and showing an inexplicable indulgence towards beer."   In its "new form" the campaign had become "a real national danger . . . absolutely deplorable for the economic life of the country." [88]

In somewhat the same vein it was claimed in the viticultural press that the competition of mineral waters with wine was "disloyal."   They were not a "national product."   They "drowned the French spirit" in a drink that had no "national character."   Mineral waters were only good for snobs; the *poilus* at the front did not drink them.[89]

These last statements accompanied a successful proposal to tax mineral waters which was enthusiastically seconded by the wine industry.[90]   Like the claims in the preceding paragraphs, these statements were gross exaggerations, but as an example of an interest trying to protect itself or gain an advantage over another they are at least understandable.   However, such statements and much of the propaganda that surrounded wine during the war intensified the twin myths that wine was somehow "French" or "patriotic" and absolutely necessary to the economy of the country.

6. *BETWEEN TWO WARS: CHRONIC OVERPRODUCTION*

"All is joy in the vineyard," the *Revue de viticulture* announced in 1920,[1] with good reason. The year before, the largest harvest since the beginning of the war (54,353,577 hectolitres) had seen prices continue to rise rapidly until they reached an average of 116 francs the hectolitre at the production level. And in 1920 a harvest (58,416,916 hectolitres) that nearly equaled 1914's bumper crop sold at the still high average of 99 francs the hectolitre. A storm cloud over the vineyards might have been seen in 1921 when this figure dropped to 98 francs while production fell an average of 17 percent.[2] As in the period before 1900, however, nobody cared to look for danger signals. With production costs estimated at 50 to 65 francs the hectolitre during the immediate postwar years,[3] the outlook was understandably optimistic. The only jarring note was an "inconsiderate campaign" in the Parisian press which encouraged consumer resistance to the high price of wine and denounced the winegrowers as "profiteers" and "hoarders." [4]

Again as before 1900, the mood of optimism was reflected in the vigor with which the vineyard was replanted. Obviously the problem of replanting was not as great as in the post-phylloxera period. If it is recalled, however, that vines do not die overnight from lack of care, and that it takes about three years for new vines to start producing, an idea of the speed of the replanting movement is possible. Since 1914 the vineyard area had declined until it reached 1,440,648 hectares in 1920. By 1922, however, the 1914 area was already surpassed with a planting of 1,526,640 hectares, and this figure rose to 1,549,860 hectares in 1924.[5] Optimism was also reflected in the prices paid for vineyard properties. They took first place in the rise in price of all agricultural properties after the war.[6] And although, as Augé-Laribé argues, the rise in general was a nominal one, there were many examples of vineyards fetching fantastic prices.[7]

Outside the vineyard proper the prevailing optimism was encouraged in many ways. On a general level there was an officially announced policy of agricultural recovery and new forms of government aid to all types of agriculture.[8] More particularly, there were lowered taxes on "the production, fabrication, and circulation of wines and other hygienic drinks."[9] The government also raised the tariff on foreign wines,[10] and at the same time there was much talk in semi-official quarters of the "export power" of French wines.[11] Finally, in 1922, as if to cap this mood of confidence, there was held a widely advertised *Semaine Nationale du Vin*—observed at Paris with imposing ceremonies and exhibitions attended by the Premier and other cabinet ministers.[12]

BUST, INFLATIONARY BOOM, AND CRISIS

Ironically, within a month after the observance of the *Semaine* the harvest of what was to be France's third greatest wine crop began. When it was finished, it was found that national production had reached over 76 million hectolitres. This quantity added to Algerian production and stocks from the previous year made a record total of more than 84 million hectolitres available for the market. Prices received by the winegrowers tumbled rapidly to an average of 65 francs the hectolitre with, for the first time, the greatest drops being registered outside the Midi. In the Bordeaux region, which was faced with a deteriorating export situation, the average drop was 59 percent; in Burgundy it was 31 percent and in the Midi 25 percent. In all areas the majority of sales were made at cost or below.[13]

The next year (1923) the harvest was lighter (59,911,210 hectolitres), but prices, although they rose, averaged about 20 percent below the 1919–21 level.   Then in 1924 the harvest once again hit the 70 million hectolitre mark, and this performance was followed in 1925 by another bumper harvest which totaled 65 million hectolitres. The national price average declined an additional 17 percent while in the Midi, where the local harvests were the heaviest since the war, drops as great as 33 percent were registered.   In 1925 the Ministry of Agriculture admitted the "seriousness" of the situation,[14] and cries of "crisis" were raised in the Chamber of Deputies.[15] There were even a few oblique discussions about limiting new plantings of the vine.[16]   But almost before limitation of plantings could be considered or the cries of crisis had died down, wine prices started up again on their dizziest spiral since the war.

Because of the heavy harvests just described, the price of wine had been relatively unaffected by the rise in prices of other commodities which, from the middle of 1925 on, had been the result of the government's inflationary policies.   In 1926, however, aided by the lightest harvest since 1917 (42,612,050 hectolitres), the price of wine recovered lost ground by shooting up an average of 120 percent from the year before.   Meanwhile, production costs lagged far behind so that 1926 and 1927 were memorable years for the growers.[17] In the Senate and the Chamber during the latter year there were now long debates on the high cost of wine.[18]

In 1928 and 1929 the seesaw pattern was resumed with two bumper harvests that passed the 60 million hectolitre mark.   Prices fell an average of 42 percent while production costs which were bridging the inflationary gap rose by almost exactly the same amount.[19]   In 1929 prices below cost were again common in the Midi.   The problems of the growers now moved to the center of the legislative stage.   A new forthrightness in these matters was shown by Léon Blum, who denounced "the rupture in equilibrium between the production and consumption of wines."[20]   And the government, following this lead, presented a program aimed at limiting production and "reorganizing the market."[21]

The program, as will be shown in more detail in a later chapter, was debated widely, with the various winegrowing associations generally objecting at first that it was too "Draconian" a solution to their problems.[22] As a result a light harvest (45,637,960 hectolitres) in 1930, which brought a 20 percent price rise, also brought some unrealistic hopes that the winegrowers could take care of the crisis themselves.[23] The observance in 1931 of the fiftieth anniversary of the replanting of the vineyard after the phylloxera may have been planned to emphasize this point of view. But on July 4, 1931, the *Statut de la Viticulture* or *Statut du Vin*, as the government project for limiting wine production was variously called, became law.

That fall, in the midst of general discontent over its provisions, which included compulsory distilling of excess wine and the holding off of part of the harvest from the market, national production reached nearly 60 million hectolitres and prices dropped 33 percent from the previous year's average. The next two years saw more normal harvests (49,569,630 hectolitres in 1932 and 51,765,860 hectolitres in 1933), but under the influence of the world-wide business depression prices remained well below the average of the previous five years. Exports were especially affected during this period, falling from 1,382,000 hectolitres in 1929 to 703,000 hectolitres in 1932.

But even more trouble was in store for the winegrowers. In the summer of 1934, while the government projected new regulations to check production,[24] the grapes grew heavy and big under ideal conditions all over France. The growers feared an overabundant harvest to such an extent that M. Queuille, the Minister of Agriculture, felt obliged to tell them that their predictions were "fantastic" and their anxiety "unjustified." [25] But in the fall, after the harvest had been gathered in, it was found that national production had reached 78,144,090 hectolitres, while Algeria had produced a record 22,043,000 hectolitres. The next year, to the continuing despair of the growers, nature again performed generously. Production for 1935 was 78,810,000 hectolitres in metropolitan France and 18,180,000 in Algeria. When these amounts were added to the record stock left over from 1934, it meant that for two years in a row 100 million hectolitres of wine had been available for a depressed market.

The *Statut du Vin* and subsequent legislation was unable to
keep prices from dropping to record lows. With production costs
averaging more than 100 francs the hectolitre, the national price
average dropped to 78 francs the hectolitre in 1934 and 64 francs in
1935. Even the *vins de cru* and champagne were "cruelly affected," [26] and responsible observers predicted the "economic ruin"
of the national vineyard.[27]

In the Midi, where selling prices 50 percent below cost were common at harvest time,[28] demonstrations were held. At Béziers, birth-
place of the uprisings of 1907, the memory of those events was invoked and in vague and inflammatory language the government was
asked to take "immediate measures." [29] In the Bordeaux region,
where a large part of production is devoted to quality wine, the average price per hectolitre for the wines of the region fell below the national average for the first time on record. Twenty thousand winegrowers marched through the city of Bordeaux on April 28, 1935,
and presented a letter to the government in which they stated "we
are about to disappear," and asked for delays in the payment of
taxes and other help.[30] Finally in the first week of June in the same
year an "extraordinary assembly" of the winegrowing associations
of France was held at Paris—again to ask the government for aid.[31]

The incidence of the crisis on the economies of predominantly
viticultural regions resembled that of 1900–1907. As early as 1931
there were complaints in the Chamber of Deputies about the stagnation of sales in the Midi of such products and goods as automobiles,
textiles, and certain types of meat.[32] Although there was some consolidation of small vineyards in the Midi due to the difficult situation
of their owners, the sale of large properties placed on the market
became "extremely difficult if not impossible." [33] The decline in
value of the best vineyards in the Midi was estimated at 70 percent,
that of an average-sized vineyard for the nation as a whole at 75
percent.[34]

The answer of the government to what was now labeled France's
third great viticultural crisis was more legislation. But before ex-
amining it and the series of laws which since 1931 had preceded it,
it should be useful to study the causes of excessive production during
the period under review.

A COMPARISON OF OVERPRODUCTION IN THREE PERIODS

Remembering that the 1900–1907 period was one of abnormal harvests, it is still interesting to compare it with the period from 1920 to 1935. If we break the latter into two eight-year periods for the sake of consistency and take the average yearly production of the three periods, we get the results indicated below. It will be seen that increases in production caused by the overabundant harvests just described are still marked.

Yearly Average of Wine Production

1900–1907	55,179,200 hectolitres
1920–27	59,095,743
1928–35	60,674,410

But production is only part of the story. During the same three periods there was a decline in exports, a great increase in imports chiefly from Algeria, and up to the middle of 1935 only a slight increase in the amount of wine distilled into alcohol. If we adjust production figures by adding imports and by subtracting exports and wine distilled into alcohol,[35] we find the following quantities of wine available for the domestic market.

Yearly Average of Wine Available for Domestic Market

1900–1907	56,172,300 hectolitres
1920–27	63,699,080
1928–34 [36]	69,551,700

While the above increases, which amount to approximately 25 percent, were taking place, the taxed consumption of wine remained relatively rigid, increasing by only 12.2 percent.[37] This meant a proportionate increase in tax-free consumption. The latter consists chiefly of the important amounts of wine consumed by the wine-grower and his family and distributed by him as part of his laborers' wages.[38] Tax-free consumption varies inversely with the price of wine and directly with the size of the harvest. Thus during the periods under study, a progressively larger part of the winegrower's product was being consumed with little or no real return to him. At the same time massive production and Algerian imports depressed his market prices.

In respect to prices, Professor Jules Milhau, perhaps the foremost authority today on the role of viticulture in the French economy, has made an interesting study for the period from 1919 to 1933.[39] He arrives at a metropolitan production figure of 42,000,000 hectolitres as the point below which the value of the harvest increases in direct proportion to production and above which demand becomes inelastic with the value of the harvest declining in an inverse ratio to production.[40]   If we accept this figure, which appears to be borne out by the consumption figures listed in Table 16, the dimensions of the overproduction problem and its effect on prices become striking indeed.

TABLE 16.   CONSUMPTION OF WINE IN FRANCE, 1900–1934

Period	Yearly Average of Taxed Consumption (*in hectolitres*)	Yearly Average of Tax-Free Consumption (*in hectolitres*)	Tax-Free Consumption as a Percentage of Domestic Production Less Exports and Distillation
1900–1907	43,287,500	11,891,700	21.5
1920–27	47,189,600	16,509,480	27.9
1928–34	48,588,100	21,255,229	36.3

Source: *Annuaire statistique.*

INCREASED YIELDS

During the 1920's and 1930's the viticultural press and the wine-growing associations tried to minimize the overproduction problem by pointing out that the vineyard area in France showed a long-term decrease of considerable proportions.   As we have seen, the same argument was used during the crisis of 1900–1907.   We also saw then that while it was true the national vineyard area was decreasing, the decrease was more than compensated for by increases in production which were largely the result of an emphasis on high-yielding grape varieties and a concentration of new plantings in the Midi. This pattern was substantially repeated during the 1920's and 1930's, as Table 17 suggests.

Back of the increases in productivity in the Midi was the wider use of agricultural machinery after World War I.[41]   The tractor especially caused a further extension of the vineyard into the rich lowlands.   And in both hillside and lowland vineyards mechanical

TABLE 17. PERIODIC YEARLY AVERAGES OF VINEYARD AREA AND YIELD
IN FRANCE AND THE MIDI, 1900–1935

	France		Midi (*Departments of Aude, Gard, Hérault, and Pyrénées-Orientales*)	
Period	*Area (in hectares)*	*Yield (in hectolitres per hectare)*	*Area (in hectares)*	*Yield (in hectolitres per hectare)*
1900–07	1,642,750	33.9	455,849	45.1
1920–27	1,524,138	38.7	433,387	57.9
1928–35	1,534,135	39.5	463,941	55.2

Source: *Annuaire statistique.*

sprayers made more efficient treatment of the vines possible. Other innovations included power-driven presses which were often mobile and new methods of spreading fertilizers.

Machinery also pushed the vine into regions where it had been little grown before. In the sandy wastes of the upper Camargue, next to the department of the Gard, a whole new vineyard sprang up after 1919.[42] There small railways ran between the vines, bringing the grape harvest to huge mechanized "wine factories," some of which could store 100,000 hectolitres a year.[43] Organized on a jont-stock basis, these "factories" and their holdings probably represented the highest development of industrialized agriculture in France up to that time.

In the other great winegrowing regions outside the Midi mechanization did not make as much progress. Nevertheless, an alarming symptom from the point of view of overproduction was a tendency to plant higher-yielding grapes in place of the quality varieties which had made these regions famous. Thus, although the Bordeaux vineyard experienced a steady if relatively slight increase in area during the three periods we have been comparing, the area devoted to the production of *grands crus* declined dramatically.[44]

Burgundy represented an even more striking example of this trend. There, although the yield per hectare increased by approximately 22 percent from 1920 to 1935, the vineyard area shrank by 21 percent. Significantly, the greatest decrease in area—nearly one half—took place in the Côte d'Or district, the home of such famous *crus* as the Clos Vougeot, Chambertin, and Montrachet.

One of the chief causes of increased yields was the spread of hybrid grape varieties. The various hybrids were descendants of the American grape varieties, the *producteurs directs,* which it will be remembered were first imported into France during the phylloxera epidemic by growers impatient of the grafting process.[45] The *producteurs directs* had not been a success. The American grapes gave a low yield of wine with a "foxy" taste. They were remarkable, however, for their ability to withstand the attacks of pests and diseases.

In the years that intervened after the introduction of the *producteurs directs,* French experimenters had patiently crossbred them with selected French varieties so that eventually the flavor and yield of the resulting hybrids as well as their disease-resisting qualities showed considerable improvement over the original American varieties. This and the prevalence of vine and grape disease of all kinds as a result of wartime shortages of insecticides and chemical fertilizers and general lack of care in the vineyards made the wider use of the hybrid vines assured. "The future belongs to the hybrids," the *Journal d'agriculture pratique* predicted in 1914.[46] And in 1919 the *Revue de viticulture* announced hybrids would be "a capital element in the second reconstitution of the vineyard." [47]

Almost immediate opposition was registered against their use, however, especially by the growers in the Midi who feared the extension of the vineyard in traditionally non-winegrowing regions, which the hardy hybrids were already making possible.[48] In other areas responsible growers feared the lowering of quality which the hybrids promised.[49]

On the other side of what turned out to be a running controversy, there were continued experiments to produce a better hybrid. Publicity campaigns were held featuring taste tests in which "experts" could not distinguish between wine coming from hybrid grapes and other varieties.[50] And even a publication, *La Revue des hybrides,* was founded to give news of all these developments.

The most authoritative statement on the precise spread of hybrids comes from the Ministry of Agriculture's *enquête agricole* of 1929.[51] That year the *enquête* found that hybrids accounted for 13.5 percent of production, or 8,486,367 hectolitres, and occupied

14.5 percent of the area of the French vineyard.[52]   The great bulk of hybrid plantings occurred in polycultural regions where, although winegrowing was practiced, it was not the chief agricultural activity. In these regions there were noticeable increases in the vineyard area,[53] although proportionately the greatest gains were registered in such improbable regions as the Alps.[54]

Professor Marres has pointed out that the planting of hybrid grapes in nonviticultural regions represented a deliberate attempt on the part of peasants in those regions to free themselves from buying wine at prices they felt were too high.[55]   Thus they undoubtedly contributed to the increase, noted earlier, in tax-free consumption which in some polycultural departments was estimated as high as 50 percent of production.[56]   On the other hand there were also important plantings of hybrids in traditionally viticultural regions.   The *enquête,* for example, tells us that the percentage of hybrids among new plantings in 1929 was 34.2 percent and 21.4 percent for the departments of Loire-Inférieure and Maine-et-Loire, respectively, in the Loire valley vineyard, and 16.4 percent for the department of Saône-et-Loire in the Burgundy vineyard, while Marres writes of a *grand domaine* in the Bordeaux region, which formerly produced *vins de cru,* being planted entirely in hybrids.[57] At all the events, the government felt that the threat of overproduction from the spread of hybrids was great enough so that from 1931 on, as will be described later, it sought to limit their planting and ended by prohibiting certain varieties.

THE ALGERIAN VINEYARD

Of all the elements contributing to the problem of overproduction, the growth of the Algerian vineyard was the most spectacular. In an earlier chapter we saw its steady development up to 1907. After that year there were fluctuations in area when a relatively mild epidemic of the phylloxera crossed the Mediterranean, and there were cutbacks in planting during Word War I.   But the long-term trend was up, and after World War I there was an uninterrupted increase in plantings until 1935.   During this period an average of 14,000 new hectares were planted each year until the vineyard area, which stood at approximately 170,000 hectares in 1920, covered 400,000 hectares in 1935.

Continuing our comparison of three periods and translating the above developments into production figures, we get the following results.

Yearly Average of Algerian Wine Production

1900–1907	7,456,400 hectolitres
1920–27	8,533,750
1928–35	15,974,500

Where France's yearly average production figured on the same basis and over the same period of time had increased by 10 percent, the increase in Algeria was 114 percent. More pertinent, however, to the alarm caused by the development of the vineyard in Algeria was the fact that where Algerian production during 1900–1907 amounted to 28 percent of the production of the four departments of Aude, Gard, Hérault, and Pyrénées-Orientales, it amounted to 60.5 percent during 1928–35.

Again, as in 1907, one of the Midi winegrowers' chief complaints was Algerian competition. All the reasons for the earlier bitterness over this competition, such as preferential transport rates for Algerian wines, still existed. What was new after 1907 were the powerful organizations the Midi growers had to back up their grievances. The result was a concerted attack by these organizations on Algeria's viticultural economy.

Although all the factors contributing to the Algerian growers' supposedly advantageous position were thoroughly debated [58] and even the status of Algeria as a part of metropolitan France called into question,[59] the main attack was concentrated on imposing tariffs or quotas on Algerian wine. The first serious proposal along these lines occurred as early as 1912 when the C.G.V. proposed limiting duty-free imports from Algeria to 7 million hectolitres a year.[60] To insure that this quota would be kept, a nominal "duty of record" of one franc the hectolitre was to be levied. Any imports above 7 million hectolitres were to be subject to a duty at the preferential rate of 12 francs the hectolitre.

Partly because of the appearance of the phylloxera in the Algerian vineyards and possibly also because of the relative peace and prosperity in the French vineyard after 1907, the proposal was never acted on in the Chamber of Deputies. The question was not really reopened until 1920 when the *Revue de viticulture* proposed limiting Algerian imports to 10 percent of metropolitan production when the latter exceeded 60 million hectolitres.[61] Thereafter various other proposals were widely discussed in the Midi press [62] and at meetings of the winegrowing associations. And on April 26, 1926, the Fédération des Associations Viticoles de France et d'Algérie met at Narbonne with the Franco-Algerian problem as the chief item on its agenda.

With the Midi delegates holding fast to the C.G.V. proposal of 1912 and the Algerian delegates refusing to compromise on any other basis than a quota which would apply equally to France and Algeria, the conference was foreordained to failure.[63] Another meeting held in 1929 at Paris was no more successful. After that the C.G.V., despairing of action through the Fédération, launched an intensive campaign of its own in favor of Algerian quotas.

In 1930 the campaign gained momentum with a mass meeting of 3,500 winegrowers at Béziers. And it continued with inflammatory broadsides in which "the wheat growers of Flanders" and "the olive growers of Provence" were warned against Algerian competition in their fields.[64] The government, for its part, tried to sponsor another meeting of the Fédération, but this time Algerian delegates refused to attend. The C.G.V., in turn, denounced this refusal and formally called upon the government for a "solution" of the Algerian problem.[65]

By 1931 the Algerian question was eclipsed by the government's project for controlling the production of both France and Algeria with the *Statut du Vin*. A partial victory for the C.G.V. campaign, however, may be discerned in the strong anti-Algerian bias of the parliamentary debate on the *Statut*.[66] Also, a quota plan backed by the C.G.V. whereby metropolitan France would supply 80 percent of taxed consumption, Algeria 18 percent, and foreign imports 2 percent, had been twice approved by the Interministerial Commission on Viticulture and pronounced "just and equitable" by the Minister of Agriculture, Fernand David.[67] It failed of incorporation in the *Statut,* however, when the latter was passed on July 4, 1931. Thereafter, the C.G.V. concentrated its efforts on amending the new law so that its provisions would apply with greater force to Algeria.

Success seemed close in 1934 when the government received a proposal to this effect from the Interministerial Commission.[68] The *Statut* called for holding off the market for a fixed period of time a certain percentage of the wine produced when the metropolitan and Algerian harvests together totaled more than 65 million hectolitres. The Commission's proposal sought to amend this provision so that "blocking" the harvest, as the operation was called, would go into effect on a separate basis for the two countries when production exceeded 55 million hectolitres in France and 10 million hectolitres in Algeria. A glance at production figures listed earlier in this chapter will show how weighted this proposal was in favor of metropolitan France and why it was denounced as a "hidden quota" by the Algerians.

The government, meanwhile, was busy with its own projects to tighten up the *Statut* and announced its contemplated measures were to be "applicable in the same fashion to all French citizens whether they cultivate their vineyards in the three Algerian departments or in the departments of the mother country." [69] The government nevertheless invited the Interministerial Commission to submit its proposal to the Chamber of Deputies, where it was defeated by a vote of 435 to 160 on July 1, 1933. In this way the Franco-Algerian struggle may be said to have ended: the integration of French and Algerian wine production remains complete to this day.

Actually, however, more disinterested and responsible heads than the *C.G.V.* recommended limiting Algerian production. The National Economic Council, in a report issued before the *Conférence Économique de la France métropolitaine et d'outre-mer* held in 1934 and 1935, stated:

There are products which should firmly be advised against or forbidden in the colonies . . . above all wheat . . . and wines. If the growth of the Algerian vineyard is not halted both the French and Algerian wine-growers will be ruined.[70]

It was also remembered that in the early days of the colony Marshal Bugeaud had written "We have not acquired this colony to create competition. . . . An ordinance should immediately prohibit the making of wine in Algeria." [71]

But with wine estimated as accounting for an average of 50 percent of the value of Algeria's exports during the period between the two wars, it would seem the Marshal's advice had gone unheeded for too long. Perhaps the final word on the matter belongs to Poincaré who, as premier in 1926, described the Franco-Algerian viticultural problem as "insoluble." [72]

EXPORTS AND IMPORTS

As briefly noted earlier in this chapter, the immediate postwar years saw great emphasis on the export possibilities of wine. On February 22, 1922, at a *séance solennelle* of the Academy of Agriculture presided over by the Minister of Agriculture, the Academy's president had described these possibilities as "without limits." [73] But at the demonstration of twenty thousand winegrowers at Bordeaux on April 28, 1935, one of the strongest demands made on the government was for "a policy of exportation for [Bordeaux] wine . . . to be adopted with extreme urgency." [74]

The two statements, however, do not measure the failure of a policy any more than they indicate possibilities missed. Wine exports had been dropping almost steadily since 1907 when, as has been noted, their decline was already a problem. If we continue our comparison of three periods, we obtain the following results.

Yearly Average of Wine Exports

1900–1907	2,053,750 hectolitres
1920–27	1,674,250
1928–35	942,375

Furthermore, during the same periods, wine had been almost without exception an object of special concern in the commercial agreements France negotiated with foreign countries. It is interesting to note, for example, that special treatment for wine was written into the Versailles peace treaty,[75] and that in 1933, when France found herself second to Italy on the quota list for imports of wines and spirits fixed by the United States for the first four months after the repeal of prohibition, she immediately negotiated to equal Italy's quota by accepting 20,000 metric tons of pears and apples from the United States.[76] Considering that the new quota was to run for only two months,[77] this does not seem an unaggressive policy and must surely have looked like favoritism to the cider producers of Normandy and Brittany and the fruit growers of central France.

Even in such important wine-producing countries as Spain, Italy, and Portugal, France strove successfully to obtain important concessions for her wines although these chiefly affected the quality varieties.[78] Of course the winegrowing associations were not satisfied, and there were contemporary observers like the National Economic Council who favored a more aggressive policy.[79] But in retrospect, given the climate of world trade at the time, it is difficult to see how the government could have done more than it did short of adopting a policy of dumping.[80]

There were also factors affecting the wine-export situation which no government policy however aggressively conceived could hope to overcome. The chief of these was the world-wide business depression which was reflected in significant decreases in the per-capita consumption of the chief wine-importing countries.[81] Of almost equal importance was the general rise in tariffs and the adoption of import quotas on all types of goods which characterized national economics after World War I. Often wine quotas were set without any real consideration of demand and raised duties on wine were frequently used as a means of economic retaliation against France.[82]

Other factors which influenced the decline in exports included the adoption of total prohibition of all alcoholic beverages in the United States and limited prohibition in the Scandinavian countries and Canada.[83] There was also a general increase in excise taxes on wines and liquors in other countries during the same period, which was at least partly sumptuary in inspiration.[84] Related to these developments and the imposition of quotas and high duties was a sharp increase in the fraudulent manufacture of "French" wines overseas. It was estimated that there was thirty times as much wine bearing the Bordeaux label and circulating on foreign markets as was exported from that city.[85]

Still another important factor in the export problem was the growth of overseas vineyards. Although the vineyard areas of Italy and Spain increased only slightly over what they had been during the 1900–1907 period, there were important increases in other countries. Thus the vineyard area of Greece, which covered 65,000 hectares in 1907, stood at 231,000 hectares in 1935. During the same period the vineyard area of the Argentine increased from 74,000 hectares to 157,000 hectares, Australia's from 25,000 to 47,000 hectares, and Chile's from 32,000 to 86,000 hectares. Chilean growth was aided by an export bounty which amounted to 95 francs the hectolitre, while Australia taxed French wines with an import duty valued at 1,500 francs the hectolitre when duties in other countries ranged from 200 to 600 francs the hectolitre.[86]

A suggested way out of the problem created by foreign vineyards was for France to concentrate on export of quality wines.[87] But parallel with a decline in their growth noted earlier in this chapter was a tendency to keep a larger portion of the production of quality wines on the home market. Thus where France exported roughly 60 percent of her production of *vins de cru* during 1869–77, this figure stood at 30 percent in 1913 and 10 percent in 1939.[88]

Accompanying the concern over decline in exports was a much more articulate concern over increases in wine imports from foreign countries. Although the balance of trade was in favor of imports, the difference between imports and exports did not average more than 1,500,000 hectolitres from 1920 to 1935.[89] What made the problem of imports such a burning one was that whereas the export problem affected the Midi growers very little, the imported wines, chiefly cheap wines of high alcoholic content, were directly competitive with the Midi product. And the Midi had a powerful spokesman in the C. G. V., which more and more during this period presumed to speak for the French wine industry as a whole.[90]

The C. G. V.'s almost unqualified opposition to wine imports, which in the case of imports from Spain, Italy, Greece, and Portugal were made mandatory by the give and take of tariff "wars," seriously embarrassed the government's commercial policies abroad. The question of imports from Italy and Spain in particular brought on a very stormy period in the relations of the government with the winegrowers.

In 1930 the impending *Statut du Vin* may be said to have brought the problem of wine imports to a head. For many growers the question of limiting domestic production was evidently acceptable only under the condition that the French borders "be closed to the importation of foreign wines." [91] The C. G. V. somewhat more moderately suggested that the "efficacy" of the impending legislation depended on the "prior resolution" of the import problem.[92] Consequently, to make the *Statut* more agreeable to the growers, the government sought to raise the minimum tariff on foreign wines from 55 francs to 84 francs the hectolitre.

To be free to do this, the government had first to come to a settlement with Italy because of the ramifications of most-favored-nation agreements based on the Franco-Italian trade agreement of March 7, 1928. This it did with a new Franco-Italian agreement of March 16, 1931, which by way of concession gave Italy a quota of 250,000 hectolitres a year at the old rate of 55 francs the hectolitre. On March 19, 1931, the government announced the new minimum tariff of 84 francs the hectolitre, but it did not publish the details of the Franco-Italian agreement until April 1.[93] Thus the complete satisfaction of the French wine growers with the new tariff was short-lived. There were to be greater causes for dissatisfaction, however. A tacit understanding entered into in the course of the negotiations over the agreement provided for a "large degree of tolerance" in enforcing Italy's quota.[94]

The latter stipulation was called "a ransom" for liberty of tariff action against other nations "which at all costs had to be obtained to protect [French] viticulture." [95] Considering that imports from Spain in 1930 had been more than ten times as great as those from Italy and imports from Greece nearly twice as great, the ransom did not seem like too great a price to pay. But the degree of tolerance was heavily exploited by Italian shippers. By April of 1931 the assigned quota of 250,000 hectolitres had already been passed. In the next four months Italy exported an additional 587,000 hectolitres, all of which were taxed under the old rate of 55 francs the hectolitre; in the month of July alone shipments totaled 287,000 hectolitres.[96]

This sudden and unexpected influx of Italian wine was blamed by the Midi growers for a summer-long drop in prices during the period when they felt the recent passage of the *Statut du Vin* (July 4, 1931) should have driven prices up.[97] The C. G. V., outraged at the lax enforcement of Italy's quota, threatened a lawsuit against the Minister of Finance, and in addition accused him of being linked with a group of wheat speculators.[98] The government for its part realized the necessity of quick action in the face of growing complaints. It could not denounce the Italian convention without three months' notice nor could it prohibit the importation of Italian wines without the assent of Parliament, then in recess. However, broadly interpreting certain powers conferred by a decree of December 26, 1926,[99] the government on August 27, 1931, adopted a system of quotas on foreign wines to be fixed each year by interministerial decree and to be arranged so that a nation's quota in any one year could not exceed the average of imports from that nation for the preceding five years.[100] The quotas were applied almost immediately; Italy's, which under the new arrangement came to 59,400 hectolitres, was, of course, already surpassed, and thus further Italian imports were effectively checked for the rest of the year.

Meanwhile the two nations entered into new negotiations and on November 16, 1931, an agreement was reached whereby a quota of 250,000 hectolitres at the 55 franc rate was once again assigned to Italy. Additional Italian imports subject to the minimum tariff of 84 francs the hectolitre were authorized when the combined French and Algerian harvest came to less than 60 million hectolitres.[101] Thus, except for the fact that the quota was to be strictly observed, the new agreement was not much more restrictive than was the one of March 16.[102] The memory of the summer's "excessive" Italian imports was still fresh; prices were low; the figure of 250,000 hectolitres compared with the quota of 54,400 hectolitres set only three months previously was provoking. And the fact that the agreement was only temporary,[103] which under other circumstances might have been a mitigating influence, probably only combined with the other factors to make the November 16 agreement the object of a particularly concentrated and bitter attack.[104]

This attack in turn reputedly led the French government to

denounce the agreement.[105] At all events a new temporary Franco-Italian trade agreement of March 4, 1932, left wine out of the list of articles to be treated, an annex to the agreement noting that "exceptional circumstances" prevented the negotiators from applying most-favored-nation treatment to each other's wines and liquors.[106] As a result Italian wine became subject to France's minimum tariff of 84 francs the hectolitre, and its importation became "very difficult if not impossible." [107] By way of reprisal Italy decreed an absolute prohibition on the importation of French wines, cognacs, and liquors. When France, in retaliation, broke off all further tariff negotiations,[108] the prohibition was lifted, but high tariffs still virtually excluded French wine from the Italian market.

The problem was somewhat resolved by an agreement of May 18, 1933 which gave Italy a quota of 10 percent of the total amount of wine imported from other nations in return for which France received quotas for champagnes and sparkling wines, *vins de crus,* and liqueurs.[109] Under this and subsequent agreements, however, trade in wine and liquors between the two countries deteriorated almost steadily until by 1938 Italian wine exports to France had declined 193 percent from what they had been in 1930, while French wine exports to Italy declined by 82 percent during the same period.

TABLE 18. FRENCH WINE EXPORTS TO ITALY, 1929–38 (*In hectolitres*)

Year	Quantity	Year	Quantity
1929	7,620	1934	1,556
1930	6,015	1935	1,115
1931	4,186	1936	532
1932	1,169	1937	1,896
1933	1,005	1938	1.088

Source: Ministère des finances, *Statistique mensuelle du commerce extérieur de la France.*

In the case of French wine imports from Spain, there was a longer history of opposition that had even more far-reaching effects on commercial relations between the two nations. During World War I in order to make up for wartime shortages the French government had sponsored a program of wine purchases from Spain to the amount of 150,000 hectolitres a month.[110] It may be imagined that this program, however necessary, was regarded with silent

TABLE 19. FRENCH WINE IMPORTS FROM VARIOUS COUNTRIES, 1928–38
(In hectolitres)

Year	Spain	Italy	Greece	Portugal
1928	3,733,640	22,805	172,337	681,953
1929	1,797,406	28,368	383,903	161,150
1930	1,587,215	144,439	277,932	115,075
1931	2,144,137	852,593	174,149	135,357
1932	624,026	15,821	206,607	176,830
1933	1,323,794	39,704	456,311	171,220
1934	262,383	19,123	83,667	109,062
1935	113,965	9,347	4,620	139,061
1936	101,486	17,216	78,724	144,886
1937	27,768	44,863	108,116	146,080
1938	4,323	8,909	6,115	113,908

Source: *Statistique mensuelle du commerce extérieur de la France.*

suspicion by French winegrowing interests, for almost as soon as hostilities ended there were demands ranging from higher tariffs to a complete prohibition of wine imports from Spain.[111]

On December 8, 1921, the extension of a system of coefficients or multipliers to the general tariff on foreign wines silenced requests of this sort—for a while, at least. A new decree multiplied the tariff on Spanish wines by 2.6, a figure which was supposed to reflect changes in the cost price of wine in Spain and France.[112] That the new tariff was weighted against Spain, however, may be surmised from that fact that it was described as a "50 percent ad valorem surtax" and hailed in the Midi as being "absolutely prohibitive of all importation." [113]

With approximately 70 per cent of Spain's wine exports going to France,[114] the Spanish government maintained that the new tariff was a crippling blow aimed at an important export, and suspended further commercial negotiations with France. The Spaniards, moreover, held to a reduction of the wine tariff as a necessary preliminary to any new trade agreement, while in France it was the opinion of the government that parliament would reject any agreement that included such a reduction.[115]

As in the case of Italy, just described, the French government sought the way out of a stalemate by a somewhat devious path. On the 8th of July, 1922, a new trade agreement between France and Spain was signed,[116] in which the coefficient applicable to Spanish

wines was reduced from 2.6 to 2.05.[117] The agreement was not presented to the Chamber of Deputies as a bill until February 26, 1923,
when it was put to the vote without discussion.[118] The vote was
favorable, but in the report that had preceded the bill's introduction,
no mention had been made of the changed coefficient.[119]

Meanwhile, in the fall of 1922 France's bumper harvest totaling
over 76 million hectolitres had taken place, and in the complaints
about the drop in prices that followed in its wake Spanish imports
figured as a prominent cause, even though they were considerably
reduced from previous years.[120] Thus before the government had
even intended to announce the reduction of duties on Spanish wine,
it was again being urged to raise them. This it avoided doing until
a law of April 4, 1926, instituted a general increase of 30 percent
on all duties. Any satisfaction the winegrowers might have received
from this raise was short-lived, however. For Spain took the increase in wine duties as a special pretext to denounce the agreement
of July 8, 1922, when it expired on July 15, 1926. The agreement
had been a profitable one for both countries, especially France,[121]
and so the French government felt obliged to reopen negotiations
which resulted in the restoration of the agreement of 1922 in all its
clauses relating to wine.[122]

Possibly because of this new settlement the French wine industry
decided to wage its war against Spanish imports from another
quarter. At all events in 1930 domestic legislation which was
described as "moral and salubrious" and an "answer to the winegrowing associations' requests" [123] aimed a real blow at imports
from Spain. A new law (law of January 1, 1930) provided that
foreign wines should be labeled to indicate their country of origin
and forbade their blending with French wines.[124] Since most of
Spain's wine exports to France were used in blending, the law was,
as one group of critics put it, a "dissimulated prohibition of
[Spanish] imports." [125]

In Spain the reaction was one of indignation; and an active press
campaign in that country urged the denunciation of the protocol
which had restored the trade agreement of 1922. Meanwhile in
France, while important economic groups opposed the law of Janu-

ary 1, 1930, for fear of the reprisals it might bring,[126] the C. G. V. defended it just as vigorously as a piece of domestic legislation which had its counterpart in other countries and in addition asked for a higher tariff on Spanish wines because of the devaluation of the Spanish peseta.[127]

Under these difficult conditions trade negotiations between the two countries were resumed in 1931, while according to one critic "the deficit in the [French] balance of trade became aggravated each month." [128] France offered concessions in the matter of blending Spanish and French wines, and trying to play a double game that would satisfy both Spain and the French growers, proposed a small quota virtually duty-free as a *quid pro quo* for raising the minimum tariff on Spanish wines from 55 francs to 84 francs the hectolitre. Spain rejected this proposal, pointing out that she still benefited from the minimum tariff of 55 francs the hectolitre because of her most-favored-nation treatment based on the Franco-Italian trade agreement of 1928.

France accordingly had to free herself from the Italian agreement which, as has been noted above, she did, following that maneuver with an 84-francs-the-hectolitre minimum tariff and the adoption of a system of restrictive quotas on all foreign wines.[129] On October 23, 1931, Spain finally settled for an annual quota of 1,800,000 hectolitres at the 84 franc rate. Possibilities for an increase of the quota in the event of a short harvest in France were given and it was also promised that the provisions of the law of January 1, 1930, against blending would be enforced with "great tolerance." [130]

The new quota system was somewhat dramatically described in the *Revue de viticulture* as "a sacrifice consented to by our [French] viticulture in order to avoid the denunciation of concluded treaties." [131] But under its successive applications, as Table 18 shows, wine imports from Spain decreased considerably, as they did from other countries. But also, as Table 17 suggests, the amounts involved were never very great in comparison with French production. The concern with which the problem of wine imports was viewed was but an extension of the larger problem of over-

production. Perhaps the best word on the subject belongs to the
National Economic Council, which in 1935 wrote:

When it comes to explaining why the available stocks of agricultural
production visibly exceed demand, peasant opinion attributes this disequilibrium to excessive imports from abroad. And when the statistics
tend to demonstrate that these importations are in process of constant
reduction, this [peasant] opinion doesn't hesitate to believe in abnormal
or fraudulent importations, the legend of which is very difficult to dis-
sipate.[132]

Certainly an attitude such as the above rather than any "invasion" of the French market by foreign wines would best account
for the differences between the government and the French winegrowers over the import question. Nevertheless it is at least arguable that these differences were settled in favor of the growers—and
that in the cases of wine imports from Italy and Spain, pressure from
French winegrowers limited the government's liberty of tariff
maneuver and prevented over-all settlements with these and other
countries which might have been more beneficial for French commerce than the ones concluded.

The period under review, however, was one of general deterioration in commercial relations between France and her overseas trading partners, and to draw up the final balance sheet of an argument
such as the above one would have to examine the effect of the
quota system on the export and import of industrial goods and
other agricultural products as well as wine. Still, in view of the
decreasing export possibilities for wine and the small percentage of
wine imports in relation to domestic wine production, it is possible
to conclude that wine occupied an unnecessarily pivotal position in
French tariff negotiations during this period.

7. *GOVERNMENT EFFORTS TO LIMIT PRODUCTION AND STABILIZE THE MARKET, 1928–38*

As has been observed in the preceding chapter, a post-World War I pattern of "boom and bust" for the wine industry gave way after the harvest of 1928 to a crisis which lasted almost uninterruptedly for eight years and which in most respects resembled the earlier crisis of 1900–1907 in its severity. A new note was struck, however, by the promptness with which the government recognized the situation. Soon after the bumper harvest of 1928, a parliamentary committee was set up to investigate the wine industry and to recommend legislation which might put it in a healthier condition.[1] When 1929 saw still another bumper harvest and prices fall below cost in the Midi and Bordeaux vineyards, the government passed emergency legislation in the spring of 1930 which set up a special fund of 250 million francs to buy, until the end of the year, alcohol distilled from wine.[2]

The latter move was a precedent-shattering form of direct aid which, as will be seen in more detail further on, was to have far-reaching consequences. But equally revolutionary was the proposed legislation based on the parliamentary committee's findings.[3] Announced on June 3, 1930, by Tardieu, then Minister of Agriculture, its major provisions included:[4]

Article 1. A tax to be levied on the average yield per hectare of a vineyard as follows—

For that part of the yield from 81 through 100 hectolitres the hectare: 5 fr. the hectolitre yielded.

For that part of the yield from 101 through 150 hectolitres the hectare: 10 fr. the hectolitre yielded.

For that part of the yield from 151 through 200 hectolitres the hectare: 20 fr. the hectolitre yielded.

For that part of the yield from 201 through 250 hectolitres the hectare: 40 fr. the hectolitre yielded.

For that part of the yield over 250: 80 fr. the hectolitre yielded.

Article 2. An annual tax of 5,000 fr. the hectare to be levied on all vine plantings made after promulgation of the proposed law.[5]

Exemptions from the tax for the following types of plantings were allowed—

1. The planting of one hectare every five years by the same proprietor.

2. The replacement in an equal area of vines pulled up by the same proprietor during a ten-year period prior to the promulgation of the proposed law provided the replanting was done with grape varieties of a yield equal to or less than those uprooted.

3. Plantings where the production of an entire vineyard was reserved for family consumption.

4. The replanting in a period of ten years following the promulgation of the proposed law of vineyards destroyed or damaged during the war.

Article 6. Under conditions of excessive production the "blocking" of part of the harvest in the cellars of the growers and its release at decreed intervals. The complete text of the paragraph read as follows:

In the case where prospects of a harvest give evidence of a dangerous overproduction for the domestic market in relation to average consumption of the three previous years, the Government may by a decree given before August 15, on the initiative of the Minister of Agriculture and the Minister of the Budget after the advice of the Interministerial Commission on Viticulture, take steps necessary to limit the quantity of wine which may be shipped from the property of viticulturists whose declared harvest indicates a production of more than 500 hectolitres with an average yield greater than 80 hectolitres the hectare.

This last article was described as the "keystone" of the proposed legislation,[6] and the three articles together promised a more direct intervention by the state in the production and marketing of wine than any that had been attempted or for that matter even seriously discussed before the crisis of 1928–35. Yet at the same time the government, in the spirit of 1900–1907, placed a great deal of emphasis on legislation which it was hoped would improve the quality of wine and thus indirectly limit its production.

Already, since the beginning of the crisis, a spate of laws directed to this end had passed through parliament. In 1929, for example, the amount of sugar that could be legally used in winemaking was reduced from the 1907 level, and in the whole of the Midi, the Bordeaux vineyards, and Algeria its use was forbidden entirely.[7] In 1930 complicated legislation which some critics said "was made to give work to the chemists"[8] regulated the minimum degree of alcohol and the amount of acidity in blended wines at 9° and 3.5 grams, respectively.[9] Blended wines falling short of these requirements could only be distilled or made into vinegar. In addition, the national vineyard was divided into seven regions and annual decrees were to regulate the alcoholic content below which unblended wines could be consumed only in the region of origin.[10] This, like the regulation that preceded it, was designed to prevent abnormally weak wines, which at best should have been used for no other purpose than blending, from having a wider circulation and use than they had formerly enjoyed. Tending to promote quality at the expense of quantity were further regulations which required that unblended wines be labeled to show their region of origin and which forbade the use of foreign wines for blending.[11] This last measure, it will be remembered, was also inspired by the winegrowers' objections to the import of foreign wines.

To complement the foregoing legislation and to introduce other measures to improve the quality of wine the government on June 3, 1930, also proposed the following, Articles 5 and 7.

Article 5. Annual decrees by the Ministry of Agriculture would fix the composition (degree of alcohol and amount of acidity) of wines suitable for consumption in the different winegrowing regions.

This was a tightening of the decree-law of April 19, 1930, which permitted wines falling below a minimum composition to be consumed only in the region where they were made.

Article 7. Agents of the Service for Repression of Frauds named by the Minister of Agriculture were to be permitted to enter winemaking sheds and cellars without accomplishing any previous formalities (notification, warrants, etc.).

Although it would have abolished a "sacred temple" enshrined by a law of July 28, 1812, this article had been decisively approved at a meeting of the representatives of all the winegrowing associations of France and Algeria held on May 11, 1930, where the government gave advance notice of its program. Objection had come principally from the delegates of central France, whose spokesman in the Chamber of Deputies, Camille Chautemps, had said that the proposed inspection would reflect suspicion of the probity of the grower visited and that "the mentality of his region was opposed to the measure." [12] Even so, a grudging acquiescence had been gained at the meeting by having anti-fraud agents responsible for the inspection instead of agents of the Contributions Indirectes, as originally proposed.

It is interesting to note, however, that in 1931 when the measure came up for debate in the Chamber, the central France deputies led a forceful attack on it that marvelously reflected the peasant psychology and narrow regional prejudices that sometimes characterize French parliamentarism. The government, already under fire for more important parts of its program, backed down and the offending paragraph was deleted. [13]

On July 10, 1930, the government proposed the following additional articles, 3 and 8. [14]

Article 3. Declarations of harvest were to be broken down into red, white, and rosé wines, and stocks from previous harvests were to be included. A tolerance of error of 3 percent for producers of more than 500 hectolitres and 5 percent for producers of less was to be allowed. A greater margin of error was to bring fines and imprisonment.

This was a tightening of the provisions of the law of June 29, 1907, dealing with the declaration of a grower's harvest. Under that law declarations were presumed to be made and also accepted in "good faith."

Article 8. Future sales (*ventes sur souches*) based on a specified alcoholic content were not to be permitted without a clause which allowed for adjusting the price to the actual alcoholic content of the wine as it was drawn from the vats.

This was entirely new legislation. In ordinary future sales growers were tempted if not virtually forced to add water to their wine if it came out stronger than the degree specified, or sugar, often beyond the legal limit, if it came out weaker.

And in the course of the debate on the government's program in 1931, the following provisions were added to the existing Articles 1 and 5.[15]

Article 1. Irrigation of vines was to be forbidden each year from July 15 until after the gathering of the harvest.

Excessive irrigation was described as "watering wine at the roots instead of in the vats." In the debate on the proposal it was brought out that the fixing of an arbitrary date like July 15 worked a particular hardship on the Midi where in some vineyards irrigation was of necessity practiced around the calendar. There was also the problem of drought.

As a result exceptions were made in the final version of the law so that by decrees applicable to individual departments and communes the irrigation season could be extended in "certain situations" or "where irrigation had been a local, loyal, and constant usage." [16]

The exemptions pulled the teeth of the law. One commentator remarked, with an acerbity reminiscent of Bastiat, that the government might just as well try to legislate against the traditionally heavy rains of August 15.[17]

Article 5. Anyone buying newly pressed wine in regions where the use of sugar was forbidden was not to add sugar to this wine unless it was destined exclusively for family consumption.

This was to prevent shippers and merchants from getting around previous legislation by moving wine from regions where sugaring was not allowed to regions where it was legal.

It is interesting to note that, with the exception of Article 7, the part of the government's program which sought more particularly to improve the quality of wine received remarkably little discussion both before and during the lively debate in the Chamber of Deputies over the *Statut du Vin* or *Statut de la Viticulture,* as the proposed legislation was variously called.

Perhaps the growers had become inured to the mass of legislation which since the end of the nineteenth century surrounded the making of their product—legislation which, as one critic sarcastically remarked, required "a library and the presence of several archivists to classify it" and "the neglect of the vines if the vineyard owners were to read it all!" [18]   Also it would appear, if only from reading the provisions presented above, that this legislation might have surpassed the limits of rational enforcement.   The standard objections to increasing government control during the period under review almost always included a request "for stricter enforcement of existing laws."   And, of course, the relative inviolability of the winegrower's plant and cellars created particular difficulties until it was finally breached in 1934.

In respect to the problem of improving the quality of wine it is interesting to note that the government's proposals and the legislation that followed from them specifically exempted *vins d'appellations d'origine contrôlées* from all production controls and tax penalties.   These wines were the well known *vins de cru* from such regions as Burgundy, Bordeaux, Champagne, etc.   Formerly, standards for their manufacture and the delimitation of the areas in which they could be grown had been fixed—in some cases rather loosely— by the growers and shippers themselves.   Since 1919, however, the government had been tightening these standards and incorporating them into a series of laws which gave a grower, if he complied with them, the right to an *appellation d'origine.*

There were difficulties in the application of the laws and some resistance to them in various localities, but by 1930 the great majority of the quality vineyards had satisfied and welcomed this new official classification.   Very likely because *vins d'appellations d'origine contrôlées* only accounted for roughly 10 percent of total wine production, their exemption from the provisions of the *Statut de la Viticulture* did not cause any special comment.   And although there were instances of fraud to take advantage of the exemptions, the exemptions did not cause any appreciable increase in the production of *vins d'appellations* during the period under review.

A DEBATE IS JOINED

No such indifference as was shown to the proposals for improving the quality of wine greeted that part of the government's program which sought to limit production by taxing yields and new plantings. From the time of its announcement it was subject to a barrage of comment and criticism both in the councils of the winegrowing associations and in the viticultural press.[19] The same was true, although possibly to a lesser extent, of the provisions dealing with "blocking" the harvest.

At first the reaction was relatively mild. The government, through the meeting of May 11, 1930, had within broad limits committed the winegrowing associations to some support. Moreover the C.G.V., undoubtedly shaken by the crisis, had lost some of its *vin d'abord* spirit. It was described now as "justly proud of its organization . . . strong from its parliamentary and administrative support . . . more concerned with practical remedies than with turns of phrase . . . influential in the Chamber, sovereign in the Commission des Boissons." [20]

In its first statement on the government's program the C.G.V. pledged itself to press for the "organizing of the metropolitan market and all other measures susceptible of saving continental viticulture." But with noticeable reserve it added that it considered the government's *projet de loi* as a "basis for discussion" only. Meanwhile, the C.G.V. added, the *projet* served a useful purpose in bringing the viticultural crisis to the attention of the nation.[21]

As the first statement reminds us, the C.G.V. was at this time carrying on a spirited attack against Algerian winegrowing and also demanding the raising of duties on imported wines. Still, in some quarters the C.G.V.'s stand appeared too approving of the government's program. Large numbers of growers and some regional groups [22] joined a new organization, the Conféderation de Défense Viticole et de Propagande du Vin, dedicated to fighting the government's program on nearly every point. Meanwhile the viticultural press repeated all the old arguments about Algeria, foreign imports, and stricter observance of existing laws, and warned the winegrowers of the dangers in "applying too often to the government." [23]

Possibly because of these developments a more critical turn in the attitude of the C.G.V. towards the government's program was shown at a meeting of its president with the Interministerial Commission on Viticulture in December, 1930. Admitting the threat of a dangerous overproduction, the C.G.V. nevertheless rejected the proposed taxes on yields and new plantings. In respect to the latter it said with surprising candor that the exemptions robbed the measure of any effectiveness and that in any case existing plantings were sufficient to cause overproduction. The only remedy the C.G.V. saw was to block part of the harvest on a progressive scale that penalized the large growers and favored the small ones. But to the principle of blocking the harvest already accepted by the government, the C.G.V. added the distillation of the blocked quantities (the resulting alcohol to be bought by the government) in the event that one overabundant harvest followed another.

Although the recommendations of the C.G.V. attacked two important provisions of the government's program, the dissidents were not satisfied. The Confédération de Défense Viticole, now organized in numerous local *comités*, launched a sustained campaign which "riddled with pitiless criticism the positions already taken, flogged the C.G.V., bullied the legislators, and railed against the government." [24] A more responsible attitude was taken at the general assembly of the Fédération des Associations Viticoles de France et d'Algérie, held between January 18 and 20, 1931, where once again the government's entire program came under the closest scrutiny and debate. Here, according to a somewhat bemused reporter, "the quasi-unanimity of viticultural opinion finally rallied, often reluctantly and not without resistance, to the necessity of limiting production." [25] But the amendments suggested by the assembly pointed to the alterations which the government's proposals would undergo in the Chamber of Deputies.

The Fédération recommended that the taxes on yields be increased so that for yields above 250 hectolitres the hectare they would be "prohibitive," while at the same time tax reductions were asked for yields of 81 to 100 hectolitres. Concerning the taxes on new plantings it was recommended that they be dropped in favor of a ten-year prohibition which would, however, include "certain exemptions" for small growers. And while the principle of blocking the harvest was approved, many resolutions were offered which would have raised the minimum production subject to blockage above the 500 hectolitre floor suggested by the government. Thus, although it could be said that the Fédération approved the broad principles of the government's program, the small grower was beginning to emerge as the party that must be spared at whatever cost to the program.

It would be unfair, however, to hold the winegrowing associations entirely responsible for this attitude. Back in June of 1930, when he announced the government's program, Tardieu had taken pains to point out that it would affect "only a small minority." [26] Speaking of the proposed taxes on yields of more than 80 hectolitres the hectare, he showed that in 1929 only 5,331 growers out of a total of 1,573,273 in France and 726 growers out of a total of 10,348 in Algeria would have come under the tax. Speaking of the proposed 500 hectolitre blockage floor, he pointed out that, again in 1929, out of a total harvest of 62,901,443 hectolitres in France, 16,600,145 hectolitres came from properties producing more than 500 hectolitres with a yield of more than 80 hectolitres the hectare. For Algeria the figures stood at 10,788,407 hectolitres out of a total production of 12,332,430 hectolitres. These last figures might have deserved some special comment, but in his remarks on blockage Tardieu limited himself to emphasizing that this part of the government's program would also "not affect too many." [27]

The attitude of penalizing only the big producers received a further boost in the report of the Chamber of Deputies' Commission des Boissons. [28] Since the Commission was charged with getting the proposed legislation through the Chamber, the language of the report is doubly significant. Its introductory statements were peppered with references to "*les landlords* [sic] *de la viticulture*" and "*les nabobs* [sic] *de l'industrie viticole*." [29] The fascinated deputies were regaled with the story of an 80 percent return on the capital of the *domaine de Kéroulis* in Algeria—an item twice repeated in debate. Further sensational disclosures included the mention of an Algerian grower who planted in the winter of 1928 "at the rate of 20 hectares a day" a vineyard stretching three kilometers in length. "He owns," the Commission breathlessly reported, "nearly four thousand hectares of vines, all in one holding." [30]   But worse, in 1928, 189 Algerian growers, individuals or corporations, harvested more than ten thousand hectolitres each. These practices were not confined to Algeria, however. "In certain parts of the Midi, notably the Camargue," the Commission continued, "the feudalism of heavy but inferior production holds sway." [31]

The spirit behind the foregoing remarks was reflected in the Commission's more concrete proposals. It was recommended that the tax on yields from 81 to 100 hectolitres the hectare be dropped, and that the tax on yields of 101 to 125 hectolitres the hectare be lowered from 10 francs to 5 francs. But by the nature of their operations, big properties often had relatively low yields, so a 5 franc tax on yields of 81 to 100 hectolitres where production was 5,000 hectolitres or more was also proposed.[32]   Moving in another direction the Commission suggested tightening up the limitations on new planting and recommended that the floor for blocking the harvest be lowered so as to include a production of 300 or more hectolitres. In respect to this last proposal, while we have seen that there was some agitation for raising the blockage floor above 500 hectolitres at the assembly of the Fédération des Associations Viticoles, the Commission felt that rather than being a penalty, blockage was a benefit which should be extended to as many growers as possible.[33]

The other committees in the Chamber of Deputies—finance and agriculture—to which the government's project was submitted were not, of course, responsible for its passage and so were freer to attack it than the Commission des Boissons had been. This they did on numerous grounds. The Finance Commission, while admitting that the fiscal aspects of the project were its only concern, sniped at the "economic Malthusianism" of the proposed law. And in something of a pique reported unfavorably on the whole project because of the "substantial" number of new tax agents it would involve and the absence of any precise details on the amount or distribution of the expected revenues.[34]

The Agricultural Commission objected to the "blanket" nature of the proposed floors for blockage and the tax on yields, and asked that regional differences in production as well as average production in preceding years be taken into account. It also followed the proposal of the Commission des Boissons to eliminate producers in the 81-to-100-hectolitre range from the tax on yields, and made a particularly strong stand against the proposed inspections of the winegrowers' property without warrant.[35] But because of the influence it had on parliamentary debate, perhaps the most important of the Agricultural Commission's objections was to the proposed limitation of new plantings. The Commission felt that in limiting new plantings the government could assure the big producers a dominating position in the market. In the words of the Commission:

The limiting of plantings will establish a formidable injustice. It will be a subsidy given to the big vineyard owners, to the capitalist companies who have industrialized the vine, who have planted extensive areas in the Midi and in Algeria and who, moreover, will now be the veritable masters of the wine market. It will, moreover, consecrate to their profit a privilege, a veritable monopoly, a legalized injustice.[36]

This sort of reasoning was echoed in the Chamber of Deputies. The following is a good example:

The winegrowers whom you will reach [with the proposed law] are not the proprietors of the great *domaines* nor the corporations whom you reproach for their dividends. They have already planted their vines; you will revalue and strengthen their holdings. Their capital will increase; thanks to your project they are assured of seeing their revenues swell in the future. . . . It is not only over a period of time but equally in its restrictive clauses that this limiting of plantings must not reach the small winegrowers and small landholders who wish to become winegrowers.[37]

Little wonder, then, that a great many deputies and small growers saw the government project as a maneuver of *les grands* against *les petits*, and that the debate in the Chamber moved from a discussion of the problem of overproduction to a spirited defense of the small grower.[38]

The debate originally scheduled for January of 1931 did not

take place until June. By this time all the positions described above had already been taken. But in eleven sittings of the Chamber, the last one of which ran for nearly twenty hours, they were all thoroughly and repeatedly restated. In addition, there was an interesting tendency to lift the debate above the immediate problems of the winegrowers to the broader level of social and economic principles. This was provoked by the threat to the idea of absolute right in property believed to be implicit in the proposed law, the specter of socialism that it raised, and the precedent the law might establish for government intervention in other sectors of the agricultural economy.

The first two of these three fears caused actual and nominal supporters of the government from the right and the center to oppose the bill. The government's defense, often repeated in varying form and emphasis, is best summarized in a statement made on the eve of the debate:

An attack on liberty and property? Certainly we would understand the objection if we recommended a text analogous to the *contre-projet* tabled by Jaurès at the second sitting of the Chamber on June 11, 1907, and of which the first lines read thus: "After July 1, 1907, properties in which vine growing constitutes the principal element of revenue are national property." But between the *étatisme* which would nationalize the vineyards and the *laissez-faire, laissez-passer,* and *laissez-pousser* which would perpetuate anarchy of production and insecurity of property we intend to practice the intervention of the state.[39]

After a reminder of the numerous forms of intervention practiced by the state in social and economic spheres which nobody could now possibly object to, after a recall of previous viticultural legislation the benefits of which were obvious, and after pointing out that in Greece, Yugoslavia, Rumania, and Switzerland planting of the vine was either limited or forbidden, the government concluded that

To guide a production wanting in foresight is to preserve it from mortal crises in the future; to avoid the depreciation of property is the best means of defending it. It is to guarantee the liberty of the grower that we wish to shield him from mortgage, loss in sales, and expropriation.[40]

If ideas such as the above were already reflected in the well-established practice of French national economics, sentiment about them was something else. In spite of the government's moderate exposé of its intentions, deputies from the right and center were still able to conjure up the bogey of socialism. As one of them put it, the government's program was nothing but "socialism manufactured by its adversaries." [41] A Radical-Socialist deputy mandated by his party to give its opinion of the bill well emphasized this gap between sentiment and reality. He complained somewhat bitterly of the deceptions he had felt in seeing "M. Tardieu, a representative of the great enlightened bourgeoisie, abandoning . . . the liberal principles which were at the base of his distinguished intellectual formation." Tardieu had opened, the deputy concluded, "a fissure in our legislation through which the whole of socialism will pass." [42]

The Socialists, for their part, had the most original objections to the government's program in that they were the only group to consider the effect it might have on the consumer. From their point of view, "to fear overproduction of foodstuffs, whatever their nature, would be an inconceivable foolishness in a period of high prices." [43] But with an eye no doubt on the rural vote they specifically attacked limitation of plantings with the same argument we have seen used by the Agricultural Commission. They did not stop there, however: there were other monopolies beside the "monopoly" of big producers; to restore equilibrium in the wine market the "monopoly" of distribution must also be smashed. The Socialist demonstration of the difference in price between wine in the vats and wine on the table must have confirmed the suspicions of both consumer and grower. And a demonstration of the lack of relation in the price of the latter to the fluctuations in price of the former [44] must have especially played on the suspicions of the small growers from the "red belts" of the Midi who had traditional misgivings about urban dealers.[45]

The representatives of agriculture, whatever their political affiliation, were unanimous in agreeing that something must be done for the winegrowers, but what to do seemed only to present problems. One of the most difficult of these was offered by the tax on yields. Given the great variations in growing methods in the different winegrowing regions, how could a single figure for an "excessive" yield be set? As a deputy from the Midi pointed out—and not without some justification—it was possible in his region to produce good wine through normal production methods on properties yielding an average of 150 hectolitres the hectare.[46] And if after all it was the small grower who was to be protected, what was a small grower? In Burgundy, for example, a production of 500 hectolitres might be big, involving paid hands and relatively extensive holdings, but in the Midi it could be the work of one family.[47] On a more general level, what was to become of scientific agriculture or good growing practices if they were only to result in taxes?[48]

The overriding concern of agriculture, however, was the precedent involved in the government's project which it was feared would spread to other branches of agricultural production. To one spokesman for agriculture in the Chamber, the situation of the winegrowers was simply "a boil to be lanced—that is to say a means of treatment entirely exceptional and entirely temporary . . . which must have no consequences for other agriculturists.[49] Interestingly enough the government agreed: what it was proposing was only "an exceptional remedy for an exceptional situation."[50] This last statement may have been sanguine, but it must have at least soothed the breasts of many growers of beets and raisers of wheat or even the Breton deputy who asked if the government might not now attempt to limit fishing and the planting of apple trees.[51]

No such conciliatory words were reserved for another group, however. The Algerian deputies, for understandable reasons, were unanimously opposed to the bill. And like the other groups mentioned above they too tried to lift their objections to the level of principles. The government's project, it was maintained, would "shatter the colonial *élan* of France."[52] What would happen, it was asked, to the *petit colon* who had bought 100 hectares covered with scrub and who could with difficulty and in "an admirable spirit of colonization" barely clear twenty of them and plant them in vines in five years?[53] And in view of the proposed taxes, what about Algeria's fiscal autonomy which was supposed to encourage settlement?[54] As might have been guessed from the anti-Algerian bias of the debate, the government stood firm against these objections. Tardieu sternly reminded the Algerian deputies that as head of the government he had fought against a quota system for Algerian wines in the name of national unity. Then all that Algeria had asked for was the same treatment as metropolitan France and this was what Algeria was getting now.[55]

LE STATUT DE LA VITICULTURE

After criticism, attack, and ridicule, and by compromise and threat, the *Statut de la Viticulture,* or law of July 4, 1931, was at last passed by the Chamber of Deputies on June 24, 1931, with a vote of 385 to 205. In its final form it was much changed from the original *projet de loi.*

The tax on yields, which began with a yield of 101 hectolitres the hectare, was reduced for yields up to 175 hectolitres the hectare and above that figure was increased by as much as 25 percent in the case of yields of 250 hectolitres the hectare or more. The suggestion of the Commission des Boissons to tax yields in the 81- to 100-hectolitre range if total production was 5,000 hectolitres or more was more than acted upon. A production of 2,000 hectolitres or more was now subject to a tax of 5 francs the hectolitre yielded if it fell in the 81- to 100-hectolitre bracket, and in addition a production of 50,000 hectolitres or more, if the yield was from 51 to 80 hectolitres the hectare, was also subject to the 5-franc tax. Moreover, a production of 400 hectolitres or less was not to be taxed unless it represented a yield of more than 151 hectolitres the hectare.

Thus the argument that yield alone was a poor basis for figuring this tax gained some acceptance. In the Midi many small proprietors had high yields and so the net of the law was loosened for their benefit. On the other hand the biggest producers in the same region, by the nature of their operations, could not get the same yield from the same variety of grapes as an entire family toiling over a few hectares. Therefore the net had to be widened and strengthened to catch them.

In the matter of limiting new plantings the recommendations of the January, 1931, assembly of the Fédération des Associations Viticoles prevailed. The annual tax on new plantings was dropped in favor of a ten-year prohibition. But an important exemption which went beyond the provision for one new hectare every five years originally proposed by the government permitted every grower owning ten hectares or less to plant an additional ten hectares.[56] The other exemptions, such as vines planted only for family consumption, proposed by the government in the first instance were left unchanged.

The minimum production for blocking a grower's harvest was fixed at 400 hectolitres which, while lower than the government's original figure, was still considerably above the 200 hectolitre floor proposed by the Commission des Boissons. Annual decrees were to announce whether blockage would be necessary or not and if so they would also fix the percentages to be blocked. These were to be calculated on a progressive scale according to production and yield. The blocked wines were to be released when the average price of wine on the markets of Nîmes, Béziers, Montpellier, Narbonne, and Perpignan exceeded the average of the previous five years.[57] All imported wines were to be blocked in the same proportion as domestic wines. Exempted from blockage were growers whose production was at least 40 percent less than the average for the three previous years provided the current yield was not more than 100 hectolitres the hectare. Losses of more than half the harvest from hail, frost, or hurricane also brought an exemption.

Compulsory distilling did not figure in the government's original proposals.[58] And when the C.G.V. recommended that the government should provide for distillation of part of the blocked wines, the Commission des Boissons in an interesting opinion rejected the whole principle of compulsory distilling.[59] It was incorporated in the new law, however, but the percentage of wine to be distilled was based on a grower's total production rather than on that part of it which was blocked. Distillation was to go into effect only when the combined harvest of France and Algeria exceeded 65 million hectolitres, and it affected only those growers producing in the previous three years an average of 500 hectolitres or more with a yield of 80 or more hectolitres the hectare. The percentages to be distilled were fixed on a progressive schedule ranging from a little less than 3.5 percent in the 500 hectolitre bracket to a fraction over 5 percent for productions of 3,000 hectolitres or more. The alcohol distilled was to be bought by the state at a price equal to that which the state alcohol monopoly charged for industrial alcohol destined for use in the *carburant national,* an automobile fuel mixture imposed on all motor-fuel refiners or importers.[60] This price represented a real loss for the winegrowers on the quantities distilled, and the provision was much criticized.[61] But if compulsory distilling was a penalty, the percentages were light.[62]

To the government its completed *Statut* was by admission "imperfect," but it was claimed that "it would nevertheless serve the interests of viticulture." [63] If by this last statement the government meant the desires of the small growers, the claim was undoubtedly correct. And it should also be noted that in general the *Statut* conformed to the recommendations of the C.G.V. and the other winegrowing associations. But reservations about its future effectiveness were in order.

As we have already seen, glimpses of these were apparent in the figures quoted by Tardieu in 1930 when he first announced the government's program. Now, under the completed *Statut,* the regular tax on yields, not counting the partial exemption for producers of less than 400 hectolitres, would have, in 1929, affected roughly one half of France's total production. The additional tax on producers of more than 2,000 hectolitres would have at the most affected somewhat less than 15 percent of metropolitan production, or about 27 percent of combined Franco-Algerian production. The tax on producers of more than 50,000 hectolitres, it is amusing to note, would have affected only six growers in Algeria, who accounted for one half of one percent of combined Franco-Algerian production. There were even larger gaps in the legislation dealing with distilling and blocking the harvest. In 1929 at least 75 percent of production would have escaped both.[64] And although it is impossible to figure exactly the area of new vines that could have been planted under all the exemptions of the *Statut,* the legislators would have done well to remember when fixing the 10 hectare exemption that in 1929 the average area of a French vineyard was less than 2 hectares and that in the department of Hérault, the Midi's biggest producer, the average was still only 3.3 hectares.[65] The weaknesses of the new law indicated by these figures were to become apparent almost as soon as it went into operation.

THE PROGRAM IN ACTION

As prescribed by the *Statut,* the Interministerial Commission on Viticulture met on September 14, 1931, to decide whether it would be necessary to block part of the approaching harvest. With the information it had on hand about the harvest's expected size, it decided against the move. Then, perhaps a little uneasily, it reminded the growers that if its prediction of "a normal harvest—without excessive superabundance" were surpassed, compulsory distillation would operate to protect sales.[66]

But on December 15, with figures coming in showing a harvest of 57,457,000 hectolitres for France and 15,380,000 hectolitres for Algeria plus about 4,100,000 hectolitres in stocks remaining from the year before, the Commission reversed itself and belatedly decided to bring blockage into play.[67] Those growers who had already sold all their wine were, of course, not affected, but those with quantities still on hand found them presumably blocked in their entirety if they happened to represent an amount of wine less than the percentage that would normally have been blocked.[68]

Since Franco-Algerian production passed the 65-million hectolitre mark the distilling provisions of the *Statut* also came into force.[69] But since the total of wine available for the market came to more than 75 million hectolitres, distilling under the provisions of the law of April 19, 1930, likewise became operative.[70] In addition it had already been decreed that growers subject to this earlier law (production of 500 hectolitres or more in 1929 with a yield of 50 hectolitres the hectare or more) were to have their percentages of blocked wine doubled.[71] The latter move, much criticized and without any precedent in either of the two laws,[72] was presumably to encourage further distillation since the decree offered exemptions from blockage for growers who would voluntarily distill beyond the required amounts. This relief proved somewhat illusory, however, as distilling facilities were swamped.[73]

The end result of these measures, all decreed within five days, was to cause a virtual halt in sales. According to one observer, "confusion, indecision, and anxiety" dominated the markets [74]—a situation further prolonged by government attempts to enforce blockage on wines already sold to dealers, which under normal conditions would have been blocked in the growers' cellars.[75] Of course these developments affected only a minority of growers, but that they created real hardships as well as confusion is undeniable, although the former were undoubtedly exaggerated.[76] To the complaints of the minority, however, were added more widely expressed dissatisfactions with the new law. These were occasioned by what was considered the remarkable fact that the price of wine was falling.

On July 4, 1931, the average price of a hectolitre of red wine on the markets of Montpellier and Perpignan had been 180 francs. By December 5 prices of 72 to 90 francs were being quoted at Perpignan; and on May 15 1932, a rough average of prices on all five of the markets named in the *Statut* would have come to around 67 francs.[77] In July, prospects of a light harvest began to push prices up, but by December of 1932 they had reached only 88 francs. Under these conditions the formula that tied the freeing of blocked wines to the attainment of the previous five years' average price proved unworkable. The wines blocked since the harvest of 1931 were finally released in February of 1933 with the average price on the five markets still below what it had been when the *Statut* went into effect. Clearly the debut of the latter had not been a success.

Meanwhile the government, remembering the last winter's confusion, decreed as early as July, 1932, that until final production figures should be known, every winegrower subject to blockage was to consider one third of his harvest provisionally blocked.[78] As predicted, the metropolitan harvest in 1932 was light (49,564,-630 hectolitres) and blockage was decided against, although Algeria produced a record 18,180,000 hectolitres and stocks from the previous year made a total of over 70 million hectolitres of wine available for the market. Compulsory distilling went into effect and the provisional blockage was not lifted until February, 1933. But the two measures failed to affect prices,[79] which remained low and went into a steady decline after April.

Similar conditions obtained after the harvest of 1933. The total amount of wine available for the market represented an increase of 2 percent over the previous year. Blockage was decreed, although on a lighter scale than in 1931, and compulsory distillation went into effect. Prices, however, continued to decline. The national average for 1932 had been 128 francs the hectolitre; in 1933 it fell to 117 francs, and in 1934 dropped to 78 francs.

Meanwhile the first experiences with the *Statut* had convinced the government that some changes were in order. A new law (law of July 8, 1933), voted after a long debate, amended the *Statut* in the following important particulars.

Blockage was to be automatically decreed when Franco-Algerian production and stocks exceeded 70 million hectolitres, and provisional blockage was made a permanent part of the law with the proportions fixed at one third for producers of 400 hectolitres or more, and one half for producers of 5,000 hectolitres or more. Some flexibility was thus taken out of the law, but at least a repetition of the previous year's confusion was avoided.

By way of compensation, flexibility was added to the compulsory-distilling provisions. The percentages of the harvest to be distilled were now to be fixed by annual decree instead of having them permanently fixed as was the case with the original version of the *Statut*. Production figures which would bring compulsory distillation into play were changed from 65 million hectolitres (combined Franco-Algerian production) to 70 million hectolitres (combined Franco-Algerian production plus stocks). Also, the price paid for compulsorily distilled alcohol was increased.

The prohibition on new plantings was shortened from ten years to five, but the ten-hectare exemption was tightened to allow the planting of only up to three hectares by those who did not have that much area under cultivation. The other exemptions remained in force as formerly, but an interesting addition specified that replanting was to be made with grape varieties approved by the departmental *office agricole*.

The new law barely lasted a year in most of its important provisions. As we have seen in the preceding chapter, the autumn of 1934 brought Algeria's greatest (22,043,000 hectolitres) and France's second greatest (78,144,090 hectolitres) wine harvest, which, added to stocks, brought the total wine available for the market to over 100 million hectolitres. Into this unprecedented glut the government rushed with more legislation (law of December 24, 1934).

The floor on growers subject to compulsory distillation was lowered from a production of 500 hectolitres to 200 hectolitres as a "temporary measure" to meet an "extraordinary year." [80] The percentages to be distilled were determined according to the law of July 8, 1933, and it is interesting as an indication of the emergency to note that they averaged about 50 percent more than those originally fixed by the *Statut*. Also a "super distillation" written into the new law increased the quantities to be distilled by 10 percent when yield was from 40 to 80 hectolitres the hectare, and progressively up to 50 percent when the yield was 150 hectolitres the hectare or more.[81]

The blockage provisions remained unchanged. But again it is interesting as an indication of the emergency to note that the percentages decreed ranged from 22 percent in the lowest production range up to 47 percent in the highest. The percentages for these same ranges had been 9 and 15, respectively, in 1933.

In the matter of new plantings the three-hectare exemption was lowered to one, and this was only allowed if there had been no increase in the vineyard area of the department concerned since 1920. The right to replace vines pulled up for any reason except phylloxera was limited to 95 percent of the area existing on Janaury 1, 1933. Thereafter the percentage diminished by one for each additional ten hectares until a floor of 80 percent was reached.

Two important innovations in the matter of plantings were the forbidding of any new plantings of certain grape varieties declared "undesirable," [82] and the granting of exonerations from distilling and blockage to growers who would pull up some vines. The exonerations were to be based on the average yield per hectare for the preceding three years of the area uprooted.

Other important innovations in the new law which in a sense reflected the crisis atmosphere were a provision against speculation [83] and the granting to agents of the Service for Repression of Frauds in the Ministry of Agriculture the right to enter the winegrowers' cellars or other buildings freely and at all times. This right, it will be recalled, had been defeated when proposed in 1931.

The law of December 24, 1934, was even more short-lived than either of its predecessors. It could do nothing to stop a now drastic drop in prices which on April 1, 1935, reached a new low of 36 francs the hectolitre on the five markets of the Midi. In the midst of the meetings, demonstrations, and general discontent that followed, the Interministerial Commission on Viticulture met on June 26 "to establish the basis of a new *Statut.*" [84] The day before, the Ministry of Finance in an extraordinary move announced that the government would buy *all* the wine alcohol offered to it beyond the amounts prescribed by compulsory distillation. The price was set at 480 francs the hectolitre (100°), the then current price of natural alcohol on the open market. And in July, the government, eschewing parliamentary debate, presented its decree-law of July 30, 1935, to the troubled winegrowers.

Both the blockage and the compulsory-distilling limits were to be lowered to include a production of 200 hectolitres if total Franco-Algerian production plus stocks was greater than 84 million hectolitres, and a production of 300 hectolitres if this total was greater than 78 million hectolitres. The tax on yields was also lowered to include a production of 200 hectolitres and one of 125 hectolitres if the yield per hectare was 150 hectolitres or more.[85]

An important new provision affected unblocked wines. In the event that the average price of wine on the five markets of the Midi fell "manifestly" below cost, the government was to fix a time schedule for the staggered release of the remaining portions of unblocked wine. Release was contingent on the reaching of predetermined prices on the five markets during two selling periods. The amount released was not to be less than 10 percent of the original portion of unblocked wine or 100 hectolitres, whichever was greater.[86]

In the matter of pulling up vines, the new law went considerably further than previous legislation. In addition to the dispensations from blockage and distilling already provided for, tax abatements and indemnities were offered for voluntary uprooting and a promised delay in replanting of thirty years. Agreements were to be entered into by November 30, 1935, and if by January 1, 1936, a minimum of 150,000 hectares in France and Algeria had not been put out of production, obligatory pulling up was to be decreed with indemnities cut by one half.

An even more surprising innovation was the government's plan to place its purchases of wine alcohol on a more permanent and extensive basis. A good part of the law of July 30, 1935, which caused it to be called the *Statut de l'Alcool,* was devoted to reorganization of the government's alcohol monopoly [87] so as to include a regular quota for wine alcohol freely offered. The quota was set at 325,000 hectolitres, which were to be paid for at a price 2.55 times the price of a hectolitre of beet alcohol. This offered the winegrowers an opportunity of distilling approximately 3,250,000 hectolitres of wine each year at a fair profit. In addition there was a quota for 300,000 hectolitres of *alcools de marc* [88] which offered further inducements to distilling. Compulsorily distilled wine alcohol, however, was to be paid for at a lower rate but one which allowed for higher prices than those offered by previous legislation.[89]

The prospect of the obligatory pulling up of vines was much criticized, and the wine-alcohol quota was denounced (not by the winegrowers, to be sure) as a subsidy and a sellout to viticultural interests. But as the summer of 1935 gave way to autumn there was little time for controversy. The official communiqués of the Interministerial Commission, first predicted a figure of 88 million hectolitres as the amount of wine that would be available for the market. Then, as the *Revue de viticulture* sarcastically put it, this figure "echelloned" to 90 and then 92 million hectolitres.[90] When the harvest was gathered in, however, it was found to be only slightly less heavy than the year before—75,810,000 hectolitres for France and 18,910,000 hectolitres for Algeria which, when added to a record total of 8,533,600 hectolitres in stocks, made more than 100 million hectolitres of wine available for the second year in a row. In addition it was estimated that there were still 10 million hectolitres from the harvest of 1934 waiting to be distilled.[91]

Blockage was decreed with the same percentages in force as in 1934 plus percentages of 15 and 18, respectively, for the newly included levels of production (200 to 300 hectolitres and 301 to 400 hectolitres). Compulsory-distillation percentages were the same as in 1934 in the lower ranges but were increased by up to 34 percent

in the higher ones.   In December the government moved to stagger
the release of unblocked wines still in the possession of growers.   The
release price was set at 72 francs the hectolitre.   On April 30, 1936,
this price having been reached, one half of the unblocked wines were
set free and the next release price was fixed at 85.50 francs.   This
price was reached in June when an additional one fifth were set free.
The remaining three tenths were released at the end of September
when the price of wine on the five markets had climbed to 100 francs
the hectolitre—a sum, it should be noted, roughly equivalent to cost
price.

TABLE 20.   WINE PRICES QUOTED ON THE PERPIGNAN MARKET
AT SELECTED INTERVALS (*In francs*)

Date [a]	Price [b]	Date	Price
July 4, 1931	18.00–19.00	Dec. 21, 1935	5.00– 6.00
Jan. 7, 1933	11.00–15.00	Jan. 18, 1936	6.00– 6.50
June 20, 1934	9.00–11.50	Feb. 22, 1936	6.50– 7.00
July 21, 1934	10.00–12.00	March 21, 1936	7.00– 8.00
Sept. 22, 1934	7.00	May 9, 1936	7.50– 8.00
Dec. 17, 1934	4.50– 5.50	July 4, 1936	9.00– 9.75
May 4, 1935	4.75– 5.00	Oct. 3, 1936	9.50–10.50
May 25, 1935	4.00– 4.25	Dec. 21, 1936	13.50–14.00
Aug. 24, 1935	4.30– 4.60	Feb. 12, 1937	14.50 (9°)
Oct. 5, 1935	4.00– 4.25	June 5, 1937	14.50 (9°)
Nov. 23, 1935	4.25– 5.00	Sept. 25, 1937	15.25 (9°)

[a] Prices are for week preceding date indicated. As markets are not held at
regular intervals it is not possible to give exactly equivalent dates for the different
years.

[b] In the Midi and Algeria prices are always quoted by the degree per hectolitre as alcoholic content is the only distinguishing feature of cheap, unblended
wines. Thus a quoted price of 8 francs for a hectolitre of 10° wine actually
means a payment price of 80 francs. In the prices listed above, the first figure
after each date generally applies to wines of 8° to 8.5°, the second figure to wines
of 12° plus. The majority of Midi wines are in the 9° to 10° category, so their
price would fall somewhere between the limits listed above.

Source: Weekly market quotations furnished by the Chamber of Commerce of
Perpignan and published in the *Journal d'agriculture pratique*.

As Table 20 suggests, the staggered-release system may well
have helped the upward turn of prices in 1936.   But these prices
still offered a miserable return.   The situation of the winegrowers
seemed only slightly less depressed than in 1935, and 1936 was
still a year of ferment.   The *Revue de viticulture* predicted a gov-

ernment wine monopoly if the harvest of 1936 should be as great as in 1935.[92] Such a measure had already been proposed by a Socialist deputy from Hérault in January.[93] But with the coming of the Popular Front government in May, agitation for something of this sort really got under way. In April Léon Blum in an address on Radio-Midi had already proposed the creation of an Office National du Vin, and in June, after the creation of the Office des Blés, he began to try to gather support for the proposal. But the opposition of the winegrowing associations was strong and there was only lukewarm support in the Socialist party itself. The Socialist members of the Interministerial Commission on Viticulture actually declared themselves against the Office, as did the Communists.[94]

The project was then dropped, and it might be said that this was an operation in which nature had a hand. The harvest of 1936 was refreshingly light, blockage and compulsory distilling were dispensed with, and the national price average shot up over 100 percent. Cautiously the government kept the staggered-release system in operation, but this brought only mild protests from the growers.[95]

In 1937 the harvest was extremely light in the Midi—nearly 40 percent less than the year before—but production was moderate to heavy in the rest of France and in Algeria. The total of wine available for the market represented an increase of nearly 16 percent over the previous year, yet scarcity prices in the Midi pushed the national price average up an additional 29 percent to 180 francs the hectolitre. After the harvest of 1938, total wine available increased by another 15 percent, but prices only dropped about 6 percent. After the harvests of 1937 and 1938 blockage and distillation went into effect without any criticism from the growers. And when, after the harvest of 1938, Algeria's second heaviest production on record added to metropolitan production and stocks made for an available total of more than 87 million hectolitres of wine, prices remained relatively firm.

The chronicle of the three years before World War II suggests the return of stability to the wine market. Shortly after the harvest of 1936, the Interministerial Commission eagerly spoke of "recovered confidence." At the same time it assured the growers "that the measures applied last season remain the basis of government action," and urged that "viticulture be not in any way projected into the adventure of new experiments." [96]

The advice was not immediately heeded. Although there were no "new experiments," a law of July 12, 1937, raised the quantities

TABLE 21.   WINE PRODUCTION AND PRICES AT THE PRODUCTION LEVEL
IN FRANCE AND ALGERIA, 1930–38

Year	Production in France (in hectolitres)	Production in Algeria (in hectolitres)	Stocks (in hectolitres)	Average Price per Hectolitre (in francs)
1930	45,637,970	12,024,000	6,185,625	183
1931	59,131,000	16,159,000	3,835,411	121
1932	49,569,630	18,180,000	4,328,921	128
1933	51,765,860	16,731,000	5,480,248	117
1934	78,144,000	22,043,000	3,631,717	78
1935	75,810,000	18,910,000	8,533,600	64
1936	43,444,000	14,127,000	——	139
1937	54,331,330	15,424,000	6,344,894	180
1938	60,332,402	21,490,000	5,569,663	169

Source: *Annuaire statistique.*

of wine that would bring blockage and distillation into play by six million hectolitres at all levels of production.[97]   After the harvest of 1937, however, a new law was passed that permitted the government to order blockage simply when "resources were greater than needs." [98]   But with prospects of a relatively heavy harvest in 1938 the new law and the six million hectolitre raises enacted earlier were both canceled, and the quantities prescribed by the law of July 30, 1935, for bringing blockage and distillation into effect were virtually restored.[99]   In addition the government reserved the right to make a production of less than 200 hectolitres subject to blockage if total wine available for the market came to more than 95 million hectolitres.

Thus the government may be said to have held the line against any relaxation of blockage and distilling regulations during the three years of recovered confidence.   The same was unfortunately not true for the program of pulling up vines.   In 1936, the target date of January 1, by when it was hoped 150,000 hectares would have been voluntarily pulled up, was changed to October 20.   Meanwhile, in the hopes of speeding the process a law of March 28, 1936, offered to growers who would uproot and agree not to replant for fifteen years the same indemnities that the law of July 30, 1935, had offered for a thirty-year delay.

Still, in December, 1936, assuming the government's unwillingness to resort to obligatory pulling up, the target date had to be postponed to October, 1937. This date was moved back another year by the law of July 12, 1937, but before it could be reached, a new law (decree-law of May 31, 1938) left the responsibility for determining the final date up to the Ministries of Agriculture, Interior, and Finance after consultation with the Interministerial Commission on Viticulture. This, according to the *Revue de viticulture,* meant "in actual fact the adjournment *sine die* . . . of the menace of obligatory uprooting." [100]

DID THE PROGRAM WORK?

The preceding description of the government's program in large part answers the question as to its effectiveness. As we have seen, from the first moment of the program's discussion it was subject to practical considerations, prejudices, and even traditions which would militate against its complete success. The vested interests of the winegrowers, the *mystique* of the vine, the sacredness of property, and the exaltation of the small grower all set limits that can be clearly traced in the *Statut* and its subsequent emendations.[101]

The most obvious limitation was that under the floor of a 200 hectolitre production were grouped the great majority of French winegrowers and about two thirds of national production. For these and some producers in the upper brackets there were also exemptions which in turn probably opened larger holes in the law than intended.[102] The latter plus evident difficulties in the enforcement of complicated legislation [103] make difficult any detailed measurement of the effectiveness of the *Statut*.[104]

There are, however, two general questions which may be asked about its operation during the period under review. One is, did the *Statut* raise prices; and the other is, did it check production? Each one of these questions is, of course, the corollary of the other. And in a large sense all the provisions of the *Statut* were aimed at these

two goals. But two provisions—blockage and staggered release—
bore directly on prices, and two others—compulsory distillation and
limiting plantings or pulling up vines—bore more directly on overproduction.

Blockage, as we have seen, was not a complete success. Although in some years it may have kept prices from going down
faster than they did, it did not bring them up. Moreover, when two
abundant harvests followed one another, it could help drive prices
down. The release *en masse* after the record harvest of 1934 of
wines blocked from the previous year would be a case in point.

The staggered release of unblocked wines, as we have also seen,
fell somewhat short of its goal the first year it was tried in that it
did not drive prices above cost. Of this system Professor Milhau
has the following to say:

The average price of wine during a certain period depends uniquely on
the quantity of wine sold during this period and not on the manner in
which the sale has been organized: staggered sale or free sale, the average price will be the same. Article 8 [staggered release] will not lift
prices unless it reduces the quantity of wine sold during the period under
consideration. To expect anything else is to invite delusions.[105]

There is still, however, the experience of the three years after
the harvest of 1936 to take into account. By any but crisis-year
standards, 1938 and 1939 saw heavy harvests, yet the price of wine
climbed for part of the period, and when it did decline remained at a
relatively high level. Augé-Laribé has attributed this to a "caprici-
ous Nature who put things in order." [106] Milhau, consistent with
his statement quoted above, said that the upward swing in prices
which began in 1936 was caused by the release of the last three
tenths of the harvest of 1935 at the end of September, 1936.[107]
Many others, however, felt that the staggered-release system was
directly responsible for the rise in prices.[108] And there were critics
who made the more general conclusion that "in the long run" the
Statut, as a whole, kept prices up.[109] The intervention of World
War II and the postwar experience, however, would seem to render
this last conclusion a very attenuated hypothesis.

Of the four chief provisions of the *Statut,* it can most certainly
be said the attempt to limit vine planting was a failure. As might
have been expected, the new planting exemptions in the *Statut*

caused a rush to take advantage of them.[110] Thus the area of the French vineyard which covered 1,526,900 hectares in 1930 before the *Statut* went into effect had increased to 1,555,830 hectares by 1934 when the voluntary-uprooting program began—and it still stood at 1,524,722 hectares in 1940. The area of the vineyard, however, is subject to considerable fluctuation from year to year. Storms, frosts, and diseases, for example, put vines temporarily out of production and off the statistics as well. New plantings, it should also be noted, are not carried in the statistics until after their third year. Nevertheless, a projection of averages over five- and ten-year periods still shows the ineffectiveness of the provisions of the *Statut* regarding the planting or uprooting of vines:

Average Vineyard Area of France

1926–30	1,516,958 hectares	1921–30	1,524,408 hectares
1931–35	1,543,854	1931–40	1,527,369
1936–40	1,510,883		

Moreover in Algeria where, because of larger-sized properties, it might have been expected that exemptions from the limitations on new plantings would be less numerous, the following almost steady advance in plantings took place:

Vineyard Area of Algeria

1930	271,000 hectares	1935	400,000 hectares
1931	312,000	1936	390,000
1932	353,000	1937	395,000
1933	373,000	1938	399,000
1934	388,000		

Compulsory distilling, on the other hand, was perhaps the most effective part of the *Statut* in that it at least removed a certain quantity of wine from the market. It should be noted, however, that the most significant amounts were distilled when the government had to take extraordinary steps to supplement the compulsory-distilling program. Of these the most effective step was the assigning of a quota for wine-alcohol purchases by the state alcohol monopoly. The relatively high percentage of wine distilled after the harvests of 1937 and 1938, which, if they were moderately heavy, were not overabundant, may be attributed to the quota, and the latter may well have been the determining factor in the high prices of those two years.

Moreover, the whole program, as Table 22 shows, brought the amount of wine distilled relatively close to the level it had reached in pre-phylloxera days before beet alcohol began to dominate the alcohol market. But in contrast to the earlier period, when distillation had acted as a natural "safety-valve" in times of over-production, the new development was an artificial one bought at a price paid for by several sectors of the national economy. It is to an examination of this price and the war waged by the grape on the beet for a larger share of the alcohol market that our study must now turn.

TABLE 22. WINE PRODUCTION AND WINE DISTILLED INTO ALCOHOL IN FRANCE
(*In hectolitres*)

Year	Wine Production	Amount of Wine Distilled into Alcohol [a]
1870–79, yearly average	54,670,800	4,998,900
1900–07, yearly average	55,179,200	2,252,900
1919–28, yearly average	58,844,052	1,979,573
1929	65,015,710	2,330,350 [b]
1930	45,637,970	2,013,620 [c]
1931	59,131,000	2,744,890 [d]
1932	49,569,630	1,619,300 [d]
1933	51,765,860	1,712,380 [d]
1934	78,144,090	11,684,870 [e]
1935	75,810,000	8,380,290 [f]
1936	43,555,000	886,160 [f,g]
1937	54,331,330	2,298,560 [f]
1938	60,332,402	6,684,720 [f]
Yearly average	58,329,992	4,035,514

Sources: *Annuaire statistique; Bulletin de statistique et de législation comparée.*

[a] Figures in this column are for the year following the one indicated in the first column. The greatest part of distillation took place in the calendar year following the harvest year.

[b] Law of April 19, 1930: special purchases of wine alcohol by state until end of year.

[c] In part carryover of the above. Includes wine delivered to distillery before December 30, 1930, but not distilled until 1931.

[d] Compulsory distilling in effect under law of July 4, 1931.

[e] Government as an emergency measure (decree of June 25, 1935) offers to buy all wine alcohol offered to it in addition to that compulsorily distilled. Price for former higher than latter.

[f] Regular quota purchases of wine alcohol (in addition to compulsorily distilled alcohol) in effect under law of July 30, 1935.

[g] Compulsory distilling lifted for harvest of 1936.

8. *THE WINEGROWERS AND THE STATE ALCOHOL MONOPOLY*

In an earlier chapter we have seen how in the period from the phylloxera epidemic to the outbreak of World War I wine alcohol lost its position of leadership in the alcohol market to the "industrial" alcohols of the North. The reaction of winegrowing interests to this situation was to urge the diversion of northern alcohols to purely industrial uses, leaving the beverage alcohol market in the exclusive possession of wine alcohol and other "natural" (i.e., fruit) alcohols. But as we have also seen, this solution to what was then the problem of a decline in the distilling of alcohol from wine involved too many conflicting regional economic interests to carry the day.[1]

With the advent of World War I, however, the proposed solution became imperative for quite different reasons. The early invasion by the enemy of important distilling regions and the growing need for alcohol in the manufacture of explosives led the government by successive stages to larger requisitions of industrial alcohol and a stricter control of the alcohol industry. A law of June 30, 1916, finally reserved for the state the entire production of alcohols other than those distilled from "wines, ciders, perries, marcs, rapes, lees, and fruits." [2] The alcohols acquired by the state were to be re-assigned for industrial uses only. First priority went to the manufacture of explosives which generally accounted for 90 percent of the total requisitioned, the remainder going to medical, pharmaceutical, or motor-fuel usages. Thus, although some natural alcohol was also requisitioned in 1917, the division of the alcohol market so desired by winegrowing interests was established by law until the end of the year in which hostilities should cease.

THE WARTIME ALCOHOL REGIME

As early as 1915, however, there was agitation on the part of the winegrowers to make this division permanent. And in the same year a bill to this effect which included a state monopoly of the purchase and sale of industrial alcohol [3] was proposed by Édouard Barthe, a deputy from Hérault, soon to be known as the *chef incontestable* of Midi viticulture.[4] Numerous counterproposals and reports followed Barthe's bill, but none of them ever came to a vote.[5] The chief areas of difficulty were the limits of the divided market and the financing of the proposed monopoly which might have involved taxing one or all of the interests concerned. And these interests, in the words of one authority, were "so diametrically opposed that it was extremely difficult to find grounds of conciliation which would have permitted the elaboration of a rational, definitive project."[6] But by the summer of 1919 circumstances and developments had somewhat changed the picture.[7]

It was, of course, manifestly in the interest of the producers of natural alcohol and their numerous representatives in parliament to continue the wartime regime. Under it the price of wine alcohol had at first outpaced and then paralleled the breakneck price rise of wine. Similar benefits accrued to the distillers of other natural alcohols. In fact the distilling of cider became so profitable that nearly the entire cider production was being consumed in this way, and the government, in the public interest, had to intervene in 1918 to assure a supply for beverage purposes.

The wartime regime was also not unprofitable for the industrial distillers, but they had a less clear-cut interest in its continuance. With their outlet in the manufacture of explosives shut off they were eager to reinvade the beverage alcohol market. On the other hand, the stopping of controls would have involved the liquidation of large stocks of alcohol held by the government. At the end of the war these comprised roughly 1,050,000 hectolitres, a quantity 25 percent greater than the combined production of natural and industrial alcohols in 1918. The release of this amount on a free market would have meant an unprecedented drop in alcohol prices and probably the ruin of producers of natural alcohols.[8] The damage suffered by northern distilleries during the war also made the continuation of state purchases attractive, however much the distillers might have looked forward to the end of the divided market that accompanied them.

Thus the industrial distillers, grudgingly to be sure, were led to favor a continuance of the wartime regime, and so a numerically formidable, if otherwise fragile, parliamentary coalition of beet, wine, and fruitgrowing interests went to work. On August 6, 1919, a hotly debated bill which provided for the regime's permanent organization under the Ministry of Finance passed the Chamber of Deputies by a close vote. But it was defeated in the Senate, chiefly because of a clause which called on the general budget of the state to furnish credits to set the project in operation. The lower house then invited the government to decree the provisional extension of the wartime regime. This was done retroactively on August 13, for a six-month period following the ending of hostilities on June 28. Subsequently one more six-month extension was voted in 1919, another in 1920, a nine-month one at the end of 1920 and again in 1921, a twenty-seven-month one in 1922, and a two-year one in 1924.[9] Finally a law of February 27, 1926, prolonged the regime indefinitely until such time as a permanent one could be set up. But given the differences of the industrial and natural alcohol distillers, differences sharpened by increasing production, these extensions might never have been carried out if meanwhile an extraordinary development had not taken place outside the halls of parliament.

THE AGREEMENT OF BÉZIERS AND THE *Carburant National*

The great impulse given to the development of gasoline-powered transportation by World War I, not to mention the experience of wartime fuel shortages, renewed France's interest in an alcohol

motor fuel.   On November 5, 1918, the Comité Général des
Pétroles set up, under the leadership of M. Barthe, a Commission
des Carburants Nationaux.   The next year the Commission carried
out experiments in which mixtures of alcohol and benzol were used
in public transport.   These experiments, however, were chiefly inspired by the state alcohol surplus and the quantities of benzol delivered by Germany under terms of the peace treaty.

It remained for winegrowing interests to see the larger possibilities of an alcohol carburant, not only in the national interest, but
as a solution to the problem of maintaining the division between
natural and industrial alcohols.   In April, 1921, the Comice
Agricole of Béziers, "persuaded that the alcohol question is of a
primordial interest to viticulture," announced a prize competition for
automobiles running on alcohol and for inventors who realized
processes "making still more practicable the use of a mixture of
denatured alcohol and gasoline as a motor fuel." [10]   The C. G. V.
quickly offered a "large sum" for the competition, and other groups
followed suit.[11]   More important, the initiative of the winegrowing
Midi was not lost on its representatives in Paris.

In July 9, 1921, M. Barthe obtained from the Chamber of
Deputies a resolution inviting the government "to organize through
experiment the perfection of the formula of the *carburant national*
and to insure the participation of interested government agencies
in the competition and demonstration at Béziers." [12]   This assured,
among other things, the important cooperation of the Ministry of
Agriculture and a government subsidy for the proceedings, which
were now fixed for April of 1922.   Further, the government on
October 17, 1921, organized a Comité Scientifique du Carburant
National which included France's foremost chemists and automotive
engineers.   Fiscal advantages were also accorded mixtures of gasoline and alcohol.   Meanwhile, the sponsors of the Béziers competition had easily enlisted the support of distilling interests in the
North, and a conference between the two groups was arranged to
run concurrently with the competition.   "Everything is thus ready,"
the *Progrès agricole et viticole* rhapsodized, "to channel industrial
alcohol toward an outlet without limits." [13]

The Bèziers competition, now elevated to *La Grande Semaine
du Carburant National,* ran from August 2–9, 1922.   It was pre-

sided over by the Minister of Agriculture, and attracted large crowds drawn by the automobile road tests and an exhibition of agricultural machinery powered by alcohol and gasoline mixtures. The *Semaine* was thus a foreordained "official" success. Much was made of the more than one hundred motors used to demonstrate mixtures from many competing firms, and of the fact that of the three thousand tins of mixture supplied to the automobilists, only three were found defective. Less was made of the fact that the Comité Scientifique, which attended the proceedings in a body, failed to give a prize to any single mixture. While some mixtures were better in some respects than others, none succeeded in being both technically and economically satisfactory. The Comité was encouraging, however, in its pronouncements. The better mixtures needed perfecting, to be sure, but this last step would not be a long one.[14]

Such reassurances were enough for the distillers of the North and the viticultural and distilling interests of the Midi. After meeting on the next to last day of the *Semaine,* they published the following order of the day.[15]

The Assembly met at Béziers, April 8, 1922, on the occasion of the *Semaine du Carburant National,* on the initiative of the Confédération Général des Vignerons and comprising notably

1. The authorized representatives of the C.G.V. and the producers of wine of the Midi,
2. The authorized representatives of the industrial distillers and the agricultural distillers of the North—

After having registered the adhesion of the producers of cider manifested by a telegram dated April 7, 1922,

1. Notes the full success of the tests organized at Béziers with a view to utilizing alcohol as a national carburant and congratulates the Comice Agricole of Béziers which has taken the initiative in this organizing;

Thanks the subscribers whose pecuniary assistance made the tests possible and who thus gave the decisive and material proof of the utility of a national carburant with an alcohol base. . . .

2. Takes cognizance of the complete accord arrived at between viticultural production, Midi distilling [interests], the Syndicat National des Vins et Spiriteux, industrial distilling and the agricultural distilling [interests] of the North on the following basis:

a) The domestic beverage alcohol market must be entirely reserved to natural alcohol except in the years when French wine production is lower, stocks included, than 40 million hectolitres and when the available stocks of natural alcohol do not surpass a third of the consumption of the preceding year, in which case industrial alcohol will be exceptionally permitted to be sold [for beverage purposes] at a price equal to the price of natural alcohol plus an additional 50 francs the hectolitre;

b) the beverage export market remains open to industrial alcohol;

c) The financial resources of the Office [Service des Alcools] will be assured by a tax of one franc the hectolitre on wine and 0.50 francs the hectolitre on cider at the retail level and by taxes levied on imports of rum, tafias [spirits of molasses] and other spirits, also by profits from the Office's sale of alcohol to certain industries. The credits thus obtained by the Office will be used by the Office to sell below cost alcohol for heating, lighting, and motor-fuel purposes so that alcohol will remain an essential fuel in France.

The Assembly unanimously decides to propose this project to parliament and appeals for a prompt and definitive vote of it in the interests of the prosperity of French agriculture and the national defense.

The delegates of the North, given their concern to insure the necessary resources for the continued existence of the Office, demand that legislation proceeding from this project include in its preamble the promise to help them obtain additional resources [for the Office] should actual resources prove insufficient, this promise having been agreed to by the deputies and senators here present.

All the members present and delegates to the reunion have signed this resolution and the minutes [of the Assembly].

Such, then, was the much commented on "agreement of Béziers." An "elegant solution," the Société des Agriculteurs de France proclaimed, which would mark an "enormous advance for all French agriculture."

No question has divided the mind of agriculture more than that of alcohol, which seemed to cause severe conflict between the interests of the winegrowers of the Midi and those of the beet producers of the North. There is no longer today any alcohol "question," or at least the question of alcohol has achieved a perfect limpidity which does not leave room for any rivalry.[16]

THE *Loi des Finances* OF FEBRUARY 28, 1923

The Béziers agreement was, of course, a mandate to parliament. On November 22, 1922, M. Barthe, supported by some three hundred deputies, offered a bill which incorporated the agreement's main features. Entering the realm of the specific where the language of the agreement had been vague, Barthe demanded that all importers of gasoline be required to mix alcohol with their gasoline in proportions of 10 percent to 90 percent, respectively.[17]

On February 26, 1923, the bill came before the Chamber of Deputies, where it was inserted in a law dealing with provisional budget credits for the next month (the so-called *douzièmes*). It was voted the same day, and approved by the Senate two days later. Although the bill was discussed, it would be incorrect to say that it was debated, so enthusiastically was it received. The Minister of Finance amidst applause took the floor to announce that the bill was in the interest both of France's domestic finances and her foreign-exchange balance.[18] M. Barthe for his part, again amidst applause, said that it was an effort "to escape the hegemony of the great world-wide trusts," and "to increase the financial and economic strength of the nation by the limitless development of the richness of its soil." [19] Another sector of agriculture was brought into the proceedings by the reminder that increased cultivation of the beet meant a better cultivation of wheat.[20] A northern deputy rose to thank M. Barthe for "the fine fight he had waged for twenty years on behalf of industrial alcohol." [21] And M. Barthe in his concluding remarks told the Chamber that the bill was a reform for which "it could surely count on priding itself before the country." [22]

In its final form, Article 6 of the law of February 28, 1923, required importers of gasoline, benzol, benzene, toluene, and coal distillation products, "in order to obtain import licenses, to buy each month from the state a quantity of ethyl alcohol . . . of 100° Gay-Lussac corresponding to a minimum percentage of 10 percent in volume of the quantity of fuel passed through customs by them in the preceding month." [23]

The law thus only required the importers to buy a certain quantity of alcohol. The percentage of mixture was left up to them. All alcohol acquired, however, had to be used for motor power (*force motrice*). And the government further increased its control over the disposition of its alcohol by reserving the right to change by decree the percentage of alcohol to be bought. Annual decrees

were also to fix the price of the alcohol sold to the importers, and
the price of the mixtures sold by them or eventually the spread between the price of these mixtures and the price of unmixed fuel, the
former to be cheaper than the latter. The right to determine technical standards for the mixtures and the manner of their storage and
handling was also reserved.

As provided for by the Béziers agreement, the consumption
taxes on wine and cider were increased by one franc and 0.50 francs
respectively, but the sums to be realized by these two increases were
credited to the Treasury. The financial balance of the Service des
Alcools was to be achieved by the diversion to its account of an
already established "temporary" surtax of 5 francs the hectolitre
on imports of motor fuels. The increase in the wine and cider tax
served then as a partial recompense for the loss to the state of the
motor-fuel import surtax.

To those who were genuinely interested in the rational development of a *carburant national,* the hasty acceptance of the law was a
disappointment.[24] The *carburant* was far from technically perfect.
A particular difficulty was the stability of the alcohol and gasoline
mixture. A few drops of water left in a gas tin after rinsing or
condensation in a gas tank or fuel line were enough to make the
carburant inoperative. The success of the Béziers trials was due to
the warm and dry weather in which they were held. Before Béziers
the Comité Scientifique, and afterwards the congress of the Société
de Chimie Industrielle, judged that a mixture of 50 percent alcohol
and 50 percent gasoline presented the maximum of stability, and
that mixtures of 10 to 15 percent alcohol "did not present a sufficient coefficient of security."[25] According to serious critics the 10
percent figure imposed on the motor-fuel importers represented the
maximum of industrial alcohol available for carburation.[26] And
although the law did not specify a mixture of that percentage, the
figure arrived at under such considerations showed that it was still
too early for a general use of the *carburant national,* and that the
hopes placed in it were deceptive.[27]

Further difficulties were presented by the fact that it was necessary to use 100°, or "absolute," alcohol in the *carburant.* In 1921
absolute alcohol was still a laboratory product, and although im-

petus was given to its processing by the *carburant national,* it was still an expensive affair. In place of absolute alcohol, solvents had been tried to homogenize the mixtures, but these too were expensive. Finally, there were difficulties in adjusting carburetors and other parts of the motor to the new fuel. All these factors combined to create consumer resistance to the *carburant* and, according to some authorities, a greater prejudice against it than was warranted.[28]

It was also observed that the whole program of the *carburant national* was principally tied to beet alcohol, which furnished at the time almost exactly 75 percent of the purchases of the Service des Alcools.[29] And beet alcohol, though three to four times as cheap as wine alcohol, was still the most expensive of the raw materials that could be used for industrial alcohol. Its yield was relatively light:

Raw Material	Litres of Alcohol per 100 Kilograms [30]
Beets	7.5
Potatoes	10.2
Wheat	30
Rye	38
Corn	39

Moreover, the beet was much less susceptible to machine cultivation than grains, and the price of beet alcohol was linked in parity with the price of beet sugar, the refining of beet sugar being a more expensive process than distilling. Still, given the pattern and requirements of French agriculture and the considerations of national economics governing them, beets offered at the time the only important source of industrial alcohol. But observations such as the preceding reflected the dismay of those who would have liked to see the *carburant national* live up to some of the promises made for it in the Chamber of Deputies. Marcel Rooy, in a contemporary monograph on the *carburant,* asked if concern for the protection of the wine-grower had not played a more important role in the vote of the law of February 28, 1923, than the considerations of national defense and economic independence that were invoked.[31] And other critics felt that the linking of the program for the *carburant national* with the interests of the beet and the vine boded ill for its success.[32]

These were small voices, however. The important fact for the moment was that two giants of French agriculture had won an important victory. Symbolic, in a sense, of this victory was the way in which they had cleared and continued to guard the sectors they laid out for themselves. Before the war the most important single source of industrial alcohol after beet alcohol was the molasses or syrup that was a by-product of beet-sugar refining. In the four years before the war, for example, the annual production of molasses alchohol averaged 40 percent of beet-alcohol production,[33] and molasses alcohol always commanded a higher price. During the war the Service des Alcools brought this price down to the level of beet alcohol but in 1920 it was paying 48 percent more for molasses alcohol.[34]

In 1922, however, the Service, in what was described as a "deliberate phase of eviction," [35] fixed the purchase price of molasses alcohol 56 percent *below* that of beet alcohol. This level was maintained for the next two years, during which time the production of molasses alcohol dropped an average of 44 percent and represented only 20 percent of beet-alcohol production. After that the production gap began to close, but in 1930 when the two alcohols had begun to approach prewar production levels, molasses alcohol was still priced 25 percent below beet alcohol.[36]

This policy was justified on the grounds that molasses for animal feed was being imported and that sugar was in short supply (it was possible to refine the molasses and obtain additional sugar). But one might ask if a concern for reestablishing sugar production, which had been badly affected by the war, was entirely served by limiting the production of the refiner's most valuable by-product. And on another level of argument, as eminent an authority as Henri Hitier noted after the war that the easy and profitable outlet given the beet growers in distillation was "strongly prejudicial to the production of sugar." [37] At least one critic suggested that the pricing policy just described was an unjust attempt to favor one alcohol at the expense of another.[38]

Grain alcohol was a more vulnerable victim of the same policy. Before the war, alcohol produced from grain closely followed and in some years surpassed molasses-alcohol production. To meet food requirements during the war its manufacture was forbidden except for those quantities obtained in the making of yeast. After the war the Service des Alcools cut the price for grain alcohol in the same proportions as molasses alcohol. The effect was drastic; whereas in 1913, 429,073 hectolitres of grain alcohol had been produced, the figure dropped to 203,306 hectolitres in 1922, and 28,376 hectolitres in 1924.[39] Again, an economic and social reason was advanced: grain for bread was in short supply. But if economic and social concerns were overriding, it is well to point out that during the bumper wheat harvests from 1932 through 1934, with the market in a depressed state, an average of only 23,965 hectolitres of grain alcohol was distilled each year.[40] It might well be argued that the government's commitment to beet-alcohol distilling, which was in turn largely inspired by winegrowing interests, deprived the Service des Alcools of an important source of cheap alcohol.

Not the slightest economic and social concern, but rather a virulent protectionism, colored the actions of the producers of natural alcohol, led by Midi viticultural interests, in their sector of the alcohol market. The Commission des Boissons, which cannot be accused of bias against the producers of natural alcohol, noted in a report the "organizing" of the latter's production after the war.[41] The first victims were the Algerian distillers of alcohol from figs, carobs, and dates. These had been encouraged by the high prices paid for natural alcohol during the war, and their production began to take on "an imposing character." [42] But a law of July 31, 1920, arbitrarily it would seem, ended the classification by earlier laws of this alcohol as natural alcohol. Thus, according to the Commission, "a budding industry was brutally suppressed." [43]

The next target was gin. Gin, although in most cases flavored by the juniper berry, is made entirely from grain alcohol. But by the capriciousness of the laws which distinguished between industrial alcohols and natural alcohols, gin was included among the latter. Its production in France had never been important compared to other beverage alcohols ranging, before the war, from 15,000 to 20,000 hectolitres a year.[44] But possibly fearing an extension of this production because of the government's policy towards industrial grain alcohol, the representatives of the Midi winegrowers and distillers pushed through some interesting legislation. By a law of December 31, 1920, distillers of gin were limited to an annual production not to exceed their average annual production from 1910 to 1913, with quantities beyond these amounts to be classified as industrial alcohol. In addition a surtax was to be levied on gin equal to the difference between the average price of wine alcohol quoted on three successive markets at Montpellier, Béziers, Nîmes, and Narbonne, and the price of industrial grain alcohol fixed by the Service des Alcools for the same year.

It was argued that this last was a prohibitive imposition, and so in 1921 the difference for establishing the surtax was changed to that between the price of wine alcohol on the four markets and the price of gin on the market at Lille quoted under the same conditions.[45] It is interesting, in view of the government's price policy towards grain alcohol, that even with the surtax on gin most of the greatly reduced production of grain alcohol went into the latter beverage, grain alcohol purchases by the Service des Alcools averaging only 250 hectolitres a year between 1924 and 1930.[46] It is also interesting that during this relatively prosperous period for the winegrowers, the viticultural press could still take time out to attack— as it often did—gin's peculiar grouping with natural alcohol as a "fissure" in the "classic separation" between natural and industrial alcohols.[47]

The next and biggest target the winegrowers attacked was rum. Before the war, rum and tafia (a cheap rum distilled from molasses) entered France freely, principally from her "ancient colonies" in the West Indies and Réunion. From 1910 to the outbreak of the war imports averaged roughly around 400,000 hectolitres a year.[48] During the war rum reached the same high price levels as metropolitan natural alcohols. Its position was the more advantageous because even though a relatively heavy duty was now levied on it, it was the only imported alcohol that was not required to be diverted to industrial uses. As a result a large amount of cheap rum was rectified,[49] the resulting neutral spirits being used in *eaux-de-vie* and *apéritifs*.

When after the war rum returned to its duty-free status, the producers of wine alcohol began to look on it as a dangerous rival.

In 1922, secure in their divided market, viticultural interests, following a now familiar pattern, attacked rum's classification as a natural alcohol. What was the difference between alcohols produced from the sugar cane and the sugar beet? And were not the tafias molasses alcohol? These arguments had some logic behind them, if the system of a divided market could be called logical, but unlike the case of alcohol distilled from figs, carobs, and dates, the classification established by the laws of 1903 and 1916 was upheld. Nevertheless the winegrowers obtained a partial victory by a decree of June 27, 1922, which allowed the free entry of only rums *consommables en l'état,* that is, not deprived of "the aromatic agents to which rums and tafias owe their specific character." It was also stipulated that the rums could not contain more than 65 percent alcohol.

These provisions effectively ruined the profitable rectification of rum. But the battle was not finished. Inspired in 1922 by the first really bumper wine harvest since 1907,· the representatives of the winegrowers in parliament were able to push through, after much debate, even more crippling legislation. A law of December 31, 1922, which was criticized as "a heresy embedded in economic barbarism," [50] fixed a quota of 160,000 hectolitres for rums as defined by the June 27 decree. Quantities above the quota were to be subjected to a surtax which roughly equaled the heavy duty levied on foreign spirits. With sugar production in the colonies always critically short of outlets, protests were such that in 1923 the quota was raised to 185,000 hectolitres, and again in 1925 to 200,000 hectolitres, where it remained, a figure roughly equal to one half that of prewar imports. [51]

Thus we have seen in brief how the beet and the vine came to dominate their respective sectors of the divided market. With the former it was the result of government policy which, if not ultimately rational, at least had a firm base in expediency. With the latter it was naked self-interest, which was to become more and more dangerous for the producers of industrial alcohol. For as the Commission des Boissons noted in the report referred to earlier, the legislator in 1923 had given "to the growers of beets and the industrial distillers a lot envied by the other producers [of alcohol] at grips with the difficulties of an unoriented free market." [52] Actually, in spite of the fine words at Béziers and in parliament, the boundary that divided the alcohol market was almost from the beginning an uneasy one.

BREAKING UP OF THE DIVIDED MARKET

The chief cause of friction between the producers of natural and industrial alcohol was the operations of the Service des Alcools. After the war, as we have seen, the functioning of the Service was indefinitely extended until it could be set up on a permanent basis. The government was thereby committed to a continued monopoly of the purchase of industrial alcohols. As has also been noted, beet alcohol made up the bulk of government purchases. During the war the principle of parity between the price of beet alcohol and sugar had been accepted. And after the war the formula was improved and annually adjusted so that the beet grower had an equal interest in sending his product to a sugar refinery or a distillery. The purchase prices of other industrial alcohols, as we have also seen, were arbitrarily fixed below that of beet alcohol.

The new problem the Service faced after the war was one of outlets. The outlets entirely reserved to it were sales, now minimal, to the Service des Poudres, a wartime munitions agency, and after 1923 sales to importers or manufacturers of fuel for heating, lighting, or carburation. Other outlets were sales to "privileged industries" as established by the law of June 30, 1915. In addition to the four outlets mentioned above the list of privileged industries comprised the following:

1. The *vinage* and *mutage* of wines used for the preparation of *vins de liqueur*, vermouth, bitters, *mistelles*, and similar products for domestic consumption. [53]

2. The manufacture of vinegars for domestic consumption.

3. The manufacture of perfume, chemical, and pharmaceutical products for domestic consumption.

4. Alcohol for export—pure, or in the form of compound spirits, chemical, pharmaceutical, or perfume products, vinegar, liqueurs, etc.

5. Manufacture of denatured alcohol for domestic consumption or export.

The Service sold its alcohol for these uses at widely differing prices determined by the cost it was felt each category of users could afford. Because of the high price of French beet alcohol in relation to world alcohol prices, alcohol for export and denaturation was sold at a small loss or slight gain. Because of cheaper competing raw materials, alcohol for heating, lighting, and carburation was sold at a loss. The lowest price was fixed for alcohol used in the *carburant national.* In the year after the law of February 28, 1923, went into effect, sales to that source represented a loss for the government of 145 francs the hectolitre, or 80 percent of the purchase price of a hectolitre of beet alcohol.[54]

The Service sought to recover these losses by profitable sales to the *apéritif* and liqueur industries (alcohol for *vinage* and *mutage*), to manufacturers of vinegar, and to perfume, chemical, and pharmaceutical industries. Theoretically, these three groups of outlets were equally open to natural and industrial alcohols. But natural alcohol was three to four times more costly than beet alcohol. By pricing its alcohol for the three outlets moderately below natural alcohol, the Service could and did reap a large profit on these sales. Typical of its concern with profits was the addition in 1920 of preserved fruits to the list of privileged industries.[55]

Sales for *vinage* and *mutage,* although sanctioned by usage and helpful for export purposes, were, in a strict sense, a break in the division between beverage and industrial alcohols. But winegrowing interests do not appear to have had anything to say about them at first. Possibly the initial necessity of keeping the Service alive kept the winegrowers quiet, for the Service from 1921 through 1923 had piled up annual deficits which totaled more than 22 million francs.[56] At all events this partial break in the divided market was implicitly accepted at Béziers, and as Table 23 shows, sales by the Service for *vinage* and *mutage* increased for awhile in considerable proportions.

With these increases came complaints from the winegrowers and demands that alcohol sales for *vinage* and *mutage* be reserved

to them.   To their mind the government was not "respecting" the
law of February 28, 1923, and was concentrating "too much" on its
sales to profitable sources.   In addition they demanded the raising
of the percentage of alcohol in the *carburant national,* and for this
suggested the possibilities of cheaper alcohol distilled from rye, buck-
wheat, and potatoes.[57]   A further irritant to the winegrowers and
one which seemed to support their case was the fact that from 1924
through 1929 the Service des Alcools showed a commercial profit
that averaged around 40 million francs a year.   In addition the
surtax on imports of motor fuel furnished revenues for the Service
which increased, almost steadily, from 74,458,277 francs in 1924
to 122,001,674 francs in 1929.[58]

TABLE 23. SALE OF ALCOHOL FOR VINAGE AND MUTAGE, 1921–30

Year	Alcohol (Wine and Industrial) Used in Vinage and Mutage (in hectolitres)	Sales of Alcohol by the Service des Alcools for Vinage and Mutage (in hectolitres)	Price per Hectolitre of Alcohol Sold by the Service des Alcools for Vinage and Mutage (in francs) [a]
1921	71,830	40,000	525–425–300
1922	75,049	87,231	300–350
1923	120,827	105,219	350–450
1924	153,610	134,164	450–550–600
1925	115,866	36,803	600–500–600–700
1926	134,918	70,689	800–850
1927	87,969	57,848	850–900–1100–900
1928	118,266	125,446	900
1929	117,940	141,152	900
1930	92,090	102,975	900–1000

[a] Figures on the same line indicate periodic price changes during the year.

Sources: for columns 1 and 3, *Bulletin de statistique et de législation comparée;*
for column 2, Weill, *Monopole de l'alcool,* Appendix B, Table XIII.

But the winegrowers did more than complain.   Critics have
pointed out that their representatives in parliament were behind the
steady increase in the prices of industrial alcohol offered the profitable outlets.   Weill speaks of a "ten-year domination" of the Service's
price policies by the winegrowers whose interest was to push these
prices to a level where natural alcohol could compete.[59]   Thus the
price of state alcohol for the preserving of fruits increased from
500 francs the hectolitre in 1922 to 1,375 francs the hectolitre in

1930.[60] For vinegar the increase over the same period was from 350 francs the hectolitre to 600 francs. For alcohol used in *vinage* and *mutage* there was a steady increase from 350 francs the hectolitre in 1922 to a high of 1,100 francs the hectolitre in 1927.[61] It should be pointed out by comparison that the weighted average price of industrial alcohol bought by the government during the same period ranged from a low of 201 francs the hectolitre registered in 1923 to a high of 336 francs the hectolitre in 1927.[62]

These manipulations and the demands of the winegrowers brought counterproposals from the beet growers. To the winegrowers' demands for a reserved outlet in alcohol sold for *vinage* and *mutage,* they answered with a demand for strict adherence to the Béziers agreement. And to criticism of the Service's operations and to check the influence of winegrowing interests on the prices of the Service they countered with a proposal of autonomy for the Service which in turn would give it more flexibility and initiative in the matter of developing outlets.[63] Those seriously interested in the rational development of the Service shared these views. To their mind the high prices described above, besides placing an unjustified burden on the industries affected, prevented greater development of the profitable outlets necessary if the alcohol sold for the *carburant national* was to equal the price of gasoline without further fiscal aid.[64]

WINE-ALCOHOL PURCHASES BY THE STATE

Friction between the producers of natural and industrial alcohol became more intense beginning with the passage of the law of April 19, 1930, which set aside 250 million francs for purchase of wine alcohol by the state. The law was, as we have seen earlier, an extraordinary measure designed to stem the wine-price crisis which broke out that year. But to the northern distillers, it looked like an attempt on the part of wine alcohol to invade the operations of the Service des Alcools. Although M. Barthe, in presenting the bill to the Chamber of Deputies, had spoken of agricultural solidarity and reciprocity between the North and the Midi, the new law had actually been the subject of a lively wrangle between representatives of the two regions at meetings of the Interministerial Commission on Viticulture.[65]

The first item of disagreement was the source of the 250 million francs. Barthe had suggested that it should come from the reserves of the Service des Alcools, but the North countered by pointing out that in the language of the law of February 28, 1923, those reserves were set aside for the "benefit" of producers of industrial alcohol. A compromise called for the Treasury to advance the 250 million francs, and although the Service was to buy and sell the wine alcohol, the financing of these operations was to be assigned to a special account, in order, as it was put, "to clearly indicate that it was a matter of an exceptional transaction which could not interfere with the purchases of industrial alcohol."

Further disagreement occurred over the disposal of the wine alcohol. Barthe, true to one of the most cherished demands of the winegrowers, proposed that it be sold for *vinage* and *mutage*. But here, invoking the Béziers agreement, the North put its foot down firmly, and Article 3 of the law specified that the wine alcohol could be sold only for those beverages in which natural alcohol was used exclusively.

The greatest preoccupation of the North, however, was with the precedent which the new legislation set. Here there was nothing to be done except to accept the extravagant pledges of solidarity, security, and other guarantees that Barthe made from the floor of the Chamber of Deputies. It is interesting to note in passing that these were capped by a remarkable plea for all "agricultural alcohol" to unite against the synthetic alcohol which was beginning to appear on the market.[66]

In spite of the oratory of M. Barthe and his presentation of what was an agreement already arrived at between the North and the Midi, the representatives of the former continued to battle from the floor. Here an uneasiness was shown not directly related to the business at hand. Beet-alcohol production was increasing—more of it would of necessity go to the *carburant national*. Could the financial equilibrium of the Service be maintained under these conditions?[67] The answer was an amendment which required that the price of alcohol sold for the *carburant* could not be less than 70 percent of its purchase price by the state,[68] a move that immediately increased the selling price of this alcohol by 33 percent.

Thus a worried North considered that it had obtained some safeguards for the continuing financial balance of the operations of the Service. But under the unrelieved pressure of the wine-price crisis it was forced to abandon, step by step, the positions described above. The first blow came with the passage of the *Statut de la Viticulture* on July 4, 1931. As we have seen, wine-alcohol purchases by the state now in great part lost their temporary character due to the compulsory distilling provisions of the new law. Worse, the financing of these purchases and subsequent sales were to be carried out by the Service des Alcools on its own account.

This last blow was in effect canceled by the fact that compulsorily distilled wine alcohol was to be bought by the state at a price equal to the price charged fuel importers for alcohol used in the *carburant national*. But the fact remained that wine alcohol had been "absorbed" into the operations of the Service where, like beet alcohol, it was, theoretically at least, as available for one use as for another. And for this new source of alcohol, the Service's already strained outlets would have to be enlarged.

On the initiative of the representatives of the beet growers, therefore, legislation previously contemplated was hurriedly inserted into the *Statut de la Viticulture*. Its Article 9 required that henceforth importers of motor fuel would be required to mix a minimum of 25 percent and a maximum of 35 percent alcohol with all grades of gasoline except that known as *tourisme*.[69] The mixture of alcohol with the latter was provided for in the event that other gasolines could not absorb within the limits set by the law the amount of alcohol importers of motor fuel were obliged to buy from the state.[70]

Also, the provision of the law of April 19, 1930, which required that the price of alcohol sold for use in the *carburant national* could not be less than 70 percent of its purchase price was repealed. Under this regime a loss of 100 francs per hectolitre of this *carburant* had developed for motor-fuel importers, which they had tried to recover by a pro-rated increase in price of 5.40 francs the hectolitre on all grades of their gasoline. This increase in the case of the *carburant national* was enough, according to the importers, to bring the sales of the latter to a standstill, thus causing new and greater losses for them in spite of the price increase.[71] To make sure that the *carburant national* would not be subject to such difficulties again, Article 9 of the *Statut* also raised the surtax on imports of motor fuels from 5 francs to 10.40 francs. The additional amount, or "surtax of equalization," as it was called, was to be applied to reducing the price of alcohol sold for carburation to the level of the *carburant poids lourds,* with which the *carburant national* now became synonymous.

The measures incorporated in Article 9 were largely effective. Where sales of alcohol for carburation had totaled 547,996 hectolitres in 1930, they jumped to 926,506 hectolitres in 1931, and after dropping to 623,322 hectolitres in 1932, shot up again to a total of 2,340,786 hectolitres in 1933.[72] Roughly 30 percent of this increase may be attributed to the inclusion in these sales of compulsorily distilled wine alcohol and wine alcohol purchased under the provisions of the law of April 19, 1930. But in spite of this extended outlet for wine alcohol, or perhaps because of it, the problem of the encroachment by wine alcohol on the industrial-alcohol sector became a difficult one.

NATURAL ALCOHOL COMPETES WITH INDUSTRIAL ALCOHOL

In August, 1932, the price of natural alcohol on the free market began to decline rapidly. That month it had been 1,200 francs the hectolitre; in September it dipped to 966 francs; by January of 1933 it reached 880 francs, and in July of the same year it had fallen to a record low of 668 francs the hectolitre.[73] With the price of state alcohol for use in *vinage* and *mutage* fixed at 1,000 francs the hectolitre during the same period, the most important profitable outlet of the Service des Alcools quickly and almost completely dried up.[74]

In an attempt to correct this state of affairs, three important measures were incorporated with the viticultural legislation of the law of July 8, 1933. The first made obligatory the purchase from the Service of alcohol for use in *vinage* and *mutage*. The second required the state to sell wine alcohol up to three fourths of the amount needed for these purposes. To boost the price of alcohol on the free market to a point where it was hoped it would not be competitive with industrial alcohol, a third measure gave the state the right to fix the purchase price of compulsorily distilled wine alcohol up to a limit of three fifths of the price of alcohol sold for *vinage* and *mutage*.

Although the three measures were designed primarily to protect the operations of the Service des Alcools, they nonetheless represented important gains for the winegrowers. The second measure in particular had long been asked for, and the third, as it turned out in practice, lightened the financial penalty attached to compulsory distilling. Paradoxically, both measures, in spite of their curative intent, also threatened the financial equilibrium of the Service. To reduce this menace a new tax for the benefit of the Service was included in the law of July 8, 1933. Henceforth a surtax was to be levied on imported liqueurs equal to the difference between the price the state paid for wine alcohol and the price at which it was sold for *vinage* and *mutage*.

The foregoing measures, however, did nothing to stop the worsening of the alcohol situation. The price of natural alcohol on the free market continued to fall. At the end of 1933 the commercial balance of the Service des Alcools showed a deficit of 381,711,000 francs, and after adding the revenue from motor fuel and other taxes there was a net deficit of roughly three million francs.[75]

This last sum, though relatively small in relation to the Service's reserves, was enough to alarm beet-growing interests with whom the financial health of the Service was almost an article of faith. Their apprehension on this score was heightened by the fact that at the same time that wine alcohol was invading the operations of the Service, the production of beet alcohol was increasing. In 1931 the refiners of beet sugar had begun a series of self-imposed quotas which diverted new quantities of sugar beets to the distilleries.

The increase in beet-alcohol production plus the new purchases of wine alcohol meant in turn an alarming increase in held-over stocks of state alcohol. By 1934 these consisted of 1,734,238 hectolitres of industrial alcohol, and 1,570,777 hectolitres of natural alcohol, or a total roughly equal to new purchases the same year.[76] Moreover, a law of March 31, 1933, had limited beet-alcohol purchases to an annual quota of 2,300,000 hectolitres. The quota, if generous, did little to allay the fears of beet-growing interests about the future of the Service. As noted previously, the price of natural alcohol on the free market continued to decline. In December, 1933, it was quoted at an average of 570 francs the hectolitre. In March of 1934 it dropped to 513 francs, and after that declined more or less steadily to a new low of 291 francs the hectolitre in November.

TABLE 24. BEET-ALCOHOL AND BEET-SUGAR PRODUCTION IN FRANCE, 1930–34

Year	Beet-Alcohol Production (in hectolitres)	Beet-Sugar Production (in metric tons)
1930	1,521,297	825,333
1931	1,783,051	1,084,129
1932	2,201,400	786,968
1933	2,404,270	920,032
1934	2,777,157	851,620

Source: *Annuaire statistique.*

In 1935 an upward swing took place, but the range was only between 316 and 438 francs the hectolitre.[77] During these two years the price of state alcohol for use in vinegar was fixed at 500 francs the hectolitre, and for use in perfume, chemical, and pharmaceutical products at 525 francs the hectolitre.[78] The sales of state alcohol to these sources graphically reflected the difference in price between industrial alcohol and natural alcohol on the free market: in 1933, 163,392 hectolitres were sold; in 1934, 117,229 hectolitres; and in 1935, 28,702 hectolitres.[79]

Thus the North in the three previous years had seen wine alcohol invade the operations of the Service and deprive industrial alcohol of all but one fourth of the most important profitable outlet for the Service. Now, because of its dual existence inside and outside the operations of the Service, wine alcohol in clear violation of the Béziers agreement was claiming other outlets as well, even though those outlets commanded prices which often fell below cost. In 1933 the North, preoccupied with assuring the well-being of the Service, had said nothing about the advantages accorded the winegrowers. But at the close of 1934, with a massive wine harvest gathered in and legislation being enacted to extend the compulsory distilling of wine, northern demands were in order.

The law of December 24, 1934—which, it will be remembered, was the second in a series of revisions of the *Statut de la Viticulture*—offered, as proposed, some concessions to the North's preoccupations. Purchases and sales of compulsorily distilled wine and other natural alcohols, although carried out by the Service des Alcools, were to be financed by a special Treasury account. Furthermore, the government, showing a new aggressiveness, was determined that it should be recompensed for lost tax revenues and that wine and cider should carry an additional tax to help assure the new account's balance. Accordingly, an amendment was offered requiring that the account be debited, in favor of the general budget and the Service des Alcools, a sum equal to the state's loss in revenue from the addition of natural alcohol to gasoline.[80] Thus for each hectolitre of natural alcohol that replaced a hectolitre of gasoline the account would be "taxed" a sum equal to the domestic taxes and the import surtax of 10.40 francs on a hectolitre of gasoline. The account was also to be credited with an increase of 5 francs the hectolitre on the *droit de circulation* of wines and 2.50 francs the hectolitre on that of ciders and perries. These surtaxes were, however, to be abolished when the account balanced.

The debit and the 10.40 franc item in particular were bitterly resented by the winegrowers. In the Chamber of Deputies M. Barthe angrily pointed out that any measure of protection, whether industrial or agricultural, involved some reduction of tax receipts. "Had it ever occurred to anyone before," he asked, "to require from the interested corporation a compensatory payment?"[81] Flandin, head of the government, avoiding what certainly could have been an interesting debate on the theory of national economics, spoke sternly instead of budget demands: the budget had given the government enough trouble; the adoption of M. Barthe's counteramendment to abolish the debit items in the special account would simply "bore a hole" in it.[82]

The counteramendment was defeated, but there still was the problem of outlets for the alcohol of the Service, compromised, as we have seen, by the low price of free-market alcohol. Here the

North offered an amendment to require each of the privileged industries to buy *all* their alcohol from the Service.[83]   In addition it was proposed that all compulsorily distilled wine alcohol and other natural alcohol purchased by the state be diverted only to the *carburant national* and *vinage* and *mutage* in the proportions specified by the law of July 8, 1933.[84] This last measure was adopted, but against the first the representatives of the winegrowers took a stubborn and successful stand.

"We acknowledge that the Béziers agreement is involved in this situation," a Midi deputy said, "and we do not want to keep a market that does not belong to us, but we cannot give it up as long as we are in a period of crisis." [85]   In spite of opportunities for charges of bad faith and a discussion of the apparent breakdown of the Béziers agreement, this reasoning gained a short-lived victory for the winegrowers. The Minister of Agriculture intervened to remind that the law of December 24, 1934, was intended to deal only with the wine crisis and should not become involved with the alcohol problem. The latter had been under long study—it involved the linked interests of the beet growers and winegrowers; action satisfactory to both was promised at the next session of parliament.[86]

THE NEW ALCOHOL REGIME

Action came in the form of the decree-law of July 30, 1935. The government, considering the seriousness of the wine crisis and the past record of opposition to a permanent alcohol regime by the budget-minded, took advantage of emergency powers to enact its solution to the alcohol problem without debate.   However, representatives of the beet growers had met at Narbonne in March of 1935 with representatives of the C.G.V. and again in May at Paris with delegates of metropolitan and Algerian viticultural associations and cider-producing interests, and a program not too different from that adopted by the government had been proposed. Although, as we have seen in an earlier chapter, a large part of the new decree-law dealt exclusively with viticultural problems, the numerous articles of its fifth part organized the Service des Alcools on a permanent basis and brought about several other important changes in its operations.

The first of these, conforming to the wishes of the beet growers and industrial-alcohol distillers expressed in 1934, tightened the quasi-monopoly of the Service in furnishing alcohol for industrial uses. Henceforth all alcohols other than *eaux-de-vie* with a right to the name of cognac or armagnac and *eaux-de-vie* of 70 percent alcohol or less, not rectified, and distilled from wines, ciders, perries, fruits, marcs, rapes, or lees, were reserved to the state, from whom the users would have to obtain them. Even *eaux-de-vie* bought by the liqueur industry for purposes of blending were subject to a tax equal to the difference between their price and that of alcohol ceded for *vinage* and *mutage* when the former should drop below the latter.[87] Thus the threat of invasion of industrial sectors by free-market natural alcohols was stopped, and an alcohol monopoly was set up in fact if not in name. Only *eaux-de-vie* as defined above remained outside the monopoly.

This did not, however, mean a return to a strict division between industrial and natural alcohol. The alcohol purchases of the Service were organized on a quota basis, with natural alcohol freely offered, figuring among purchases for the first time in its own right. The quotas, generously calculated on the whole, were fixed as follows:

Alcohol	Hectolitres	Price Coefficients
Beet	2,300,000	0.00
Sugar-beet molasses	600,000	.68
Wine	325,000	2.55
Alcools de marc	300,000	1.60
Apple and pear	300,000	2.20
Synthetic and grain	28,000	.60
Cider and perry	25,000	2.55

The price of beet alcohol, still figured in parity with the price of sugar, determined the price of other alcohols according to the coefficients listed in the last column above. Alcohols in excess of their quotas would be bought at a price equal to the sale price of alcohol for carburation.

To the latter use all alcohol resulting from the compulsory dis-

tilling of wine was now diverted. Its price per hectolitre was figured
on a progressively descending scale in an inverse ratio to quantity
offered, with the highest price limited to three fourths of the wine-
alcohol quota price. The financing of the purchase and sales of
compulsorily distilled wine alcohol was to be carried out by the
Service des Alcools, but in a separate account known as the *caisse
annexe de la viticulture.* This account was credited with the return from sales of compulsorily distilled wine alcohol and the
revenue from the surtax on the *droit de circulation* of wines and
ciders as established by the law of December 24, 1934, plus a 20 percent increase in the same which would be canceled when the reserves
of the account reached 300 million francs. The 20 percent increase
was in the meantime to be drawn on to furnish indemnities for the
pulling up of vines as prescribed by the law of July 30, 1935. The
account was also credited with an annual subsidy not to exceed 125
million francs from the profits realized through the regular operations of the Service. The account was debited, in addition to purchases of wine alcohol and attendant expenses, an amount equal to
domestic taxes on gasoline lost to the state through adding wine
alcohol to motor-fuel mixtures.

The regular operations of the Service, now grouped under the
rubric of *caisse générale,* were credited in much the same way as
they had been since 1923. The chief source of revenue in addition
to sales continued to be the 10.40 franc surtax levied on motor-fuel
imports. In addition to the subsidy to the *caisse annexe,* however,
one half of the remaining surplus of the Service was to be returned
to the general budget, the other half, going into what would be
greatly reduced reserves. Finally, decrees of September 29 and
December 18, 1935, converted the Service into a *régie commerciale*
with a legal and financial personality, thus making its prices and
operations less susceptible to political pressures than they had been.

In reviewing the main provisions of the new alcohol regime, it
is possible to say that in general they consolidated the inroads that
natural alcohol and wine alcohol in particular had made on the industrial sector of the divided market. The winegrowers, for example, now had an assured and profitable annual outlet in the
Service for a quantity of their wine alcohol roughly 33 percent

greater than their average annual distillation from 1920 through
1930.[88] Supplementing this outlet was the not unimportant
quantity of *alcools de marc* that the Service was also pledged to buy
each year.

Compulsory distilling, to be sure, still involved a financial
penalty. But gains had also been made in this quarter. In 1931, it
will be remembered, compulsorily distilled wine alcohol had been
paid for at a price equal to the sale price of alcohol for carburation
or 250 francs the hectolitre. Under the pricing system of the new
regime, compulsorily distilled wine alcohol was paid for in 1936 at a
rough average of 355 francs the hectolitre, while the sale price of
alcohol for carburation was between 129 and 190 francs the hectolitre.[89]

True, to assure the balance of the *caisse annexe* there were
measures which were not entirely to the liking of the winegrowers.
But the increase in the *droit de circulation,* steep as it was, was at
least divided between grower, middleman, and consumer. As for
the *caisse* reimbursing the state for lost gasoline taxes, it might be
pointed out that in 1936 this sum was estimated at 53,856,000
francs,[90] or less than half the 125 million franc subsidy received
from the *caisse générale.* It should also be remembered that the reimbursement was for domestic taxes only and did not include the
import surtax as originally proposed in 1934.

Compared to the gains listed above, the advantages accorded the
beet growers and the industrial distillers by the new regime seem
relatively minor. True, the Service had assured the latter good
profits even during the dislocations caused by the wine and wine
alcohol crises, and now the Service was organized on a permanent
basis almost completely monopolistic in character. But the ransom,
it seemed, for this permanent organization was the inclusion of
natural alcohol in the Service's purchases and sales. And even the
monopoly was really a belated remedy for an emergency that should
not have occurred if the spirit of the Béziers agreement had not been
violated almost from the beginning by winegrowing interests. Moreover, beet alcohol found its production checked by the quota system[91]—not too seriously perhaps, but with the sugar refiners
practicing quotas themselves, a disquieting anxiety was created

which need not have existed if natural alcohol had not been included among the quota alcohols.

Finally, the *caisse annexe de la viticulture* answered the beet growers' preoccupation with the financial health of the Service by removing the purchase and sale of compulsorily distilled wine alcohol from the Service's regular operations, even if this alcohol was all destined for an outlet that one northern deputy reminded the Chamber had been exclusively set up for industrial alcohol.[92]   But the advantage of separate accounts was mitigated by the annual 125 million franc subsidy. This sum could, of course, be taken care of by fixing higher selling prices for the alcohol of the Service.   But remembering viticulture's aggressiveness in the years of crisis just ending, could one be sure that the subsidy would stop at the agreed sum?   Even supporters of the *caisse annexe* admitted that its balance presented "certain difficulties." [93]

Thus, although beet alcohol's protected position was still a strong one, much ground had been lost to wine. This was not overlooked by outside observers.   There was criticism in the Parisian press of the added burden on the Treasury which it was felt regular wine-alcohol purchases by the Service would create. The reaction of the C.G.V. is interesting.   Its delegates visited the Premier to call his attention to a "press campaign." [94]   The extension of the regular purchases of the Service to include all alcohols was to the C.G.V.'s mind simply giving wine and fruit production the same advantages granted beet-growing interests, advantages which had secured the latter "ten years of prosperity." [95]   It would appear that the enviable position of beet alcohol, which had been in large part engineered by the winegrowers themselves, had become too much for them to bear.

THE DECREE OF APRIL 21, 1939

The structure of the new alcohol regime remained unchanged until 1939. Then for a while its very existence seemed threatened. The government, faced with greatly increased defense expenditures, began looking for ways of increasing tax revenues and cutting expenses.   One of the first targets was the collection of autonomous organizations subsidized by the state. A decree-law of March 20, 1939, entitled "reorganization and suppression of offices," decreed that "receipts of a fiscal character now attributed to offices, public establishments, autonomous services, and special funds, are carried in the returns of the general budget on and after January 1, 1939, and cease to have any special appropriation." [96]

Although the Service des Alcools was not included in a list of numerous organizations immediately "absorbed" by the state, the provision just quoted brought a storm of protest from the various viticultural associations and even a "state of alert" in winegrowing communities in Algeria.[97] The treatment of the Service, as later embodied in the famous decree-laws of April 21, 1939,[98] was mild, however, compared with that given the Office des Blés [99] or the virtual halt of the public-works program and the withdrawal of important subsidies to municipal organizations.

The government noted in the April decree-law dealing with the Service that the intervention of the state as practiced through the alcohol regime had had a beneficial effect on beet, wine, and cider culture, and should be continued. But the Service des Alcools, in conformity with the decree of March 20, 1939, was to assure its equilibrium "with its own resources," and could not appeal for a contribution from the general budget or for fiscal receipts.[100] The working out of this mandate, however, was nothing more than a bookkeeping operation which, outside of the removal of the possibility of government subsidies, promised to do little to affect the Service's operations or financial health. Briefly, by the suppression or reduction of various taxes on the alcohol sold by the state, the Service was enabled to get higher prices for this alcohol, the taxes in some cases being completely "integrated" in the selling price. The price of alcohol sold for carburation was fixed at 85 francs the hectolitre above the cost price of a hectolitre of gasoline. Other changes were greater demands on the profits of the Service by the government, and the reduction of the subsidy from the *caisse générale* to the *caisse annexe de la viticulture* from 125 million to 100 million francs. The latter account was no longer debited for compensatory payments on lost gasoline-tax revenue and the *droits de circulation* on wines and ciders formerly credited to it were now of course credited to the general budget, as was the surtax on motor-fuel imports which had been such an important source of revenue for the *caisse générale.*

A BACKWARD GLANCE

The effect of the alcohol regime between the two wars on France's economy is difficult to estimate. Can a policy of protection such as the regime accorded to viticulture, beet growing, and the alcohol industry be considered only in terms of favorable cash balances? If not, at what point do losses to the state become intolerable? And to what extent can these losses be shifted to the nation as a collectivity? These are some of the questions that must be considered even if they cannot be completely answered in a brief review.

Turning first to the question of the balances of the Service des Alcools, it will be remembered that in the three years preceding the advent of the *carburant national,* the Service ran up annual deficits. After that, sales through high-priced outlets, combined with relatively light sales for carburation, permitted the Service to show a favorable commercial balance for the period from 1927 through 1931. This, combined with increasing revenue from the motor-fuel import surtax, gave the Service credit balances which averaged around 144 million francs a year during the same period.[101]

In 1932 there was an estimated net deficit of approximately 73 million francs,[102] probably for the most part due to the compulsory distilling of wine which, it will be remembered, had to be carried out on the Service's account under the law of July 4, 1931. Also in 1932, the government made an extraordinary levy of 700 million francs on the reserves of the Service in favor of the general budget. But when a new regime (decree-law of July 30, 1935) went into effect on September 30, 1935, the reserves of the Service still totaled 231,895,000 francs.[103] At the same date, although unrelated to the Service's operations, the emergency purchase of wine alcohol by the government in 1935 and the operation of the special account set up by the law of December 24, 1934, had cost the Treasury after sales a net loss of 302,952,000 francs.[104] After 1935, there were

no more commercial profits for the Service. The subsidy to viticulture's account and the return of one half of the surplus of the
general account to the state all took their toll, so that the reduced
credit balances of the Service were maintained largely by the revenue from taxes, and those of the *caisse annexe de la viticulture* by
bookkeeping arrangements.[105]   Still, in the three years of the 1935
regime's existence the Service returned 800 million more francs to
the Treasury than the latter advanced to it.[106]   The financial condition of the Service was much weakened during these years compared with pre-1931 standards, and had not wine harvests been
moderate the viticultural account might have presented problems.
But at least up to the outbreak of World War II, the Service had
apparently managed to balance its books with the resources assigned
to it.

These resources, as just noted, came increasingly from taxes.
But in the Service's good days as well as its bad ones, revenues
from these taxes were objects of envy by governments in budgetary
difficulties.   They explain both the 700 million franc levy in 1932
and the regime of 1939.   And they were what Paul Reynaud, Minister of Finance, meant when, defending the April, 1939, decree, he
said that to assure the balance of the Service, the Treasury had had
"to give up" 1,200 million francs.[107]   It should be pointed out that
Reynaud's estimate, which was for the three years beginning in
1936, did not include the regular customs duty on motor fuel lost
by mixture, losses on domestic taxes for the amount of industrial
alcohol mixed with gasoline, or the special tax exemption of 25
francs the hectolitre to make the *carburant poids lourds* cheaper
than the *carburant tourisme*.[108]   One student of the alcohol regime
has estimated that had the Service been able to supply the 15 percent
of alcohol that motor fuel importers were obliged to acquire, lost
revenues on these last items would have to run to more than 420
million francs a year,[109] adding another 1,260 million francs to Reynaud's figure.[110]

Offsetting such figures, however, were 2,538 million francs in
taxes on wine and and ciders and 6,570 million francs in alcohol
taxes which went directly to the state during the same period.[111]
One might ask, at this point, if the taxes and import duties lost to

the Service were not a fair price to pay for the protection of industries that gave the state such important revenues. But such a question leads us back to one asked earlier: Can a policy of protection and the different considerations that determine it be squeezed into a simple financial statement? In 1939, at all events, the government felt it needed the lost revenue and also felt that the continuity of the Service could and should be assured by the new regime introduced that year.

Whether taxes were paid to the state or to the Service, their cost in the end was borne by the consumer. Each change in the alcohol regime brought increased taxes on wine and motor fuel. Taxes aside, the alcohol-price system, resting illogically, one critic felt, on the price of sugar like a "pyramid turned on its point," [112] meant alcohol costing three to ten times the world market price for those industries which constituted the most profitable outlets for the Service.[113] The assigning of wine alcohol to some of these outlets was, of course, a contributing factor. Again, taxes aside, alcohol sold for carburation was priced above the cost price of gasoline except for the period from 1931 to 1935. In addition there were the costs of handling, storing, and mixing what the gasoline refiners always felt was an unwelcome addition to their product.

Were these costs too heavy to bear? If they were, gasoline was already heavily taxed,[114] and so one cannot place the entire blame on the alcohol regime. But in any case it is interesting that a commission of the Chamber of Deputies pointed out in 1937 that "in the last several years" the volume of motor traffic in France had not kept up with its increase in other countries. The consumption of gasoline per vehicle was 2,900 litres in Great Britain, 2,800 litres in the United States, 2,700 litres in Germany, and 1,700 litres in France.[115]

Such, then, are some of the costs passed on to the consumer for which viticultural protection was at least partially responsible.[116] But as Professor Shepard Clough has suggested, low prices have not been the chief object of the protectionist phase of French national economics.[117] Security and stability are probably more important— a view mirrored by a thoughtful article on the alcohol regime in the

Revue d'économie politique. According to the author, the regime saved viticulture by imposing "a hard and ineluctable discipline on all branches of agriculture touching alcohol production." But this discipline also "demanded sacrifices and contributions from the entire collectivity: it was only a question of distributing the burdens as rationally and equitably as possible." [118]

In looking back over the two decades between 1919 and 1939, it can be said that viticulture gained two very important advantages. The first, reviewed in an earlier chapter, was legislation which attempted to protect the winegrowers by what might loosely be called stabilizing their production and prices. True, the legislation was not perfect nor did it please all winegrowers alike. But in concentrating on its faults one is liable to overlook the fact that it represented an extraordinary effort on the part of the government. One jurist, commenting on the law of July 4, 1931, called it "the most important legislative measure consecrating the intervention of the state in the domain of economic life since the French Revolution." [119] If there may be a touch of exaggeration in this claim, we have nevertheless seen that the 1931 law was only the beginning of a series of laws that carried this intervention further and further. And as we have also seen, after 1935 this legislation at least seemed to have a beneficial effect on prices.

The second advantage was the one just reviewed: the fastening of a good part of the burden of viticultural protection on to the national collectivity. For those who saw the viticultural problem only in terms of keeping France's one and a half million winegrowers gainfully at work in their vineyards, these advantages were in the national interest. Others flatly opposed them in the name of *laissez-faire,* although wishing the winegrowers well. A smaller group of critics was also opposed, not because it was against government intervention, but because it felt that this intervention had been misdirected. The most economic producers had been penalized, the most inefficient made secure in their inefficiency. This was bad both for viticulture and the national economy.

Professor René Courtin of the University of Montpellier has

well expressed this point of view. Writing in 1931 of the *Statut de la Viticulture,* he called it a solution of "laziness." [120]

Rather than probe the secrets of the future they [the government and the winegrowers] try to revive a past still recent but which it is in the power of nobody to resuscitate. Thus the Commission of Investigation received a petition from the barrel-makers protesting against the substitution of tank cars for the traditional casks. One should not think to find a simple anecdote here, for all of viticulture is imbued with this state of mind. In taking up again the erring ways of mercantilism it strives to create fetters which will permit it to keep the privileges which threaten to escape it. . . .

France is not rich enough either in material assets or men to permit any such wastefulness, and at a time when the whole economy is marked for rationalization, one can only denounce such an attempt at social parasitism.

A shift towards this point of view and a slackening of government indulgence towards the winegrowers are two important themes in the chapters that follow. But they are not the most obvious ones, because in the period after World War II viticulture finds itself again faced with much the same difficulties of overproduction and much the same remedies for them as during the period just reviewed.

9. *THE WINEGROWERS AND THE GOVERNMENT,*

1939–53

In August, 1939, French delegates to the International Congress of the Vine and Wine at Bad Kreuznach, Germany, heard Walter Darré, the Reich's Minister of Food Supply and Agriculture, express his hopes that the work of the Congress would go beyond professional limits and advance "the mutual understanding of peaceful peoples." [1] But on the day of the official closing of the Congress, the French delegates were ordered home and a week later France was at war.

As in 1914, the first wartime wine harvest was an abundant one; nearly 70 million hectolitres were produced in metropolitan France, with the total of wine available for the market passing the 90 million hectolitre mark. Again as in 1914 an extraordinary effort was made to get the harvest in. The government granted delays in calling the winegrowers to the colors, military labor detachments were sent to the vineyards, and the farm horses of small growers were not to be requisitioned before the end of the harvest. [2]

Other events were also reminiscent of 1914. In July the government had enacted legislation against alcoholism, [3] and by September there were complaints that "certain prefects" had forbidden the sale of wine to the troops. [4] But when the troops reached the front there was a generous wine ration waiting for them, inspired by official propaganda which called for increasing quantities of *le vin chaud au soldat*.[5]

In comparing 1939 with 1914 there was one outstanding difference to be noted. To the surprise of many, the bumper wine harvest of 1939 did not unduly depress prices. True, the now familiar mechanisms of the *Statut* did their work; 7 million hectolitres of wine were distilled into alcohol. But remembering the low prices they had received for their wine when the large harvest of 1914 could not be immediately moved, many growers were apprehensive.[6] From the beginning, however, distribution of the harvest actually went more smoothly than the year before,[7] and although there was an almost complete halt of sales in June, 1940, prices remained firm throughout the year.[8] With a 15 percent increase in production, the average price received by the growers showed a drop of 12 percent from the year before.

TABLE 25.   FRENCH WINE PRODUCTION AND YIELD DURING WORLD WAR II
(*In hectolitres*)

Year	Production	Yield per Hectare
1939	69,015,071	46.2
1940	49,427,910	33.6
1941	47,585,638	32.7
1942	35,022,362	24.4
1943	41,014,552	28.8
1944	44,303,687	31.6
1945	28,617,225	20.0

Source: *Statistique agricole annuelle.*

In 1940 production fell off 28 percent and an unbroken series of short harvests began, lasting to the end of the war and for several years after. After 1941 labor became increasingly scarce, chemical fertilizers were "practically nonexistent" and rations of insecticides were "inadequate."[9] In addition German military authorities carried out an unusually severe requisition of farm horses. It was estimated that 30,000 of the latter disappeared in the four chief winegrowing departments of the Midi alone.[10] Production on the whole, however, did not drop as abruptly or as far as it did during World War I,[11] yet wine was subject to rationing and did not have the liberty of production and sales that it enjoyed during the earlier war.

VITICULTURE AND THE VICHY REGIME

In July of 1940 the new government at Vichy announced that maximum prices would be set for all agricultural products.[12] A law of October 21, 1940, set up the machinery for doing this and expressly noted that prices would be fixed at the production, wholesale, and retail levels, thus providing for a closer control than had been the case with previous legislation.[13] Responsibility for price fixing was to be shared between the Ministry of National Economy and Finance and the Ministry of Agriculture, after advice by a Committee on Prices in which figured a Groupe Spécialisé Viticole de la Corporation Paysanne.[14] This centralized organization marked another departure from existing legislation, for the prefects who formerly exercised wide powers in price fixing were limited to petitions concerning prices on the production level, and if the latter were granted, to the fixing of profit margins on the local wine markets and in the stores.[15]

The Vichy price-fixing system has been criticized as authoritarian and rigid; the viticultural experts were not listened to enough. Prices resulted which "the unanimity of winegrowers" considered "a veritable persecution." Prices did not take into account either the decline in production or the decline in value of money and the purchasing power of the winegrower. The interests of the latter were subordinated to those of the consumer to an unjust degree.[16]

On the basis of an absolute comparison, however, wine prices rose in very nearly the same proportions as during World War I. And against claims such as the above must be balanced the difficulty, even in normal times, of working out a price policy that equally satisfies producer and consumer. Add social and economic unrest plus the aura of patriotism that surrounded the "black market," [17] and the Vichy regime may appear as more sinned against than sinning. M. Daniel Combes, the critic quoted above, has admitted that given the need that existed for a directed economy on the national level, Vichy's centralized price-fixing structure was justified, but it could not be disassociated from German needs or a pro-German policy.[18] Also, it is interesting to note, this structure was adopted with only minor changes by the post-liberation and provisional governments.

TABLE 26. COMPARISON OF INCREASE IN WINE PRICES AT THE PRODUCTION
LEVEL IN FRANCE IN WORLD WAR I AND WORLD WAR II

Years	Average Price per Hectolitre (in francs)	Percentage of Increase
1909–13	30	
1918	102	240
1934–38	126	
1944	561	345

Source: *Annuaire statistique.*

Looking optimistically beyond the immediate problems of price fixing and short harvests, the Vichy government in 1941 announced a forthcoming "review and simplification" of the *Statut de la Viticulture*. At the same time its supporters called for the creation of a Corporation Viti-vinicole "entirely composed of technicians and practitioners, to the exclusion of all politicians." [19]   On February 11, 1941, a law was passed which called for the distillation of one third of the harvest if wine available for the market as defined by earlier laws amounted to 84 million hectolitres or more. Producers of more than 5,000 hectolitres were to distill one half their harvest, and only those growers with a yield of less than 20 hectolitres the hectare were to be exempted from compulsory distillation. Regardless of the amount of wine available for the market, growers with a yield of 120 hectolitres the hectare or more had to distill one half of their production.

These provisions were much stricter than any incorporated in earlier versions of the *Statut*. The lowest yield, for example, subject to compulsory distilling had been 40 hectolitres the hectare, and a distilling of one third of their harvest had affected only the biggest producers. Still, in its reliance on compulsory distillation as a means of checking production, the Vichy legislation offered little new in the way of a solution to viticulture's chief problem.[20] The new law, however, is only of academic interest. The Vichy government's chief problem was to insure an adequate supply of wine in the face of diminishing production. To this end it issued more than fifty laws, decrees, and ministerial orders, which undid most of the pre-1939 viticultural legislation.

In the autumn of 1941 the minimum alcoholic content tolerated by law for wines used in blending was lowered,[21] as was that for "local wines" (*vins du pays*) which could only circulate in the region where they were produced.[22] *Piquettes,* or "second wines," were also allowed.[23] And the following year the watering of wine was encouraged by an ingenious pricing schedule which fixed the highest prices for wines with 8 percent alcoholic content and lower prices for wines of less or greater alcoholic content.[24]

In November of 1942 the continued production of wine from the so-called "undesirable" or "prohibited" grape varieties was allowed.[25] Earlier, all other provisions of the *Statut de la Viticulture* which "hindered the recovery of production" were indefinitely suspended.[26] These included the program for pulling up vines, the limitation of new plantings, the prohibition against watering the roots of vines after July 15, the tax on yields, and compulsory distillation. In connection with the last a law of September 25, 1942, specifically suspended the *caisse annexe de la viticulture.*

Compulsory distilling and the *caisse annexe* had, of course, been dead letters since 1941.[27] But the Vichy government did require the distilling of *alcool vinique.* Unlike direct distilling, this did not cut wine production appreciably. *Alcool vinique* was distilled from the residues left after pressing, being in this sense identical with *alcool de marc* except that the former was "boiled" to a point of greater alcoholic strength and tastelessness. This process did cut down the possibility of making *piquettes,* but the requisitions of *alcool vinique* determined by annual decrees were not heavy and were only levied against producers of more than 200 hectolitres of wine.

The requisitions were entirely the result of a program for the rational utilization of the by-products of winemaking in the face of a lack of certain other foodstuffs and products. Thus concentrated musts took the place of sugar in winemaking,[28] oil was pressed from grape seeds,[29] and the roots of dead vines were burned as motor fuel.[30] One measure which did cut into the supply of wine was the obligation for producers of more than 500 hectolitres to furnish a quantity of concentrated musts representing one fifth of their harvest for conversion into grape sugar.[31] An estimated 4 million hectolitres of wine were lost to the market this way, and the

measure caused some discontent among the growers.[32]   But it did
not affect the majority.

Of much greater moment to all winegrowers was the adoption
of rationing.   A law of August 31, 1942, required the state to take
in charge "the totality of wines, musts, and derived products produced in or imported into the metropole."   Organizations were set
up to direct distribution and transport.   Priorities of shipment were
established, whole trains of tank cars being sent directly to regions
where the need was greatest.   Individual citizens were issued ration
tickets, and dealers and shippers were issued purchase certificates
which were binding on the grower.   To close possible loopholes in
this last measure the government reduced the generous amount of
wine which immemorially the growers had been allowed to keep for
tax-free "family consumption." [33]   In the same spirit, quality wines
(*vins d'appelations d'origine contrôlées*) were also absorbed into
the rationing and price-fixing system.[34]   These measures, if they did
not stamp out a flourishing black market, at least made illegal sales
more difficult—and they just as surely produced more discontent
and defiance from the winegrowers.

The concern of the government over the latter attitude, and its
helplessness before it, was well symbolized in 1942 by the spectacle
of Marshal Pétain stumping the Midi to upbraid the winegrowers
for not planting other crops.   Encouragement had been offered them
to do this, and a law of August 20, 1940, had required growers with
more than five hectares in vines to plant 10 percent of this area in
vegetables and grains.   But even in the opinion of supporters, the
law was ineffective.[35]   Discontent and defiance, however, were not
unique to the Vichy regime.   A full measure was still on hand when
the winegrowers faced the post-liberation and provisional governments.

CONTINUED SHORTAGES AND SHORT-RANGE POLICIES: 1945–49

After the liberation there was as much need as before for price
fixing and rationing.   The harvest of 1945 was the lightest since
the beginning of the war (28,617,225 hectolitres).   And the harvest
of 1946, while heavier (36,159,582 hectolitres), was still consider-

ably below wartime levels, with the exception of the harvest of 1942. After 1946, production increased, but although aided by the resumption of imports from Algeria which began in 1945, it supplied with difficulty the demands of the market for a period which ended only with the harvest of 1950.

TABLE 27. WINE PRODUCTION AND YIELD IN FRANCE AND ALGERIA, 1946–49
(*In hectolitres*)

Year	Production in France	Production in Algeria	Yield per Hectare in France
1946	36,159,582	8,200,000	25.18
1947	44,170,244	8,100,000	30.67
1948	47,437,141	12,500,000	33.08
1949	42,934,749	14,500,000	29.87

Source: *Statistique agricole annuelle,* Gouvernement général de l'Algérie, *Annuaire statistique de l'Algérie.*

During this period the government, while trying to assure an adequate supply of wine at reasonable prices, was faced with pressures which made the job extremely difficult. Not the least of these was an atmosphere of relief and relaxation after the liberation which expressed itself in a desire to be rid as soon as possible of all restrictions and controls. This desire seemed a real necessity to winegrowers facing the problems of increased costs in labor, farm machinery, chemical fertilizers, and sprays. In addition there was the very real problem of reconstituting the national vineyard, much affected by wartime neglect. The winegrowers were not slow in pointing out that the cost of this operation was beyond their means or those open to them through the channels of regular agricultural credit. The government, on the other hand, was faced with similar demands from other sectors of the national economy which it was trying to meet under the twin handicaps of inflation and straitened finances. Hence the government's feeling that part of the cost of recovery should be borne by the interests concerned. Whence more discontent, especially in the Midi, which felt it had suffered more than other regions because of its devotion to the monoculture of the vine.[36] Finally, while most winegrowers clamored for freedom from controls, others—more responsible—began to ask for the return of the *Statut de la Viticulture* which the government, following the preoccupation of Vichy with the supply of wine, was holding in partial abeyance.   The result of all these conflicting demands and pressures was a stormy period in the relations of the government with the winegrowers, and much legislation which was vacillating and even contradictory.

As early as the autumn of 1944 the *Progrès agricole et viticole* was writing of "a surge of violent opinion in the Midi."[37]   And the Committee of Liberation of the little winegrowing community of Cournonterral (in Hérault) was advising the government of the possibility of demonstrations "as in 1907," adding that it could not check a current of opinion which it shared.   The government must fix a higher price for wine and relieve it from abusive taxation.[38] More important was the formation of the extremist Comité de Salut Viticole which in January of 1945 demanded "with the briefest delay" a payment to cover the losses of all winegrowers whose receipts did not meet their expenses.[39]

Within three weeks the Minister of Agriculture was in Montpellier promising the winegrowers farm horses, feed, fertilizers, insecticides, and—equally important—subsidies.   The latter promise was incorporated in an *ordonnance* of March 3, 1945, granting 250 francs for each hectolitre by which a grower's harvest in 1944 was more than 15 percent short of his average annual production from 1939 through 1943, providing that due to sickness of the vines his yield in 1944 was less than 60 hectolitres the hectare.   To qualify for this subsidy the grower had to have 95 percent of his production in *vins ordinaires* and winegrowing had to be the principal activity of his property.   An additional subsidy, subject also to the last two requirements, gave growers in the departments of Aude, Bouches-du-Rhône, Hérault, Pyrénées-Orientales, and Var a sum of 140 francs the hectolitre for that part of their harvest of 1944 resulting from a yield of less than 50 hectolitres the hectare, regardless of whether the total yield per hectare of their vineyard was greater.[40]

Even the first of these two measures principally affected the Midi,[41] and they both applied only to the harvest of 1944.   By contrast a more ambitious program was planned to give annual subsidies to all growers in the form of surcharges on the fixed price of wine at the production level.   Thus the price of 75 francs the degree-hectolitre [42] fixed for the harvest of 1945 in the Midi was only a base price.   To it were to be added a premium of 15 francs the de-gree-hectolitre for winegrowers in "exceptional difficulties," and a premium of 10 francs the degree-hectolitre for all growers, to be devoted to the reconstitution of their vineyard.[43]   This last sum, popularly known as the "viticultural nest egg," was to be withheld from payment to the grower and deposited to his account at the local *caisse régionale de crédit agricole*.   Here he could withdraw his money for purposes of planting new vines to replace sick or old ones, and the buying of agricultural machinery or implements.[44]

The *Revue de viticulture* enthusiastically noted that the "nest egg" would show the peasant the way to the bank, help the organ-ization of farm-machinery cooperatives, and lead to modernization of the vineyard.   For the government it was an "extremely supple means" of orienting viticulture towards better quality wines and a more rational production.[45]   But within less than a year the "nest egg" was broken up.   Not that the grower lost by this; the "nest egg" was henceforth incorporated in the price he received for his wine.   But the Assembly had been presented with the plight of the *petit vigneron*—so often the case in debates on viticultural policy.

The smaller grower's vines did not necessarily need to be pulled up.   Because of the size of his property there was not much occasion for this anyway.   Furthermore, the small grower did not have many tools in need of replacement.   But he did need money to pay his debts requiring interest, whereas the "nest egg" drew none.   Also, he needed money for fertilizers and insecticides, but he could not draw on the "nest egg" for any of these.   If he could qualify for a draft on his money, the formalities were still "irritating."   He also feared that another devaluation of the currency and the rise in cost of living would make his "nest egg" lose value.[46]   For all these reasons a law of May 7, 1946, gave the winegrower his money back and the right to do what he pleased with the 10 franc premium—a move, it is worth noting, reported on favorably by the Commission Agricole which had approved the "nest egg" in the first place.[47]

Closely following the problem of subsidies was the problem of taxes.   In the hopeful name of "agricultural solidarity" a tax of

8 francs the hectolitre was imposed on the harvest of 1945,[48] and a law of April 27, 1946, raised this sum to 70 francs for the next fall's harvest. In the face of protests and technical objections by the C.G.V., the government in a ministerial order of September 10, 1946, issued a redefinition of the complicated exemptions from the tax, which resulted in shifting the burden of the tax onto the wholesalers and those growers who shipped their own wine. There were misunderstandings, however: the C.G.V. felt compelled to advise flatly all growers that they were not obliged to pay the tax; yet as late as October the levying of the tax on growers produced "incidents" in several winegrowing communities.[49] In 1947 this tax was raised to 130 francs the hectolitre,[50] and the same year the *droit de circulation* on wine was also increased.[51] At the same time the government, returning somewhat timidly to the path it had followed with the "viticultural nest egg," ordered a sum of two francs the hectolitre to be withheld from the price the grower received for his wine, this sum to be paid to a Fonds de Progrès Agricole: Section Viticulture.[52] The fund, however, was to be concerned with general projects and did not constitute an account on which the individual grower could draw. In addition the fund received the revenue from a tax of five francs the hectolitre paid by dealers and specifically assigned to improving the quality of wines produced by cooperatives.[53] Necessary or praiseworthy as these taxes may have been, they were received with something less than enthusiasm, and their proliferation within a period of less than two years contributed to the uneasy relationship between the government and the winegrowers in the immediate postwar period.

But by far the greatest amount of friction between the two groups was generated in the realm of price fixing and rationing. The extremely light harvest of 1945 put a severe strain on the whole system which was aggravated by a continuously flourishing black market. The Fédération des Associations Viticoles (F.A.V.) at its annual congress held on July 6, 1946, taking note of this and the increasing costs of production, asked for what would have been roughly a 50 percent increase in the price of wine (145 to 150 francs the degree-hectolitre).[54] Later in the month the economic section of the Fédération met to take account of the government's objection to the proposed raise and offered by way of compromise a price of 120 francs the degree-hectolitre, but with an uncontrolled sector amounting to 25 percent of the harvest. This meeting was followed by a conference between representatives of the F.A.V. and the government, the latter agreeing to a price of 130 francs the degree-hectolitre and an uncontrolled or "free" sector depending on the size of the harvest.

The harvest of 1946, as has already been noted, was light, but before it had barely started the government settled on a price of 140 francs the degree-hectolitre and abandoned the idea of a free sector.[55] In view of the now unmistakable prospect of a short harvest, there was widespread dismay. On October 4 a delegation of winegrowers called on the Minister of Food Supply, and after what was called "stormy bargaining" [56] guaranteed him 18 million hectolitres of wine on condition that the rest of the harvest be left free of controls. Two days later M. Bidault, the head of the Government, hurried down to an aroused Midi to assure the officers of the C.G.V. and representatives of other viticultural associations that he was in favor of a free sector. But by October 17, when nothing had been done to change the government's original decree, the C.G.V. in an extraordinary assembly urged the winegrowers to hold back all except one fourth of their wine, the latter amount being considered sufficient to supply normal consumer demand for the first three months after the harvest.

Before this show of force, the government backed down and established what came to be known as the double sector. By a ministerial order of November 7, 1946, which incidentally kept the price of wine at 140 francs the degree-hectolitre, a grower was allowed to sell wine on the free market to the amount of 5 percent of the quantity of wine he sold at fixed prices, providing that he had sold one fourth of his available harvest before December 31, 1946. In addition, however, he was allowed to sell free of controls all or part of his wine reserved for family consumption if he paid the regular taxes on it. Although this part of his harvest was still determined by the Vichy percentages (12 percent for the lowest production range), the new law permitted the grower to figure the percentage on the basis of his most abundant harvest from 1939 to

1943 inclusive, providing his 1946 harvest was less than 25 percent of the former. The near totality of Midi winegrowers were able to qualify for increased percentages under this provision.[57]

As a *quid pro quo* for this new liberty the government instructed the agents of the Contributions Indirectes to be severe in investigating harvest declarations, and there were some squabbles because prefects tried to prevent winegrowers from getting around price fixing by barter.[58] Also, there were complaints that winegrowers were holding back their wine, but a parliamentary committee of inquiry shifted the blame for ostensible shortages onto the dealers and a widespread black market.[59] The government did, however, try to channel the free sector wines towards the individual citizen's ration by proposing that no *vin ordinaire* be sold in cafés or restaurants. But this brought a storm of opposition, especially in the Midi, and the proposal was dropped. An appropriately named Comité "Marcellin Albert" even threatened the Minister of Food Supply with a strike of local officials and a ban on the payment of taxes.[60] On the whole, however, the year that followed the harvest of 1946 brought a relief in tension. There were, first of all, increased receipts for the winegrowers: the average price of wine showed a 17 percent gain over the previous year. In addition the government successfully transacted for foreign sulfur, horses, and tractors; and German prisoners were assigned to work in the vineyards.[61]

An even easier atmosphere developed with the beginning of the 1947 harvest. The government, noting a decline in the price of wine in the free sector during August, and with all signs pointing to a more abundant harvest, decided in September on complete liberty of prices and sales.[62] This was more than the winegrowers had expected, for during the annual congress of the F.A.V. in February they had asked for a predominant free sector, but it was to be conditional on the furnishing of 4 million hectolitres to the Ministry of Food Supply at a fixed price. In addition some control of free-sector prices and supply was suggested through use of the staggered-release system of the *Statut de la Viticulture*. But the government had evidently had its fill of the double sector, or at least in the words of André Philip, the Minister of National Economy and Finance, had declared for "either complete control or complete liberty." [63]

By the next September, however, the government may well have regretted its decision. Where the average price of wine had been about 300 francs the degree-hectolitre in 1947, it had climbed to 500 francs before the 1948 harvest.[64] The latter was slightly more abundant than the year before in France, and there was a substantial 50 percent increase in production in Algeria. But prices were not significantly affected. The government, suspecting withholding, ordered the winegrowers to place 35 percent of their harvest and stocks on the market before December 31, 1948, and made the purchase of this quantity binding on the dealers.[65] Furthermore, if within fifteen days prices had not of themselves declined by 10 percent from those quoted on October 28 (430 francs the degree-hectolitre for 8° wines, 470 francs the degree-hectolitre for 11° wines), the government was to order forced sales at the reduced level.

This threat had to be carried out on November 18,[66] but the next day the government took indirect action which had a far more telling effect on wine prices as well as on those of some other commodities. This was the restriction of bank credit by the Bank of France, which according to one critic "cut down seriously the most moderate commercial speculations"[67] and according to the Société des Agriculteurs de France brought a four-month stagnation in viticultural transactions.[68]

By February of 1949, prices were being quoted at 330 to 350 francs the degree-hectolitre and the C.G.V. was calling for overhaul of a policy which had resulted in a "marasmus"—sales were being made below cost in the Midi and the wine remaining in the growers' cellars had been devalued by 10 billion francs.[69] M. Pflimlin, the Minister of Agriculture, declared that panic was not justified and promised that the government would take every step to bring wine prices into line with production costs.[70] The duty-free imports of wine which the government had been ordering to make up shortages were stopped. And on May 18 the government decreed the blocking of 30 percent of the harvest, but prices dropped to around 305 to 350 francs the degree-hectolitre.[71]

In July a sudden swing upward, attributed to a "speculative wave," took place.[72] At the end of the month prices had climbed to 420 francs the degree-hectolitre. The government, reversing itself, reordered the importation of foreign wines and released the blocked wines. But with the prospect of a less abundant harvest to come, prices were still being quoted at 420 to 450 francs the degree-hecto-litre in August. Although the season thus ended auspiciously for the winegrowers, tension had reappeared. The government had been accused of causing a "hostile climate." The price slump was an "artificial" one created by a government "haunted by the fear . . . of an exaggerated rise." [73]   In the opinion of one authority govern-ment policy had been too concerned with driving prices down by psychological pressures instead of trying to insure their stability.[74] The result had been a year of widely fluctuating prices.

TABLE 28.   AVERAGE PRICE OF WINE AT THE PRODUCTION LEVEL
IN FRANCE, 1945–49 (*In francs*)

Year	Average Price per Hectolitre
1945	1,380
1946	2,680
1947	3,131
1948	4,061
1949	3,943

Source: *Annuaire statistique.*

Somewhat the same tactics were employed after the harvest of 1949. Daniel Combes has described that year as one in which prices were "cleverly manipulated by the permanent threat of im-portations." [75]   The government did, however, try to bring both stability and reasonable prices to the market by a variant of the staggered-release system known as the Bonnave plan.

At the beginning of the harvest 70 percent of the grower's pro-duction was to be blocked.[76]   Beginning with February 1, 1950, 20 per cent portions were to be released every two months providing prices remained between 360 and 400 francs the degree-hectolitre.[77] But if in the month preceding the release of a portion, prices dropped below 360 francs on two consecutive markets,[78] the liberation of that portion was to be put off one month. If during two consecu-tive markets prices remained above 400 francs, the next portion was to be released immediately with following portions to be released every fifteen days until prices dropped below 400 francs. If, on the other hand, prices went above 410 francs, the whole amount of blocked wine was to be immediately liberated. As in the earlier *Statut* only productions of 200 hectolitres or more were subject to blockage, with the minimum portion to be released at any one date set at 100 hectolitres regardless of the percentages decreed.

Although the plan raised some criticism from the viticultural associations, it worked smoothly during its first year of operation. Of course the threat of imports may have played a part in this, but they amounted in fact to only 1 million hectolitres more than the year before, while the total of wine available for the market was about 4 million hectolitres less. At all events, prices stayed within the desired range and the blocked portions were released on schedule.

CRISIS

Like its predecessor of 1900-1907, the crisis which began with the harvest of 1950 broke out with disconcerting suddenness. Where annual production had averaged 42,675,429 hectolitres for the 1946–49 period, the harvest of 1950 produced a postwar record of 65,132,600 hectolitres. Thereafter sizeable harvests which, if they did not approach the peaks reached during the 1930–39 period, in combination with Algerian production and large stocks left over from previous harvests gave France a six-year period during which wine available for the market came to more than 80 million hectolitres each year. At the same time, in comparison with the 1930–39 period there was a noticeable drop in taxed consumption.

During the same period the vineyard area in production, after reaching a low of 1,403,000 hectares in 1944, jumped rapidly in 1945 and then continued a steady climb until, account being taken of yields, it was possible to say that by 1953 the metropolitan vineyard had approached its prewar production potential. This phenomenon is all the more apparent, as Table 30 shows, if vines not yet in production are included in the total.

The bumper harvest of 1950 had an immediate effect on prices. The Bonnave plan, it will be remembered, called for a platform price of 360 francs the degree-hectolitre, but by September 15 the price of wine in the Midi had fallen to 290 francs the degree-hectolitre.[79]

This last figure was made the new platform price, but by April, 1951, prices had dropped below it. M. Pflimlin, the Minister of Agriculture, in a speech at Épernay, then called for the "compulsory

TABLE 29. PRODUCTION, STOCKS, AND CONSUMPTION OF WINE, 1949–55
(*In hectolitres*)

Year	Production in France	Production in Algeria	Stocks in France	Taxed Consumption in France
1930–39, yearly average	58,885,000	17,298,800	6,200,626	49,307,400
1949	42,934,749	14,500,000	4,221,862	35,274,000
1950	65,132,600	14,300,000	4,231,100	37,626,000
1951	52,858,000	13,700,000	15,093,257	38,750,000
1952	53,884,500	12,300,000	13,245,900	42,113,000
1953	59,113,300	18,300,000	12,610,583	42,099,000
1954	60,858,100	19,300,000	12,950,000	45,140,000
1955	61,051,124	14,400,000	15,356,000	46,640,000

Source: *Annuaire statistique; Statistique agricole annuelle, Annuaire statistique de l'Algérie.*

and immediate" distillation of 2 million hectolitres of wine.[80]   In addition a decree of April 28, 1951, called for the eventual distillation of 40 percent of the blocked wines.

These measures affected prices somewhat, but in August 60 percent of a grower's harvest was still blocked (less the amount of wine distilled), and stocks were estimated at 19,273,555 hectolitres.[81]   Meanwhile the government had ordered the reinstitution of the tax on yields,[82] and was being invited in the Assembly to consider additional means of warding off what was now officially labeled "a viticultural crisis." [83]

The harvest of 1951 was relatively moderate, but with stocks from the year before still in excess of 15 million hectolitres the amount of wine available for the market was nearly the same as during the 1950–51 season.   In view of this situation the F.A.V. asked for emergency measures—the immediate distillation of remaining stocks and the liberation of no portion of the new harvest before October 1.[84]   Before the first of these demands the government had to take a cautious stand.   In 1951 the Service des Alcools had made a record purchase of 3,390,000 hectolitres of beet alcohol (the prewar quota limit had been abandoned); stocks of alcohol

TABLE 30.   VINEYARD AREA AND YIELD IN FRANCE AND ALGERIA, 1944–53

Year	Area of Vines in Production in France (in hectares)	Area of Vines in Production Plus Area not Yet in Production in France (in hectares)	Area of Vines in Production in Algeria (in hectares)	Yield per Hectare in France (in hecto-litres)
1930–39, yearly average	1,529,300	unavailable	357,000	38.41
1940	1,470,000	1,545,000	391,000	33.62
1944	1,403,000	1,454,000	350,000	31.57
1945	1,434,000	1,488,000	341,000	19.96
1946	1,435,000	1,492,000	333,000	25.18
1947	1,440,000	1,506,000	327,000	30.67
1948	1,433,000	1,511,000	331,000	33.08
1949	1,434,000	1,522,000	335,000	29.87
1950	1,453,000	1,536,000	350,000	42.40
1951	1,450,000	1,533,000	361,000	35.50
1952	1,454,000	1,536,000	367,000	37.00
1953	1,454,000	1,538,000	371,000	40.40

Source: *Statistique agricole annuelle, Annuaire statistique de l'Algérie.*

and losses for the Service were accumulating at an alarming rate, and the government was committed to a policy of reducing its alcohol purchases.[85]

Still, compulsory distilling for the new harvest was decided on, and the amount of wine distilled was nearly equal to the year before, although the government in March of 1952 had had to cut down on the distilling which was still going on under the terms of the decree of April 28, 1951.[86] To improve the situation of the market the government relied chiefly on a tightened version of the Bonnave plan.[87] The initial portion of the harvest to be released was reduced from 30 percent to 10 percent and the minimum quantity to be released regardless of percentages was reduced from 100 hectolitres to 50 hectolitres. The platform price was upped to 330 francs the degree-hectolitre, although the F.A.V. had asked for a figure of 377 francs because of increased production costs. Prices soon dropped below 330 francs, however. A new platform of 290 francs was adopted, but in spite of this action there were delays in the liberation of blocked portions of the harvest which carried over the release of the last portion into the next season. And at the end of the year there was a discouragingly large stock of more than 13 million hectolitres still remaining from the 1951 harvest.

THE CRISIS IS DEBATED

It was generally held that the overabundant harvest of 1950 and the accumulation of stocks that followed it were the result of the fragmentary and tardy reapplication of the *Statut de la Viticulture* after its suspension by the Vichy government. It was not until 1949, for example, that after much confusion, a decree definitely repealed Vichy legislation permitting the watering of wine, the sale of substandard wines, and the making of *piquettes*.[88]

The same decree also reinstated the prohibition against the circulation of wine coming from the forbidden hybrids. In 1947, however, the Ministry of Agriculture had designated a committee to study the "behavior" of hybrids and the quality of wines which they might produce. This action, not blameworthy in itself, was evidently taken by the winegrowers as a signal to plant any type of hybrid they wished [89]—this in spite of the fact that in 1947 a decision of the Contributions Indirectes had allowed that until a definite regime for new plantings was established, growers could plant new vines equal in area to the area of vines to be pulled up within a delay of three years, *provided* these plantings were made with grape varieties approved by the *Statut de la Viticulture*.[90] The government's failure to formulate the definite regime until 1953 further inspired the growers to take a dim view of regulations and led to charges of widespread illicit plantings, the extent of which is difficult to determine.[91]

Governmental procrastination also contributed to an understandably relaxed, if not demoralized, attitude on the part of the agents of the Contributions Indirectes and the Ministry of Agriculture who were supposed to enforce the law.[92] Under such conditions it is not hard to believe that the momentum gained during seven years practice of liberties in planting and "approved" fraud carried beyond 1949. As a result there were some urgent demands in responsible quarters before, during, and after that year for the reapplication of the *Statut de la Viticulture* in its entirety.

The development, however, of a large stock after the relatively moderate harvest of 1951 may be said to have marked a turning point in thinking concerning the viticultural crisis. It was increasingly felt that the mechanisms of the old *Statut* did not offer a permanent solution to viticulture's perennial problem of overproduction. Compulsory distilling for the past two years had signally failed to absorb what were beginning to appear as chronically abnormal stocks left over after each season.

Consequently the year 1952 was marked by discussion of many plans for viticulture's future, and demands for what was now being referred to as a new and definitive *Code du Vin.* This does not mean that some of the plans did not cover old ground with old arguments, or that the motivation of others was commendable. But the best plans anticipated the orienting of the national vineyard towards quality production at the expense of quantity on a scale not attempted before.

In respect to this last consideration an interesting lead was given by the F.A.V. itself. Elaborating on its attachment to "a policy of quality" proclaimed the year before at an annual congress, it asked, in December of 1951, for

1. Division of France into viticultural and nonviticultural zones (a) by forbidding new planting or replanting beyond the northern limits of the [normal] area of viticulture; (b) by immediate measures discouraging the extension of viticulture in those regions and zones where it is not desirable, or where it is propagated in a way contrary to quality and at the expense of true professional winegrowers; (c) by the immediate establishment of a viticultural cadastral survey, the utilization of the information obtained by the commissions concerned, and the inventory and verification of rights to replant, used or unused.

2. Control over reconstitution of the vineyard by orienting it towards a production of better quality by the judicious choice of lands, vines, and grafts.

3. Attribution of indemnities for voluntary and permanent pulling up of vines.

4. Encouragement of replacement crops by the allocation of subsidies and divers advantages.

5. Establishment of a timetable based on a hierarchy of quality for the suppression of grape varieties [hybrids] destined to disappear from use.[93]

Several months later, in May of 1952, the Ministry of Agriculture also declared "for a policy of quality." "In those regions," it added, "which produce large quantities of often mediocre wine, it should be possible to raise other crops essential for the French economy, the return on which should be at least equal to that of wine." According to the Ministry:

Viticulture is now undergoing a crisis all the more serious in that it does not result from extraordinary circumstances but from a disequilibrium between resources and demands, a disequilibrium that can only accentuate itself in the years to come because of the constant augmentation of the production potential of the vineyard.

This situation can certainly be improved by the development of domestic consumption, which is still well below what it was before the war, and by the increase of our exports, but it remains nonetheless true that an influence on production itself is indispensable in view of adapting it to the qualitative and quantitative demands of the market.

Then treading on some dangerous ground, the Ministry pointed out that actual legislation was insufficient for the above purposes.

It rests . . . essentially on the elimination of surpluses by compulsory distillation. Now this procedure, valid for correcting an accidental excess of production, is no longer acceptable when it becomes one of constant application, first because this results in the destruction of a noble product, and second because it is very costly—as much for the winegrowers as for the state.

In addition, in the actual circumstances and account being taken of existing legislation, compulsory distillation does not permit, even independently of all financial considerations, the disappearance of the totality of surpluses.[94]

The above exposé was followed by a detailed plan for the orienting of viticulture towards quality production through control of new plantings, a program for pulling up vines, and a policy encouraging of new crops—the whole to be administered by a special organisation under the Ministry of Agriculture endowed with a legal personality and financial autonomy.

The C.G.V., nettled no doubt by the attack on compulsory distilling, admitted "that it is said that the [Ministry's] project rests on excellent principles," and that its method of application, although "imprecise," deserved to be studied. But in the C.G.V.'s mind the project was too long-range. It could not pretend to ward off "a situation that could become dangerous tomorrow." From this point of view the interests of the winegrowers were better served by the Sourbet and Chevalier plans.[95]

The Sourbet plan, one of eight viticultural *projets de loi* presented to the Assembly in 1952, was based on the principle that obligations already incumbent on the winegrower (compulsory distilling, blockage, and the tax on yields) should be calculated on the basis of the *individual* grower's *normal* production and yield, and the changes in area of his vineyard since January 1, 1933 (exonerations for a decrease; penalties for an increase).[96]

The starting point for these calculations was to be a production of 50 hectolitres, and this led the plan's supporters to claim that it would bring a great many more winegrowers under its control than the old *Statut*. There was, however, a blanket exemption from all obligations, except the replanting regulations of the *Statut,* for those growers who could qualify as "viticultural artisans." A viticultural artisan was defined as a grower who owned and cultivated his own land, who produced 300 hectolitres or less for a gross revenue of "about" 900,000 francs or less, and who could prove that winegrowing constituted his principal source of income. An additional provision further defined the viticultural artisan as one whose vineyard was located in a region "traditionally viticultural," whose land had been planted in vines before January 1, 1933, whose vineyard area had not increased since then, and whose yield per hectare was 120 hectolitres or less.

The Sourbet plan, like the first provision of the F.A.V.'s project quoted above, was inspired by a relatively small but significant increase of the vineyard area in some polycultural and traditionally nonviticultural regions. The Midi viticultural press tended to place this increase high on the list of causes of the crisis, but in the opinion of serious observers it was much exaggerated.[97] Moreover, critics of the Sourbet plan were not slow to point out its "political" implications.[98] The plan was nothing more than an attempt to

secure the established winegrowing regions in a quasi-monopoly of
the market. These tactics, it will be remembered, had been used
against Algeria in the 1930's by the C.G.V., although they had then
principally taken the form of proposals for regional blockage and
distilling schedules—proposals, incidentally, which were revived in
1952 and 1953. The small-grower bias of the Sourbet plan was also
familiar and obvious.

The Chevalier plan, proposed by a former deputy from Algeria,
had as its main point the reestablishment of the *caisse annexe de la
viticulture*.[99] In its new form the *caisse* was to be a *caisse autonome*
endowed with a legal personality and directed by members of the
viticultural profession under the supervision of the state. Its chief
resources would come from a special tax imposed on *all* winegrowers based on the area of the vineyard and yield per hectare.
Further resources were to come from a tax on sugar used in winemaking and fines from infractions of the various laws regulating
winemaking (minimum alcoholic content and the like). Although,
as noted, the plan had the support of the C.G.V., its all-inclusive tax
levy produced some opposition. As one critic put it, echoing senti-
ments familiar to the 1930's, the vast majority of winegrowers
"could not make ends meet" and "were in no way responsible" for
the current crisis.[100]

By the summer of 1952, with prospects already evident of a
harvest at least equal that of 1951, the F.A.V. was also swept up
in the trend toward revival of old nostrums. At its annual congress
held from July 1–3, it approved the principles of the Ministry of
Agriculture's project, but like the C.G.V. it reserved its full support
until further study. Meanwhile it urgently demanded the "immediate application" of existing laws, and most especially the revival of
the *caisse annexe*. This last was to be done "as a preliminary step
to its eventual transformation in which viticulture would take an
important share of the financing." But for the coming harvest it
was more important to have the old *Statut* and such recent additions
to it as the Bonnave plan functioning efficiently.[101]

On the day following the end of the F.A.V. congress, a long-
awaited debate on the viticultural crisis began in the Assembly. The
debate unfortunately was not on a very high level, dominated as it

was by the Communist deputies who had obtained representation on the Commission des Boissons. The Communist argument emphasized the "social character" of the old *Statut,* and it was larded with references to the "spirit of 1907" and the peculiarly "national" qualities of French wine. Red herrings were introduced, such as an attack on Coca-Cola, "a noxious and poisonous drink," and there was a demagogic appeal to give the wine that would have to be distilled to the poor (i.e., those people earning less than 84 francs a day).[102]

More specifically, the Communist program called for a complete return to the *Statut,* and placed the party on record against lowering the blockage and compulsory-distilling production ranges. It also asked for a reduction of taxes and government encouragement for the consumption of wine. The Socialists in their turn revived their prewar project for an Office du Vin.[103] But beyond these limits the debate abandoned party lines, revolving fruitlessly around the numerous *projets de loi* that had been proposed during the year. Despite an appeal from the Minister of Agriculture to the F.A.V. to promote "unity," [104] and a last-minute demand from the floor of the Assembly for a "synthesis," [105] the debate ended inconclusively. The Ministry of Agriculture project was not even put to the vote, and the best the deputies could do was adopt a resolution asking the government [106]

1. To reestablish immediately the *caisse annexe de la viticulture* in its functions and with all its resources.

2. To absorb surpluses, notably (a) by the blockage and distillation, within the framework of the *Statut de la Viticulture,* of the surplus wines which weigh heavily on the market; (b) by the creation of a special domestic market supplied by *vins de consommation courante,* freed from taxes and compulsory distilling; [107] (c) by moving back to October 1, 1952, the beginning of the 1952–53 season, once the above measures have been realized; (d) by a correlative moving back to the same date of the declaration of stocks now fixed for August 31; [108] (e) by the development of the export of wines.

The government replied with a decree of July 25, 1952, which raised the compulsory-distilling percentages for the remainder of the 1951 harvest, and which introduced a change in the Bonnave plan for the harvest of 1952. No fixed date was set for the release of the first portion (10 percent) of the harvest; it was simply to occur when prices reached 320 francs the degree-hectolitre. Thereafter, if prices stayed between a floor of 290 francs and a ceiling of 330 francs, the release of 20 percent portions of the harvest was to take place at three-month intervals starting on January 15. Since the release of the first portion did not take place until October 10, this change, in effect, answered the request of the Assembly about moving back the beginning of the new season. But it brought to a head a new difficulty.

It was increasingly being demonstrated that the Bonnave plan was prejudicial to the grower with a low yield per hectare. Thus, as one critic pointed out, the lowland grower with a yield of 120 hectolitres the hectare who in July of 1952 found 50 percent of his harvest still blocked could count on selling 60 hectolitres the hectare, which would permit him to meet his fixed charges on schedule. On the other hand his rival with a hillside vineyard yielding 40 hectolitres the hectare, where growing costs were in the first instance higher, would only be selling 20 hectolitres a hectare, which would run him into debt and, at the end of several years, into bankruptcy.[109]

The Bonnave plan, however, only affected growers with a production of 200 hectolitres or more, and these were a minority, although in respect to their number they were the most important economically.[110] At all events, by November of 1952 there was talk of "misery and unemployment" in the Midi because of the low price of wine and the expense of holding important quantities of wines in the growers' cellars.[111] And as early as July, 1952, the F.A.V. was asking for release of blocked wines on a yield-per-hectare basis in order at least to assure what one observer called "an equality of misery." [112]

MISERY AND GOVERNMENT ACTION : THE *Code du Vin* OF 1953

In 1953, after another moderate harvest, the price of wine reached a new postwar low (account being taken of the revaluation of the currency). The drop from the average price of the year before was not great—only 2.5 percent, but the total amount of wine available for the market had decreased in nearly the same proportions (2.4 percent). In the Midi, moreover, price drops were much greater, and the Bonnave plan, tied as it was to Midi prices, became unworkable and was in fact, if not in principle, scrapped. There was no need to speak of ceiling prices, and the blocked portions of the harvest were simply released when prices reached a predetermined level as had been done during the crisis of the 1930's.

As noted, the release of the first portion of the 1952 harvest did not begin until October 10, but prices at that date had only reached 290 francs the degree-hectolitre instead of the 320 francs intended. Thereafter prices dropped so low that it was only through pressure from the Assembly that the government was persuaded not to lower the price for the release of the next portion. This meant that the next release did not begin until February 12. But worse, the release of the following portion did not begin until six months later, on August 12, which meant that 50 percent of the harvest still remained blocked after that date.

With so large a quantity of wine to be unblocked in so short a time the government raised the minimum amount that a grower could release, regardless of percentages, from 50 hectolitres to 200 hectolitres in France and 300 hectolitres in Algeria.[113] This minimum could also be figured on the basis of 25 hectolitres per hectare—an attempt to answer the criticisms of the Bonnave plan described above. On September 2 these amounts were increased again to 300 hectolitres, 400 hectolitres, and 35 hectolitres, respectively.[114]

The price fixed for unblocking remained at 290 francs the degree-hectolitre for the rest of the season except on August 12, when it was 300 francs, and on September 18, when the last 30 percent of the harvest was unblocked without any price formalities.[115] But with the Bonnave plan out of operation, prices fell after every release date and remained below 290 francs a good deal of the time. An estimate for July, for example, put them between 240 to 270 francs the degree-hectolitre.[116] And the same month it was being claimed that the small and average growers were nearly all in debt and that many had mortgaged their next fall's crop.[117] That prices on the whole did not sink any lower was due to the fact that the levels touched were close to cost and in many cases below. They represented, in short, "misery prices" obtained in a market that was described as being in a state of "complete disorganization." [118]

To bolster the sagging market the F.A.V., at its 1953 congress held from June 29 to July 2 at Bordeaux, made an unprecedented demand. Amid much talk of a "social price" for the suffering wine-growers, it asked, with all urgency, for the government to intervene and buy wine on the Midi markets. In return the F.A.V. pledged itself to support the government's project for the orienting and disciplining of viticultural production. [119]

Meanwhile, in the first week of June, the Assembly had launched another debate on the viticultural crisis, equally inconclusive as the one held the year before as far as legislation was concerned. A summary, however, of viticulture's predicament presented to the Assembly by the Commission des Boissons makes an interesting winegrower's *cahier de doléances* for the summer of 1953. Announcing that "crisis was now a brutal fact" and that "wine prices had never been so low," the Commission pointed out that

1. The price of wine (at the production level) was only fifteen times greater than before the war.
2. Taxes on wine which amounted to 27 francs the hectolitre in 1938 were now 1,195 francs or forty-four times greater.
3. Copper sulfate and sulfur (insecticides) were forty-five and forty-two times more expensive, respectively.
4. Industrial products used by winegrowers were thirty-two times more expensive.
5. In four years the price of wine had dropped 50 percent.
6. During the same time the retail price had not gone down. There was no advantage in this crisis for the urban consumer. [120]

The above statement was followed by a demand for reestablishment of the *caisse annexe de la viticulture,* reduction of taxes on wine to a total of 500 francs the hectolitre, return to the *Statut de la Viticulture,* and a 25 percent reduction in shipping costs by rail for wine.

With the newly formed Laniel government evasive about both F.A.V. and Assembly proposals, the extremist faction of winegrowers moved on to the scene. The Comité de Salut Viticole, on July 12, held a giant demonstration at Béziers, the announced purpose of which was "to revive the spirit of 1907." [121] One concrete proposal, however, did emerge from the meeting even if it was framed in threatening language.

The government in March had lowered the quota price of wine alcohol regularly purchased by the Service des Alcools to a level of approximately 22,000 francs the hectolitre.[122] This was a price which actually meant a loss to the grower—a practice followed in compulsory distilling, but not before this with quota alcohols. The reduced price was, however, inspired by the deficits and stocks which the Service was continually piling up. Nevertheless the Comité demanded the raising of the price of quota wine alcohol to 30,000 francs the hectolitre to bring it in line with the price of wine.

On July 27 the government flatly refused to do this. And the next day, as threatened, winegrowers barricaded roads in all parts of the Midi while, true to the tradition of 1907, the mayors of many communities handed in their resignations. On July 29, M. Laniel consented to receive delegates of some viticultural *syndicats*,[123] who then confronted him again with a demand for a wine-alcohol price of 30,000 francs and such vague demands as "the abolishing of privileges," the reorganization of the wine market, and the repression of fraud.[124]

On July 31 Laniel was again visited, this time by delegates of other Midi viticultural groups who asked for the immediate distillation of blocked wines and the purchase by the state of wines already on the market. To these requests Laniel answered that the blocked wines would be released as scheduled provided the determined price levels were reached. He added that many of the reforms that had been asked were already included in his government's projected program, and that others were the object of exchanges of view between the ministers concerned. But he flatly refused to have the state buy wine on the open market.

The C.G.V., undoubtedly worried by the groups that were bypassing it, urged the winegrowers to stay calm and listen only to official organizations, adding that the government was determined to act in the near future.[125] But the next week, on August 6, when France was already suffering from a general strike, the barricades went up again in the Midi.   Further dissatisfaction was caused by the announcement on August 9 of cuts in the regular quota purchases of alcohol,[126] a move justified by a law of July 11, 1953, which had given the government broad power "to realize a new distribution of the finances and resources of the nation."   A long summer of complaints and an even longer period of suspense was suddenly ended, however, on September 30 when, in the form of a decree, the government presented its long-awaited *Code du Vin*.

The first part of the new *Code* attacked the problem of the marketing of the harvest. The most notable departure from the experience of the previous few years was the final abandoning of the Bonnave plan.   Instead of having a grower's entire harvest blocked and then releasing portions of it, the *Code* simply called for the "definitive" blockage of a determined percentage. The latter was to be figured on the extent to which French and Algerian production and stocks plus Moroccan and Tunisian import quotas exceeded the needs of the market. The percentage thus determined was binding on all growers subject to blockage alike.

Compulsory distillation was to operate only on blocked wines. The percentage of these to be distilled was to be prescribed at the same time as the blockage percentage, and like the latter could be binding on all growers alike.[127] The release or additional distilling of the blocked wines was not to be determined until the amount of wine available after the next harvest was known.

The minimum production subject to blockage and compulsory distilling was lowered from 200 hectolitres to 100 hectolitres, with, however, a grower being allowed to dispose of 100 hectolitres regardless of percentages.   Also, before blockage was decreed a grower could dispose of 15 hectolitres per hectare or a total of 50 hectolitres, whichever was greater.

A grower whose yield was less than 20 hectolitres the hectare was exempted from compulsory distillation, as was one whose harvest was less than 50 percent of his average production for the preceding three years, provided his yield was not more than 50 hectolitres the hectare.   A yield of more than 100 hectolitres the hectare was blocked regardless of whether blockage was decreed or not.

Other measures included in the first part of the *Code,* while they mainly tended to improve the quality of wine, also affected the volume of production. These were increases in the taxes on yields [128] and the raising of the minimum alcoholic content and the lowering of the degree of maximum acidity of wine to prewar levels. A most important and controversial measure in the same category required all growers, irrespective of the amount or quality of their production (growers of *vins d'appellations d'origine contrôlées* were included) to furnish a quantity of *alcool vinique* corresponding to 12 percent of their harvest expressed in terms of pure alcohol and figured on the basis of the minimum alcoholic content prescribed for wines of their region.[129] The price paid for this alcohol was not to exceed 70 percent of the quota price for *alcools de marc.*

Thus the government in the first part of the *Code* brought an extension of compulsory distilling and blockage, achieved complete flexibility in decreeing them, and greatly simplified their application. That this program should have brought protests on behalf of the small grower is not surprising. *Les petits,* or at least *les moyens,* were now penalized, it seemed, nearly as heavily as *les grands.*

"We think," the *Progrès agricole et viticole* editorialized, "that provisions inspired by a less liberal [economic] tendency would have better organized the equalization of profits among the wine-growers." [130] And later the same paper invited the legislators "to protect the small grower by establishing a [better] graduation of financial and economic burdens." [131] But a more valid argument would seem to be that aside from matters of detail the first part of the *Code* did not offer any radical departure from the principles of the earlier *Statut.* Distilling still carried the major part of the burden of reducing surpluses—and this at a time when the government was actively carrying out a policy of reducing its other alcohol purchases. Also the dangers of definitive blockage during a series of overabundant harvests had been demonstrated by experience with the law of July 4, 1931.[132]

The answer to these objections might be that the government was here trying to solve an immediate problem and gambling on a short cure. The long cure, on which the government placed certain reliance, was the reduction of the area of the vineyard and the orienting of it toward quality production through control of planting.[133] To the latter end the bulk of the *Code du Vin* and its most interesting provisions were directed—and these, it is only fair to note, were for the most part supported by the F.A.V., the C.G.V., and the viticultural press.

Conforming somewhat to earlier recommendations of the F.A.V., the *Code* divided the viticultural area of France into (1) regions qualified for viticulture as defined by their anteriority and their aptitude for producing wines of quality, (2) regions of reconversion characterized by the possibility of substituting productive crops for wine.

The *Code* next called for the establishment of a list of grape varieties for each region, distinguishing between (1) recommended varieties; (2) authorized varieties; and (3) temporarily tolerated varieties, the sale, planting, and grafting of which was forbidden. In addition even the giving away of wine from the following varieties was forbidden: the Noah, the Isabella, the Jacquez, the Clinton, and the Herbemont.[134] Wine coming from these grapes could only circulate to be distilled, and vines bearing them, if planted before January 18, 1935, had to be pulled up within five years of December 1, 1953, or, if planted before the former date, within two years.

Although the right to replant existed, it could be fully exercised only if recommended grape varieties were used. If authorized varieties were used there was to be a 30 percent reduction in the area replanted. In the event that there should be a right to replant in vineyards containing the temporarily tolerated varieties, this right could only be exercised under certain conditions with grape varieties agreed to by a special order of the Ministry of Agriculture.

The right to replant existed only where an equivalent area had been pulled up. The *Code* thus went further than previous legislation in forbidding new planting. The only exceptions were the right to plant new vines for tax-free family consumption, provided the area thus planted did not exceed one fourth of a hectare. Also, the right to plant new vines to produce *vins d'appellations d'origine contrôlées* was permitted, but under such strict conditions as to make abuses virtually impossible.[135]

An important part of the *Code* was devoted to incentives for the voluntary pulling up of vines. Indemnities were to be provided for winegrowers who pulled up all or part of their vineyard and definitely renounced their right to replant. In addition growers received subsidies if they replanted their land in more economically productive crops. For those who pulled up part of their vineyard, proportional reductions in the percentage of wine subject to compulsory distilling were also offered, with an additional 25 percent reduction if the land thus made available were planted in an approved crop. Another important item in the *Code* provided for a cadastral survey of the national vineyard which would provide a base plan for the proposed shift to quality production. Finally a comprehensive clause threatened that

If the provisions enacted in the present decree do not cause resources to be brought down to the level of needs by December 31, 1958, the abnormal surpluses will be excluded from the market and from the benefits of the regime of the absorption of surpluses [i.e., compulsory distilling and regular quota alcohol purchases].

The pulling up of vines necessary for the elimination of these abnormal surpluses will be carried out under the control of the Institut des Vins de Consommation Courante under conditions which will be the object of a decree by the Council of State.

The Institut des Vins de Consommation Courante (I.V.C.C.), it remains to be noted, was one of the foundation stones of the *Code* and represented the latter's most interesting innovation. Patterned on the professionally organized Institut National des Appellations d'Origine des Vins et Eaux-de-Vie (I.N.A.O.) which had had a successful record in policing its own market, it was an attempt to shift onto the winegrowers some of the responsibility for improving the quality of their product.

The mission of the I.V.C.C., as defined by the *Code,* was

1. To study and suggest all measures of an economic and technical nature for orienting viticulture toward quality production.

2. To organize the technical control of plantings of the vine, in particular through the control of the production and distribution of vines and vinestocks.

3. To participate in the investigation of infractions of legislative and statutory provisions in the matter of planting and pulling up [of vines].

4. To establish for each vineyard a record of the variety of vine plantings in view of the cadastral survey [of the national vineyard].

5. To establish a list of the permitted grape varieties.

6. To establish the basis for determining the subsidies and indemnities provided for in articles . . . [pulling up of vines and replacement crops], and to propose the organization of corresponding expenditures.

7. To follow the same procedure in that which concerns the execution of all measures for the rehabilitation of the vineyard.

Thus the enforcement and execution of a great many of the provisions of the *Code* were assigned to the I.V.C.C. The *Code* also gave the I.V.C.C. a legal personality and financial autonomy such as that accorded the Service des Alcools, but left its organization and the prescribing of rules for its functioning to the Council of State. The functioning and organization of the I.V.C.C are still in a process of evolution. Since the organizing of its permanent committee in 1954, however, the representation of the winegrowers in that body has been predominant.[136]

To finance the operations of the I.V.C.C. and the cost of the indemnities and subsidies provided for in the *Code,* a special Treasury account was opened. Although the *Code* placed this account under the administration of the Ministry of Finance and National Economy, a committee of control was set up to which, as one of its duties, the I.V.C.C. designated representatives of the winegrowers to sit with those of the interested government agencies.

The legislation of 1953 marks the end, for the time being, of the series of laws by which successive governments have tried to regulate winegrowing. Writing a month after its passage, Professor Branas of the National Agricultural School at Montpellier has declared that now "everything happens as though the journey were ended, and the critics who are not lacking cannot conceal a general sentiment of relief, analogous perhaps to that which the arrival at a halting place produces." [137]

But, according to Professor Branas, the halting place is only a stage in a journey that goes on. Certainly there is nothing in the history just accomplished to show that the problems of the winegrowers and the government are definitely solved. Meanwhile, however, the most serious criticism one can make of the new *Code* at this date is that it came so late.

As early as December of 1946 the first Monnet plan called for the reduction of France's vineyard area to 1,350,000 hectares by 1950.[138] In 1947 a report by the National Economic Council also favored this figure and asked for a proportionate reduction of the area of the Algerian vineyard.[139] Writing in 1951 Daniel Combes has pointed out that the immediate postwar years were "years of lost opportunities" in these respects.[140] But the government, faced with what Combes has called the "clamour of thirsty consumers," [141] not to mention the demands of the great majority of winegrowers themselves, turned so far from these opportunities as to undo much of the good that had been accomplished by the legislation of the 1930's. The lesson of the too-rapid recovery of the productive potential of the national vineyard after earlier periods of shortages and deprivation was apparently ignored.

On the other hand, when the government finally did act to check production, it gave promise of more than making up for lost ground. Although the sections of the *Code* dealing with blockage and compulsory distilling represent a continued reliance on a system that has its disadvantages for both the government and the winegrowers, it may at least be said that by eliminating some of the bias in favor of the small grower from this system, the *Code* is more efficient than previous legislation in these respects. Also, as we have suggested earlier, blockage and compulsory distillation are perhaps the only solution to the immediate problem of overproduction. In addition it may well be that their extension, if we can believe the complaints of the viticultural press, will work a cruel necessity in discouraging some smaller proprietors from winegrowing.

In respect to the other parts of the *Code,* it remains only to be said that the I.V.C.C. is enjoying the full support of the viticultural associations and that, as will be seen in more detail in the next chapter, the program for pulling up vines has produced some encouraging results. Also, outside the operations of the *Code* there are developments and new currents of thought that may effect a more complete subordination of winegrowing to the needs of France's economy. These too will be examined in the chapter that follows.

10. *LATER DEVELOPMENTS AND THE FUTURE OF WINEGROWING IN THE FRENCH ECONOMY*

It is, of course, too soon to make any quantitative measurements of the effectiveness of the new *Code*. Moreover, its debut has been troubled by a succession of overabundant harvests— 59 million hectolitres in 1953, over 60 million in 1954, and 61 million in 1955. During the same period Algerian production reached its postwar peak—19,300,000 hectolitres in 1954—and large stocks have continued to remain after the end of every season. As Tables 31, 32, and 33 show, compulsory distilling remains an expensive and wasteful means of absorbing surplus wine production, and wine prices have remained discouragingly low,[1] failing, as they have, to share in the rise in prices of other foodstuffs.

The harvest of 1956 was relatively moderate—approximately 51 million hectolitres—but with the previous season's stocks plus Algerian production, total wine available for the market still came to about 74 million hectolitres. This represented a drop of 22 percent, however, from the previous year's total. A three-year period of stagnation, during which prices in the Midi had remained at a level of 290 to 300 francs the degree-hectolitre, was thus broken by midsummer of 1956. And by March of 1957 prices were approaching 400 francs the degree-hectolitre.

The harvest of 1957, predicted as "catastrophic" and accompanied by talk of ceiling prices and rationing,[2] resulted in a total

TABLE 31.   AMOUNT OF COMPULSORILY DISTILLED WINE IN FRANCE,
1950–55 (*In hectolitres*)

Year	Quantity Distilled
1935–39, yearly average [a]	6,360,000
1950	6,100,000
1951	5,900,000
1952	4,200,000
1953	6,400,000
1954	6,200,000
1955	10,500,000

[a] Includes emergency purchase of wine alcohol outside compulsory distilling limits in 1935.

Source: Ledermann, *Alcool*, pp. 20–21.

TABLE 32.   INDEX OF WHOLESALE PRICES OF FOODS AND FOODSTUFFS
IN FRANCE, 1949–56
(*1949 = 100*)

Foods	1950	1951	1952	1953	1954	1955	1956
Entirety of foods and foodstuffs listed	103.2	119.7	135.5	125.3	124.6	122.6	129.3
Farinaceous foods and starches	112.9	124.0	143.5	146.3	138.3	123.8	137.1
Cocoa, coffee, sugar	130.7	143.9	152.0	153.5	168.1	153.6	137.5
Meat	95.0	130.9	143.6	123.8	130.6	134.8	144.5
Eggs and dairy products	101.2	108.8	134.7	120.7	112.2	114.7	121.2
Fats and oils	99.5	127.9	120.8	113.5	113.3	112.9	107.8
Alcoholic beverages including wine, cider, and beer	99.5	89.6	102.6	93.0	90.4	90.3	96.8
Midi wine (at the production level)	97.3	79.0	83.0	77.9	77.1	75.5	87.4
Animal feed	105.2	125.1	161.2	161.2	145.3	149.6	156.1

Source: *Annuaire statistique*.

TABLE 33.   INDEX OF THE AVERAGE PRICE OF WINE AT THE PRODUCTION
LEVEL IN FRANCE, 1949–57 [a]
(*1949 = 100*)

Year	Index	Year	Index
1950	103.8	1954	76.1
1951	74.2	1955	74.2
1952	81.1	1956	80.8
1953	76.2	1957 (March)	93.8

[a] Computed on the basis of monthly averages.

Source: "Indice des cours du vin à la production," *Revue de l'économie méridionale*, V (January-March, 1957), 26.

production of only 32,125,000 hectolitres. On the market at Béziers, the price of wine (*vin rouge ordinaire* of 10° to 10.5°), which in August of 1957 had stood at 455 francs the degree-hectolitre, climbed steadily until it settled around 1,000 francs the degree-hectolitre for the six months preceding the harvest of 1958.[3]

The harvest of 1958, with a production of 47,012,000 hectolitres, must be classified as light. Yet prices took a steady drop, reaching, at Béziers, 600 francs the degree-hectolitre by the end of the year. For the first six months of 1959, on the same market, they have averaged 500 francs,[4] and the winegrowers are complaining about the paradox of low prices and a shortage of wine.[5] Although this last development may be disturbing,[6] prices are still well above those of 1953–56. Any conclusions about a permanent depression of wine prices must await the completion of the harvest of 1959 which, as this is being written, is described as both "great" and "unique," because of an unusual conjunction of quality and abundance. Meanwhile, it may be said that at the very least the short harvests of 1957 and 1958 have had a beneficial effect in clearing out stocks that have weighed on the market.

THE PROGRAM FOR PULLING UP VINES

If nature can take a hand in setting things right in the market place, it is government plans which may still offer the only hope of avoiding future crises of overproduction. In respect to this last consideration the program for the voluntary uprooting of vines with payment of indemnities already offers some interesting results. In February, 1957, M. Roland Maspetiol, president of the I.V.C.C, was able to report to the Academy of Agriculture that applications for indemnities covered a total of more than 100,000 hectares of vines either pulled up or about to be pulled up.[7] This figure represents 5.17 percent of the 1955 vineyard area in France and brings the present area close to that which the first Monnet Plan called for by 1950. M. Maspetiol has also pointed out that applications continue to arrive at a "satisfying rate," [8] so that it is possible to envisage the 10 percent reduction in area which the I.V.C.C. would like to see carried out in the near future.

In Algeria, it is interesting to note, applications for indemnities represent 8.48 percent of the 1955 vineyard area. But as M. Mottard, inspector general of the I.V.C.C., has pointed out, uprooting in Algeria is due more to economic than agronomic considerations and represents the "mobilizing" of viticultural capital for transfer to the mother country.[9] At this point it is possible to predict that whatever solution to the "Algerian problem" occurs, a large-scale abandonment of the vineyard there may result.

Administrators and planners from France have long been concerned that wine, Algeria's most important food crop, is of slight interest (for religious reasons) and of questionable nutritional value to an undernourished Moslem population. Solution of the undernourishment problem in the face of a rapidly increasing native population is typical of the vigorous measures France will have to take if Algeria is to remain attached to the mother country. On the other hand, should Algerian independence be granted sometime in the future, it is a question as to how long the government could resist the pressure for a stiff tariff on Algerian wines which the Midi growers would undoubtedly bring to bear in spite of any obligations the government might feel towards the *colons* who had been left behind.

Returning to the problems of the metropolitan vineyard, it remains to be noted that new plantings there for 1956 totaled 30,000 hectares. The agricultural economist Pierre Fromont has attached great significance to this figure since new plantings for the normal upkeep of the vineyard at its present extent should have totaled 40,000 hectares.[10] This phenomenon may represent a tendency to cut down the vineyard area which is not directly inspired by the incentives of the pulling-up program.

If the structure of the vineyard in Hérault, France's greatest wine-producing department, is any indicator, important areas of vines were destined to go out of production even before the *Code du Vin* was promulgated, and, in spite of new plantings after both wars, the vineyard has continued in a process of long-term reduction and degeneration. As Table 34 shows, more than half the vineyard area of Hérault has passed the age limit of maximum productivity— twenty years—and an important part of it may be said to be in a

TABLE 34.   VINEYARD AREA OF HÉRAULT IN 1948, CLASSIFIED ACCORDING
TO DATE OF VINE PLANTINGS

Date of Planting	Area (in hectares)	Percentage of Total Area
Before 1903	74,781	37.0
1903–07	14,738	7.2
1908–14	25,185	12.4
1915–19	6,947	3.5
1920–31	43,867	22.0
1932–36	10,463	5.2
1937–39	6,171	3.1
1940–45	5,241	2.6
1946–48	12,131	6.0

Source: "La Structure et les rendements du vignoble de Hérault," *Etudes et conjoncture, économie française* (Tirage à part extrait du n° 2, Mars-Avril 1951; Paris, Presses Universitaires de France, 1951), Tables VI and VIp.

state of degeneration.   The latter area suggests the possibility of a rapid extension of the pulling-up program.

Such possibility, however, in Hérault or other areas is now in abeyance.   Payment of indemnities for the uprooting of vines has been suspended since August 1, 1957, in anticipation of an increased demand for French wines on the European Common Market.[11] French agricultural economists, it is worth noting, have not been optimistic, so far, about prospects for France's wines on the Common Market, where they will be in competition with the lower-cost wines of Italy, and this first year's experience with the Common Market seems to be bearing them out.[12]   French shippers are apparently feeling competition in new markets that have been opened up for Italian wines by the lowering of trade barriers.   Where this development might leave the program for pulling up vines cannot, of course, be foretold now.   It should be pointed out, however, that provisions exist for resuming the pulling-up program if the expectations born of the Common Market are not realized.

A NOTE ON EXPORTS

As the experience with the Common Market may suggest, the export situation is not encouraging.   It will be remembered that exports have been in a long-term decline.   After the postwar period of shortages, they reached approximately 900,000 hectolitres in 1950, a level roughly equivalent to that maintained during the 1930–39 period. After 1950 they increased steadily, reaching 3,500,000 hectolitres in 1955 and 3,300,000 hectolitres in 1956, figures not registered since the fat years of exporting before the phylloxera epidemic.

The increase is illusory, however, and probably transitory. It is the result of what might loosely be called "forced" exports since 1950 to France's overseas territories. In 1954 and 1955 roughly one half of exports went to these areas, principally French West and Equatorial Africa.[13] The exports to Africa have been severely criticized in responsible quarters. They are against previous colonial policy, and exports of wine alcohol (*eaux-de-vie,* liqueurs, etc.), which have increased in very nearly the same proportions, are in violation of a convention signed by the African colonial powers.[14] Now that the African territories are gaining independence, it may be that this situation will not exist much longer. Although the short wine harvests of 1957 and 1958 were undoubtedly a factor, it is still interesting to note that out of a total exportation in 1958 of 1,458,000 hectolitres, 500,000 hectolitres, approximately only a third, went to the overseas territories.[15] With the demand for wine in these areas reaching an even more normal level and failing an increased demand from the European Common Market, wine exports could settle at a level of approximately one and a half million hectolitres, roughly equivalent to that of the 1920–29 period.

This is admittedly not an impressive figure. It is true that France's quality wines are a valuable export item with a ready and relatively noncompetitive market. But the very nature of the conditions under which these wines are grown and made renders a large-scale increase in their production impossible. If exports are to contribute to a solution of the overproduction problem, they must be brought to bear on larger amounts of *vin ordinaire*. Shippers still believe in a large market for a good, low-priced, standardized wine. The bulk of French *vins ordinaires* do not meet these specifications. And the agricultural experts do not believe they will, unless there can be better selection of grape varieties, elimination of marginal producers and too-small properties, increased use of farm machinery, and lowered costs and improved methods in winemaking brought about by an increase in cooperatives.   Meanwhile, although the *Code du Vin* promises the achievement of some of these objectives, the words of a parliamentary commission written in 1930 are still in large part applicable to the export situation today.

One of the causes of the slump in [wine] sales abroad as well as at home can be directly attributed to the winegrowers.   Our Spanish, Italian, and even our Portuguese neighbors export more than we do with a production which is, however, smaller and above all less varied— this with a geographic location incontestably less privileged and a reputation less good and more recent than ours, *vins de liqueur* excepted.

What our winegrowers, especially the harvesters of *vins ordinaires,* have looked for is above all quantity.   Prices on the French market being higher than world prices, these winegrowers have an interest in working for the French market.   No winegrower would agree to accept two prices for his harvest, one for France and another, lower, for exportation.   Everybody is convinced of the necessity for exporting wine, but nobody wants to make a move towards abandoning [the privileges of the home market] which would permit the exportation of his wine.[16]

THE PLACE OF WINEGROWING IN A RATIONALIZED FRENCH AGRICULTURE

Since the war, agriculture, like all other sectors of the French economy, has been undergoing extensive study with the aim of increasing its production through modernization.   From the point of view of national economic welfare, it has seemed deplorable that agriculture employs one third of the occupied population to produce one fifth of the national product.[17]   Considered equally shocking is the fact that France, with the richest agricultural potential in Western Europe, has yields on an area basis equal to one half those of most of her neighbors and is a net importer of food.[18]   In 1952 the deficit occasioned by the imports of food products, foodstuffs, and raw materials of agricultural origin totaled 575 billion francs.[19] Generally, the value of food imports has been twice that of exports. Among imports have been important quantities of butter, meat, and sugar—food products that are extensively grown, produced, and processed in France.

Such facts and considerations have led André Philip, Minister of Finance and National Economy in various governments of the Fourth Republic, to declare that the maintenance of a numerous peasant class is no longer desirable.[20] And they have led the *jeunes agronomes* in government service or occupying chairs in the agricultural institutions to blast French "microfundia" and outmoded and inefficient agricultural practices, especially the irrational use of land. And they have, of course, inspired the broad outlines of the agricultural sections of the Monnet Plan. In the face of these criticisms and trends, the presence of over 1,500,000 winegrowers tending nearly 1,500,000 hectares of vines has seemed something less than desirable. It should be of interest, therefore, to see what one of the outstanding spokesmen of the "new agriculture" has to say about the place of winegrowing in France's future agricultural economy.

Professor René Dumont[21] has denounced the "baneful influence" of the "myth of the beet and the vine" on French agriculture, has called for the pulling up of 300,000 hectares of vines, and has continually pushed the primacy of milk and meat in agricultural production schemes.[22] But in his book *Le Problème agricole français,* the manuscript of which served as one of the documentary bases for the work of the Commissariat Général du Plan, he has advocated intensive viticulture, albeit of a different sort from that understood by the term in the Midi.

There Dumont would convert part of the lowlands to the irrigated production of both vegetables and pasture. The new pastures would be first turned over to farm horses and oxen, and then after the development of mechanized agriculture to milk cows.[23] Among the remaining lowland vineyards an increase of cooperatives would overcome the handicaps imposed by the existence of small properties. Cooperative wineries would produce wine both better in quality and lower in cost than that coming from the individual growers' own presses. Vineyard machinery cooperatives would also reduce growing costs, and their use should be preceded not only by the widening of rows between the vines to admit tractors (narrowly spaced vines naturally give a greater yield per hectare, but this advantage is lost through the human exertion wasted in harvesting) but also by aerial surveys which would indicate the most general direction of plantings which in turn would become the rule for new plantings, so as to utilize agricultural machinery more effectively.[24]

Meanwhile, Dumont would also encourage the return of the vine to the abandoned hillsides, which are useless for growing anything else and give a wine of good quality. In this respect he has criticized the *Code du Vin* as being too *fixiste* in that its replanting provisions chain the winegrower to his original vineyard.[25] To counter the higher growing costs of the hillside vineyard, or for that matter to reduce costs wherever intensive viticulture is practised, Dumont has advocated the increased study and use of hybrid grapes. These, as we have seen, have been the object of deserved criticism in the case of some varieties. But as has been also pointed out, other hybrids give good wine. Their yield is high and regular and they require little or no treatment against many plant diseases. Dumont notes that important sums have been devoted to the study of hybrids in Germany; Russia has eleven centers for the same purpose, Chile three, and France none.[26] In California the use of hybrids is almost universal.

It remains to be noted that Dumont has not been an overly harsh critic of the Midi's devotion to vine monoculture. True, as we have seen above, he has urged replacement crops in irrigated areas there, and more lately has suggested the possibilities of growing fruit.[27] But his attachment to a rational use of French soil leads him to conclude that it is impossible to suggest a better crop than wine for numerous regions of the Midi.[28] He has not been specific about the pulling up of the 300,000 hectares of vine he has requested. But it is possible to guess that although he would propose that the volume of uprootings in the Midi should be high, the greater percentage would be recommended for those vineyard regions where France's vast and costly system of protection for wine and wine alcohol permits the inefficient and marginal polycultural farm to survive.[29]

Dumont's preoccupation with rationalizing French agriculture also leads him to believe that it has export possibilities beyond those even touched today. He has placed wine at the head of those products offering the best immediate possibilities, and has urged a vig-

orous export policy for it[30] His proposed changes for Midi viticulture should, in effect, produce the good, standardized, low-cost
wine which, as noted earlier, the exporters have asked for. He has
also envisaged increased domestic consumption and export of grapes
and grape juice, both negligible up to now, but which with a proper
processing and distribution system could become important.[31]

Bearing in mind the ideas presented above and the long-range
aims of the *Code du Vin,* and given an effective rationalization of
French agriculture, it is possible to project the future of winegrowing in the following terms.

1. An increasing restriction of the vineyard to the traditional
viticultural areas.

2. Outside of these areas, greater emphasis on the quality of the
vins du pays with an established reputation. This is being encouraged by the creation of a new classification, *vins délimités de
qualité supérieure* ranking between *vins d'appellations d'origine
contrôlées* and *vins ordinaires*.[32]

3. In the Midi, intensive production on a reduced scale of a good
vin ordinaire under the conditions described earlier. These will
permit the Midi grower a better return and a steadier yield. They
will also permit him to supply both the bulk of the domestic demand
for *vin ordinaire* and a new export market. Because of the improved quality of his wine the export market should be susceptible
to enlargement in the event of a bumper harvest.

4. In the quality vineyards of Burgundy, Bordeaux, Champagne,
etc. with an assured market, a continued emphasis on traditional
methods of viticulture, although rising labor costs may bring some
changes.

5. In the nation as a whole, a smaller number of winegrowers
cultivating a greater share of a vineyard reduced to weed out inefficient producers and to eliminate need for most forms of government economic assistance.

If these conditions can be achieved, government intervention
should be mainly limited to the control of quality, and winegrowing
should occupy a stronger, if less diffuse, position in the French
economy.

THE ANTI-ALCOHOL CAMPAIGN

One of the interesting postwar developments in France is the increasing seriousness with which the government is looking at the problem of alcoholism and the excessive consumption of alcoholic beverages including wine.

As we have seen in an earlier chapter, World War I produced the first government-sponsored study of these problems and brought attempts to control the sale of alcoholic beverages. But between the two wars, with the government supporting the Comité National de Propagande en faveur du Vin by tax money, and with the Service des Alcools itself supplying the beverage-alcohol industry, alcoholism and related problems received little public discussion. Practically the only voice to be heard on the subject came from the modest headquarters on the Boulevard Saint-Germain of the privately supported Comité National de Défense contre l'Alcoolisme.

With the advent of the Vichy government, however, a whole series of laws were promulgated to control the sale and consumption of alcoholic beverages.[33] These consisted of tighter regulations concerning places were liquor was sold, such as enforced closing three days a week. They forbade *apéritifs* with an alcohol base and those with a wine base if they contained more than 18° alcohol. Although these regulations were popularly attributed to shortages of natural alcohol and wine, they were at least as much inspired by a spirit of *redressement,* as is suggested by the fact that distilled alcoholic beverages were forbidden to persons of less than twenty-one years of age, and especially by the fact that all advertising of *apéritifs* was forbidden and the display in bars of nonalcoholic drinks was made compulsory. It is also interesting in this connection that the National Council of the Resistance pledged itself to continue the Vichy laws and proposed a ten-year plan to add to them. A similar decision was taken by the Provisional Government at Algiers in 1944, where it was further proposed to limit the number of places where wine and liquor could be sold.

But with the return of peace, the alcohol lobby and postwar euphoria were too strong. The Algiers proposals were rejected by the National Constituent Assembly in 1946, while the Vichy laws fell into disuse and were finally repealed in 1951.[34]   Meanwhile the Comité Nationale de Propagande en faveur du Vin had been reconstituted in 1948.

Since 1945, however, the government has been supporting studies of the economic, social, and physiological consequences of the heavy consumption of alcoholic beverages in France. This work is being done by the National Institute of Hygiene, which has already published a report under the auspices of the Ministry of Public Health,[35] and by the National Institute of Demographic Studies. At the latter organization a team of young experts under the direction of the noted demographer, Alfred Sauvy, is busy at work. A report by M. Sully Ledermann on excessive mortality and other effects of the heavy consumption of alcohol in France was published in 1956.[36] As the first in a series, Ledermann's work also treats to some extent the economic and social aspects of the problem of excessive wine and alcohol production, but a more detailed study on this subject by M. Georges Malignac, another member of the Sauvy team, is in preparation.[37]   Meanwhile, a report on the cost of alcoholism to the state has been made for the government by M. J.-S. Brunaud, still another member of the Sauvy team.[38]

With the accession of M. Mendès-France to the premiership, such scholarly activity was integrated into a popular campaign. In 1954 Mendès-France, whose ubiquitous glass of milk became a well-known symbol of his own feelings about the alcohol problem, set up a Haut Comité d'Information et d'Étude sur l'Alcoolisme, which is still functioning.[39] As its title indicates, the mission of the Comité is twofold. First, it is to act as a clearing house for the work being done by other groups on the alcohol problem. It is also to give these groups subsidies [40] and publish and propagandize the results of their findings. In 1955 it began bombarding the Assembly with data on the controversial question of the *bouilleurs de cru.*[41]

The second mission of the Comité is to study all aspects of the alcohol problem. And to this end numerous subcommittees have been formed. Inevitably some of this work will overlap that of other groups, but the Comité is looking at its problem from a broad point of view. The subjects contained in the names of two of its subcommittees, "Milk and Fruit Juices" and "Transformation of the Vineyard," for example,[42] suggest the breadth of its approach—one from which it is possible further legislation affecting the excessive production of wine and wine alcohol may result.

In 1954, the Mendès-France government also pushed through a whole set of regulations which it was hoped would reduce alcohol consumption. Returning to the path followed by Vichy, laws governing the opening of wine and liquor shops were tightened up.[43] Later, the annual license fees were increased by 30 percent, and an opening fee of 100,000 francs was imposed.[44] The alcohol content of *apéritifs* and some spirits was reduced, and a 20 percent increase of the purchase tax on spirits was instituted.[45] Also, a series of regulations were introduced to cut down the activities of the *bouilleurs de cru*.[46] New measures included a program for distribution of free sugared milk in the schools,[47] and forbidding the sale of all alcoholic beverages (wine included) on credit or at cut-rate prices in factory or shop canteens.[48]

DIMENSIONS OF THE CONSUMPTION OF ALCOHOLIC BEVERAGES

What are some of the findings concerning the French consumption of beverage alcohol that have already been made? Turning to Sully Ledermann's work, we find, first of all, that France drinks far more alcohol than any other nation for which statistics are available.

The figures in Table 35 give the lie to the myth of moderate consumption in wine-drinking countries. Wine accounts for 68

TABLE 35. ANNUAL CONSUMPTION OF ALCOHOLIC BEVERAGES IN DIFFERENT COUNTRIES, GIVEN IN TERMS OF PURE ALCOHOL PER ADULT [a]
(In litres)

Country	Consumption	Country	Consumption
France (1950–54)	30.0	Western Germany (1951)	5.1
Italy (1951)	14.2	Sweden (1951)	5.1
Switzerland (1950–54)	12.0	Denmark (1951)	4.9
Belgium (1951)	8.8	Finland (1954)	4.8
United States (1951)	8.8	Norway (1953)	3.0
Great Britain (1951)	8.5	Holland (1946–48)	1.8

[a] Of twenty years or more.

Source: Ledermann, *Alcool,* p. 68.

percent of the 30 litre figure quoted for France. *Eaux-de-vie,* rum, *apéritifs,* and liqueurs account for only 13 percent, while beer and cider make up the remaining 19 percent.[49]

How excessive is French consumption of alcohol? Research by the National Institute of Hygiene has determined that an active manual worker in good health can safely absorb a maximum of 100 c.c. of pure alcohol per day.[50] Sedentary workers and women can absorb half this amount. Working from a rough division of the French population into these categories, Malignac demonstrates that annual consumption per adult of pure alcohol should be at the most 23.2 litres, and is therefore actually over 20 percent greater than warranted. Studying the question in more detail, Ledermann concludes that those who drink more than double the maximum allowed an active manual worker probably number at least 2 million.[51] These people are not necessarily alcoholics. Professor Dérobert has pointed out that it is common for workers to drink three or four litres of wine a day.[52] Projected on an annual basis, this consumption is equal to 110 to 146 litres of pure alcohol a year.[53]

And what are the physiological effects of French alcohol consumption? Here again Ledermann makes some interesting comparisons with other countries (see Tables 36, 37, and 38).[54]

TABLE 36. RATE OF DEATHS FROM CHRONIC OR ACUTE ALCOHOLISM
IN DIFFERENT COUNTRIES, 1950–54
(*Average number per 100,000 inhabitants*)

Country	Deaths	Country	Deaths
France	15.2	Denmark	1.1
Switzerland	10.3	Holland	1.0
United States (colored)	5.8	Norway	0.9
Italy	3.6	Finland	0.7
United States (white)	3.1	England and Wales	0.3

Source: Ledermann, *Alcool,* p. 147.

From figures such as the tables show, a comparative loss of national productivity could be deduced. And from research under way it should be possible eventually to draw up a balance sheet of the total cost to the nation resulting from excessive consumption of alcoholic beverages. Meanwhile M. Brunaud, in the report mentioned earlier, has estimated the cost to the state directly attributable

TABLE 37. ESTIMATED RATE OF DEATH FROM ALL FORMS OF CIRRHOSIS [a]
IN DIFFERENT COUNTRIES IN 1952
(*Deaths per 100,000 inhabitants, aged 45 to 64 years*)

Country [b]	Deaths	Country [b]	Deaths
France	85.3	Denmark	10.6
Switzerland	44.8	Norway	8.4
United States	33.9	Sweden	7.5
Western Germany	28.0	Finland	6.7
Holland	10.8	England	5.9

[a] The percentage of alcoholic cirrhosis in relation to all forms of cirrhosis is 84 percent for men; 74 percent for women.

[b] The original table gives statistics for eighteen countries from all over the world, but in the interests of consistency only countries included in Tables 35 and 36 have been listed. Portugal topped France with a rate of 88.6.

Source: Ledermann, *Alcool*, p. 150.

TABLE 38. ESTIMATED RATE OF SOMATIC OR MENTAL ILLNESS OR NEAR ILLNESS
AMONG ADULTS IN DIFFERENT COUNTRIES ATTRIBUTED TO
CONSUMPTION OF ALCOHOL
(*Illness per 100,000 inhabitants*)

Country	Number Ill	Country	Number Ill
France (1953–54)	5,700	Sweden (1947)	700
Italy (1952)	2,100	Norway (1947)	400
Denmark (1952–53)	1,280	Finland (1947)	350
Switzerland (1952)	1,000	England (1948)	300
United States (1952)	900		

Source: Ledermann, *Alcool*, p. 146.

to alcoholism alone at 152 billion francs in 1952.[55] Against this sum can be credited receipts of 54 billion francs from taxes on wines and other alcoholic beverages, license fees from establishments selling these beverages, and profits from the sale of alcohol by the Service des Alcools to the *apéritif* and liqueur industries. But Malignac has pointed out that the resulting difference does not give a true picture of the net cost.[56] For one thing, only a part of the total alcohol consumed is responsible for alcoholism. For another, most of the production of alcohol by the *bouilleurs de cru* escapes taxation, yet is an important cause of the alcoholization of the rural population. Malignac prefers to work from a comparison of what might be done if alcoholism were reduced to a "residual level."

He hypothesizes a reduction by three quarters of the production of *eaux-de-vie, apéritifs,* and liqueurs, with the greatest part of this reduction being brought to bear on the production of the *bouilleurs de cru;* a reduction by one half for the production of cider, and 15 percent for that of wine. If these reductions were accompanied by a rise in taxes on these products, Malignac believes that the state might still draw between 20 and 30 billion francs in revenue. He also believes that these production cuts would bring the public cost of alcoholism down to 20 billion francs, thus effecting a gain of around 100 billion francs over the present situation. This last figure, Malignac maintains, is the best indication of the minimum net cost to the state caused by alcoholism.

At this writing it is being claimed, although mostly by the winegrowers, that the anti-alcohol campaign is causing a decrease in the consumption of wine as well as spirits. A more important cause could be the over 100 percent increase in wine taxes carried out by the De Gaulle government as part of its budget-balancing program. But the new taxes must be considered as at least partly social in inspiration. The Haut Comité d'Information et d'Étude sur l'Alcoolisme has "congratulated" itself on their passage as well as other more social legislation adopted since December, 1958.[57] The latter includes important new limitations on the licensing of liquor shops and the sale of wines and spirits to minors.

It is possible to hope that the anti-alcohol campaign linked with continuing legislation will bring about a decrease in the consumption of wine and other alcoholic beverages. But it would be optimistic to predict that propaganda, statistics, or even legislation will profoundly, or at any rate immediately, change the drinking habits of the French people.[58] As Alfred Sauvy has admitted, the anti-alcohol campaign does not involve a question of "abstinence, austerity, or asceticism." [59] Rather, its chief importance to date would seem to be the questioning of the social value of state encouragement of the consumption of wine [60] and the social and economic value of legislation which by encouraging the excessive production of wine and alcohol "drowns the consumer," as Jules Romains has put it.[61] The keystone of this excessive production, as we have seen in an earlier chapter, is the Service des Alcools, or, as it has been officially styled since 1939, the Régie Commérciale des Alcools. It is to the recent history of this body that we now turn.

THE RÉGIE DES ALCOOLS AND THE PROBLEM OF EXCESSIVE ALCOHOL PRODUCTION

The recent history of the Régie des Alcools suggests some parallels with that of the wine industry. Wartime alcohol shortages led the Vichy government in 1942 to buy all the alcohol offered it at quota prices.[62] This regime was continued until August of 1950, when the Régie once again started paying for alcohols in excess of their quotas at the same price (below cost) as alcohol sold for carburation.[63] The result of what might be called eight years of "decontrol" was that alcohol production bounded back as suddenly and even more spectacularly than that of wine.

Although the production of all alcohols stayed within quota limits until 1949, it was apparent before then that output was increasing rapidly. By 1950 a record production of 3,177,862 hectolitres of beet alcohol was registered, and alcohol from all sources came to 5,320,625 hectolitres, a figure second only to the record output of 5,862,782 hectolitres in 1935.[64] Meanwhile the Régie's unsold stocks, which had totaled 540,000 hectolitres in 1948, jumped to 2,889,000 hectolitres in 1949, and a record 3,471,000 hectolitres in 1950.

A critical situation was relieved by unanticipated sales of 3,682,000 hectolitres in 1950 and 1,337,000 hectolitres in 1951 to the United States.[65] Stocks dropped to 1,994,000 hectolitres the latter year. But by 1952 they had climbed to 2,292,000 hectolitres, and in 1953 once again reached more than 3 million hectolitres.

Back of this rapid congestion was the shrinkage of the Régie's former indefinitely extensible outlet—alcohol for carburation. As early as 1946 the Monnet Plan was asking that the motor-fuel industry be freed from "the yoke of distillation."[66] And since then representatives of the motor-fuel industry have been carrying on what winegrowing interests have called a "systematic plot" against mixing alcohol with motor fuel.[67] Moreover, in 1949 and again in

1953 the National Economic Council criticized alcohol carburants on both economic and technical grounds.[68] In 1953 the Council also published a note from the Ministry of National Defense reminding all concerned that France by her adherence to NATO had accepted a standardization of motor fuels among member nations which excluded an alcohol carburant.[69] The note also called attention to the wasteful duplication of pumps and storage tanks which the use of an alcohol carburant involved, thus depriving the latter once and for all of justification in the interest of national defense.

Arguments against an alcohol carburant were in a sense academic until the rapid recovery of alcohol production in 1950. Sales before then were small, averaging around 300,000 hectolitres a year. The obligation to mix alcohol with motor fuel was not imposed, and sales were mostly for a supercarburant (*carburant ternaire*), comprised of a mixture of alcohol, benzol, and gasoline, which has lately had a certain popularity.[70] In August, 1950, however, the state, in spite of objections by the motor-fuel industry, returned to the obligatory mixture of gasoline and alcohol. Motor-fuel importers and refiners were required to buy each month a quantity of alcohol equal to 10 percent of the gasoline declared by them as having been sold in the previous month.[71]

In 1951, 1,007,000 hectolitres of alcohol were sold in this way. With news of massive exports of alcohol to the United States, opposition of the motor-fuel industry so stiffened, however, that sales for carburation dropped to 353,000 hectolitres in 1952. After that they began to climb again, reaching 705,000 hectolitres in 1953, 800,000 hectolitres in 1954, and an estimated 1,050,000 hectolitres in 1955.[72] If it is remembered that an average of 2,300,000 hectolitres were sold for carburation each year from 1932 through 1939, it will be seen by how much this outlet has shrunk, alcohol production from 1950 through 1955 being roughly the same as during the earlier period.

It is doubtful, though, that if there had been no opposition by the motor-fuel industry or even the extraordinary exports to the United States, sales for carburation could have been substantially increased. It is becoming increasingly impossible, as gasoline becomes relatively cheaper than alcohol, for the Régie to equate the price of alcohol with that of gasoline.[73]   Moreover, the Régie, stripped of its fiscal revenues in 1939, has been unable to balance its books since then, and has piled up large deficits even in the years when its sales for carburation have been minimal.

The National Economic Council has produced some interesting revelations about the size of these deficits, since, according to the Council, their true value does not show up in the Régie's books.[74] This is because since 1943 the Régie has been applying the value of its unsold stocks, figured at average cost price, against its loss from sales and its operating costs.   Formerly this value had been figured on the basis of the selling price for carburation (below cost), which the Council maintains is a closer approximation of the true worth of the stocks.   By the Régie's method, the Council points out, "the more intense inflation is, the more the accounting of the Régie improves; . . . the more its tanks fill with alcohol, the more beneficial its financial situation appears." [75]

Adopting the Régie's method of calculating, we get the following results:

	Value of Unsold Stocks at Average Cost Price	*Operating and Sales Deficit of the Régie*
1949	18,350 million francs	12,671 million francs
1950	31,107	8,895
1951	17,745	3,805
1952	22,605	5,686

Thus, although there is a long-term deficit, the books of the Régie show a favorable balance each year.

To measure the long-term deficit properly, the Council adjusts the total operating and sales deficit to the value of the franc in 1953, bringing this deficit to 38,705 million francs.   From this sum is subtracted the value of the stock of 1952 figured at 4 billion francs on the basis of the price of alcohol sold for carburation, thus leaving a total deficit for the four years of more than 34 billion francs, or one more than twice as great as the Régie's bookkeeping would allow. Covering this deficit were nonreimbursable advances from the Treasury totaling 48 billion francs during the same period.[76]

But the Council does not stop with deficits in determining the cost of the Régie to the nation.   In an interesting demonstration prepared for the Council, Alfred Sauvy has pointed out that the alcohol regime should not be judged on its own merits but from the point of view of alternatives. These in turn should be figured on the basis of excess alcohol because certain quantities of the Régie's alcohol are obviously needed. Thus Sauvy suggests five alternative solutions for the problem of excess alcohol: [77] (1) to use surplus alcohol for carburation, (2) to export it, (3) to replace surplus alcohol with an equivalent production of sugar, or (4) milk, or (5) meat. [78] Using a production of 100,000 hectolitres of beet alcohol as a basis for his figures, and including a return of 403 million francs from by-products obtained in the distilling of this alcohol, Sauvy gets the following gross returns for each one of his five alternatives:

Alcohol for carburation	513 million francs
Alcohol for export	633
Equivalent production of sugar	1590
Equivalent production of milk	990
Equivalent production of meat	1500

Thus, taking the spread between the most and the least remunerative of his alternatives, there is a direct loss in gross national income of 1,077 million francs [79] for every 100,000 hectolitres of excess alcohol produced. If we accept the Council's estimate of two million hectolitres of alcohol as the normal amount of alcohol the Régie should buy in a year and remember that from 1950 through 1954 it brought an average of more than four million hectolitres each year, it is possible to envisage an annual loss in income of over 21 billion francs on the basis of Sauvy's calculations.

But Sauvy also demonstrates that the production of excess alcohol affects the national income indirectly. To give one example, he points out that butter, meat, and cheese constitute a very sensitive market. Each time the national income—and especially salaries —increases, the demand for these foods increases. Falling on an insufficient supply, demand drives prices up. Faced with this phenomenon the government has to contract credit expansion in order that demand may not completely outstrip supply of these products. Thus Sauvy concludes that the butter, meat, and cheese "bottleneck" obliges all industry to remain beneath its maximum productive capacity.

The production of 2,500,000 hectolitres of alcohol—the amount Sauvy considers in excess of actual needs—effectively contributes to this bottleneck because on the basis of Sauvy's earlier figuring of alternatives, it prevents 37 billion francs of output from being diverted to butter, meat, and cheese production, a sum equal to 21 percent of the retail sales value of the latter products. Suppose what would happen, Sauvy next asks, if industry, deprived of credits under the conditions described above, was able to increase its production by 5 percent. This would mean salary increases totaling 200 billion francs, approximately 20 percent of which, according to various surveys, would go to butter, meat, and cheese, for a total of 40 billion francs—roughly equivalent to the 37 billion franc figure quoted earlier. Thus if the production of excess alcohol were suppressed, Sauvy sees industry, stock farming, and the growing of fodder crops helping each other in a parallel increase of production:

The gain for the national income would be enormous, on the order of at least 300 to 400 billion francs—at the same time fiscal receipts would increase without supplementary taxation, social security (costs and expenditures) would be in balance, the deficit of the railways would be reduced.

Distillation therefore involves for the national income considerable losses unsuspected up to now.[80]

It remains to be noted that the National Economic Council's survey of the alcohol regime blasted the myth that the Régie constituted an essential base of agricultural support. For each 100 francs paid by the state for its alcohol, agriculture (i.e., winegrowing, beet raising, and fruitgrowing) receives 45 francs; the distilling industry the rest.[81] If agricultural support is in question it would be cheaper for the state to pay the 45 francs directly.

The myth that the *alcool carburant* saves France important amounts of foreign exchange was also attacked. The Council pointed out that the exchange lost in importing chemicals for insecticides and fertilizers to keep one hectare of vines producing 600 to 800 litres of alcohol exactly matched that saved by incorporating this alcohol in gasoline. Moreover, "everything else is lost: coal for distillation . . . the energy consumed in cultivating the soil, transportation, replacement crops, and what is worse, the labor of highly civilized men who devote themselves to this type of agriculture." [82]

None of this need occur, the Council concluded, if French agriculture were rationalized—and this could be accomplished in the long run by especially cutting down on the production of beet alcohol and wine. Shorter-term solutions proposed by the Council to resolve the problem of excess alcohol production were the reduction of alcohol quotas to a total of two million hectolitres, the planned development and encouragement of beet-sugar production, the abolishing of parity between beet-alcohol and sugar prices, and the placing of the operations of the Régie des Alcools under the scrutiny of the general budget.[83]

In 1953, the same year that the Council published its recommendations, the government took the first steps in the direction described above. A decree of August 9, 1953, provided for the gradual reduction of alcohol quotas until by 1958 they should total 2,775,000 hectolitres instead of the 3,770,000 hectolitres provided for in 1954. Supplementing this measure, the government ordered production cuts of 8 percent based on average production during 1951 and 1952 for beet alcohol distilleries not attached to sugar refineries and, by way of encouraging sugar production, cuts of 29 percent for those that were. The price coefficients of other alcohols were reduced with the result that in the case of wine alcohol, as we have seen in the previous chapter, the quota price fell below cost.[84]

In November of 1954, the Mendès-France government enacted further production cuts for all beet-alcohol distilleries, 5 percent of 1955 production for 1956, and 7 percent for 1957.[85] In addition, distillers who exceeded these quotas were to have the price of their alcohol reduced by 4 percent. On the other hand, a premium of 3,000 francs the hectolitre was offered to distillers who would give notice before February 15, 1955, of a definite intent to cease operating. Loans were also offered beet growers who might have to plant other crops as a result of the cutback in the production of the distilleries.

Previously, another decree had given the government the right to transfer all or part of the sugar beets destined for alcohol produc-

tion to sugar refineries, two thirds being the part decided on for
1955.[86] In Mendès-France's own words, this operation did not save
the state any money. Indemnities were offered the distillers based
on their fixed operating costs, which came to 1,500 francs for every
ton of beets diverted from their distilleries to the sugar refineries.
And in either case the price received by the grower for his beets was
the same. Thus, concludes Mendès-France, "for the producer nothing is changed—but for the nation there is an immense difference:
more sugar and less alcohol." [87]

Obviously these measures do not go all the way towards a solution of the alcohol problem. In deference to the "alcohol lobby,"
they were probably something less than the Mendès-France or
earlier governments would have liked to have seen achieved.[88] But
they point the way to further legislation. Meanwhile the Régie des
Alcools continues its operations. In 1955, it received a 4 billion
franc advance from the Treasury, and its operating deficit for that
year was estimated at 5,600 million francs.[89] Contributing to the
latter were over one million hectolitres of alcohol mixed with gasoline [90]—the process that the National Economic Council has characterized as in the long term "ruinous" for the state.[91] Also in 1955,
under the Régie's *caisse annexe de la viticulture* a postwar record
total of 10,500,000 hectolitres of wine was compulsorily distilled into
alcohol.[92]

Since then the situation has improved. For 1958 the Régie
actually showed a credit balance of 1,700 million francs after reimbursing the state for 10 billion francs in advances and paying out
1,600 million francs in indemnities to distillers. It should be pointed
out, however, that although the reduction of alcohol quotas and administrative and productive economies played their part in this
profit, it was largely due to the short wine harvest of 1957. According to M. Frappart, director of the Régie, "the balance achieved
remains precarious." In the event of an overabundant wine harvest
it could disappear.[93] Thus it is probably still too early to say that
surplus wine production and the state monopoly that encourages it
will not be a drain on the state's finances and the national economy
for some time to come. On the other hand, the compelling logic of

the arguments reviewed in the preceding pages makes it also possible to hope that this time will not be long.

WHICH WAY?

We have seen, then, how, especially from 1953 on, events, legislation, research, and even attitudes may produce a solution to the problem of winegrowing's place in the French economy. It remains to point briefly to some of the factors which might work against such a solution, at least in the immediate future.

For those who associate winegrowing's problem with the larger one of rationalizing French agriculture, the failure of the first Monnet Plan, where agriculture was concerned, was a bitter disappointment. Describing this failure summarily, one might say that none of the important over-all objectives of the plan were achieved. And running down the list of quotas for the principal agricultural products, it is possible to conclude, as one critic has, that this part of the plan also resulted in a "complete checkmate." [94]   In this last respect it is interesting to note that the plan proposed reductions for wine alone in the three categories into which its targets were divided (yield, production, and acreage), yet wine alone surpassed its quotas in all these categories. To continue the catalogue of failures, the Monnet Plan called for consolidating 3,500,000 hectares of fragmented holdings by the end of 1950, but by October 1, 1952, only 1,350,000 hectares had been assembled into more compact units.[95] This failure bears on the difficulty of achieving a rationalization of the vineyard on the order projected earlier in this chapter. A small vineyard generally producing poor wine is very often the mainstay of the marginal and inefficient polycultural or mixed farm.

There are good reasons for these failures—chiefly the niggardliness of the credits and public investments allocated for modernization of agriculture in comparison with those earmarked for industry, the details and causes of which are beyond the scope of this short summary.[96] This discrepancy has, however, produced an opinion, the prevalence of which should be interesting to measure, that the Monnet Plan has not lived up to its designation of agri-

culture as an *activité de base,* and that the plan, in the words of the
monthly *Agriculture pratique,* is "nothing more than a pretext for
lowering agricultural prices with the view of unilateral increase in
the purchasing power of the urban wage-earning mass." [97]

Politics also plays its part in the attack on rationalization of
agriculture. The Communist party has unequivocally dedicated itself to the preservation of the "small working proprietor," [98] while
a publication reflecting the views of the Catholic-oriented Mouvement Républicain Populaire (MRP) has in effect attacked "mechanized agriculture" and declared that "French agriculture will be a
peasant agriculture or it will cease to exist." [99]   Representing the
same attitude was the consecration of an issue of *Agriculture
pratique* in 1952 to the memory of Jules Méline with the admonition
that his books *Le Retour à la terre* and *Le Salut par la terre* are
"capital works worthy of attention, today more than ever." [100]   But
probably the best expression of peasant desires (the French peasant
after all would like a tractor and is avid to increase the size of his
holdings) is found in the words of M. Philippe Lamour, secretary-
general of the powerful Confédération Générale de l'Agriculture.
Commenting on the government's intentions announced in 1953 to
convert some beet and winegrowing regions to other crops, he had
this to say:

It is of small importance to us if guarantees [i.e., supports] are given
us in one form or another. We are the first to recommend the reconversion of some crops, but only on the condition that guarantees similar
to those offered by the alcohol regime are given to the replacements.[101]

As we have inferred, it is impossible to weigh exactly the significance of the ideas and statements quoted above. They have
different motivations and hold different promises. But from them
it is possible to guess that a large part of French agriculture favors
the preservation of the *status quo* and that there are powerful groups
ready, for one reason or another, to support such sentiment.

It would, of course, be unfair even in so short a summary to
overlook the progress that has been made since 1953 in modernizing
and rationalizing French agriculture. The Second Plan for Modernization and Equipment, or Hirsh Plan, which went into operation

in 1954, has through more concern and increased investments for agriculture produced some remarkable results, particularly in the wider use of agricultural machinery and increased production of milk and meat. But in those areas which bear more directly on the problem of guiding winegrowing to its proper place in a rationalized agriculture, the results have been less impressive.

According to the final report on the Second Plan, which carries the record through 1957,[102] winegrowing again appears to have surpassed its quotas, which called for reductions in acreage, yield, and production.[103] And with the consolidation, at the end of 1957, of 2,700,000 hectares of scattered farmlands into larger units,[104] the result achieved is still well behind the target set for 1950. Only 8 percent of French farms have an area greater than 50 hectares; 50 percent have an area less than 20 hectares,[105] and the agricultural pressure groups continue to be vocal in their concern for the small peasant proprietor who remains, most often, a winegrower.

Another factor working against the solution of the viticultural problem is the continued existence of the powerful "alcohol lobby." On the parliamentary level it unites representatives of beet, wine, and fruitgrowing districts, whatever their party label. This group derives additional electoral support from the existence of 438,671 establishments where wine and liquor are sold, and an army of 2,880,000 *bouilleurs de cru*.[106] More importantly, it receives the financial support of the powerful and wealthy *apéritif*, liquor, and distilling industries. The influence of these industries on the press, among other things, is immense.[107]

Thus, as we have seen, the alcohol lobby has been able to defeat the anti-alcoholism measures enacted by the Vichy government which the provisional government at Algiers and the Resistance had pledged themselves to validate. Also, as we have briefly noted, measures from 1953 on to reduce alcohol production have had their effectiveness limited by "backroom" concessions to the lobby. More recently the lobby effected the repeal of Mendès-France's decrees to control wine and liquor shops [108]—this, it is interesting to note, within one month after the fall of his government. The same year, 1955, a private-member's bill was introduced to restore the quota alcohol purchases of the Régie des Alcools to their pre-1953 level.[109]   The bill was not acted on, but since the close of 1957, when the alcohol quota cuts initiated by Mendès-France terminated, no action appears to have been taken to carry them further, although alcohol quotas are still considerably above the 2,000,000 hectolitre figure recommended by the National Economic Council.   Also since 1955, the alcohol lobby has waged a successful battle against any further limiting of the *privilège des bouilleurs de cru;* this in spite of intensive propaganda against the *privilège* by the Haut Comité d'Information et d'Étude sur l'Alcoolisme.   Finally, it should be noted that the alcohol lobby has not limited itself to direct action to protect its privileges.   According to some observers, it has not hesitated to attack, on issues other than alcohol, governments that have displeased it, and has played a capital role in the fall of many of them, the overthrow of the Mendès-France government being the most recent and perhaps the most pertinent case in point.[110]

The alcohol lobby, however, does not sin alone.   The selfishness, *immobilisme,* and often the the sheer obstructionism of many economic, political, and social interests assumes unusual proportions in present-day France.   These attitudes are the greatest obstacle to that modernization and rationalization of France's economy which thoughtful critics maintain are imposed on France by world conditions and commitments, no matter how attached the French might be to a once viable policy of autarchical social and economic equilibrium.

How far can government go in overhauling the French economy to meet these challenges?   Mendès-France, so often accused by his enemies of being too addicted to *planisme,* has said that the government has a great responsibility to break "the artificial support given to excessive or useless production which wastes, for selfish reasons, the productive capacity of the country."   But social and economic recovery cannot depend entirely on government.   It must come rather from "the nation as a whole, from a thousand initiatives, a thousand individual wills, and from thousands and thousands of small, medium, and big enterprises who by and of themselves must find the route to success." [111]

To which the historian is permitted to reply that governments and peoples have both succeeded and failed to meet external economic challenges. If France is to succeed in meeting hers, the resolution of the problem of her one and a half million winegrowers and the alcohol regime that supports their excessive production will play a capital part. Although, as we have seen, progress has been made, the problem is still one of the greatest magnitude.

11. SUMMARY AND CONCLUSIONS

In our first chapter we have seen how the phylloxera epidemic influenced winegrowers to turn toward quantity production of low-grade wines, a development that was accompanied by increasing wine imports from Algeria and decreases in exports and the amount of wine distilled into alcohol. These were all factors in the severe crisis that shook the viticultural economy from 1900 to 1907. But in addition, during the same period, production of fraudulent wine was so great that its regulation after 1907 helped, for the most part, to restore confidence to the wine market.

After World War I, while fraud remained under control, development of the other factors that had contributed to the crisis of 1900–1907 was such that overabundant harvests again became commonplace. This brought the government, from 1930 on, to enact a series of laws by which it tried to control the winegrower's production and regulate, at times, the price he received for his wine. As we have seen these laws were not sufficient to prevent viticulture from undergoing two more great crises, one lasting from 1930 to 1936 and the other from 1950 to 1956.

It may be argued that the failure of government legislation to prevent these crises was due to the methods employed. The methods were primarily (1) valorization of the price the grower received for his wine and (2) restriction of his production.[1] The first method, as practiced through blocking part of the harvest, was a particularly unfortunate experiment. Since *vin ordinaire* is unsuited to long-term storage, the blocked portion of the harvest was released the next year when, in some instances, its liberation coincided with or followed another abundant harvest. This led the government to supplement blockage with the staggered release of blocked portions of the harvest during the crop year. But, as we have seen, this shorter-term valorization proved unworkable on the whole. Floor prices often had to be lowered and when they were not a glut of wine had to be disposed of during the last selling period. The staggered-release system could regularize current prices around the average price for the year but it could not affect the latter.[2] Moreover, valorization schemes, as Professor Milhau has pointed out, cannot correct a deep-seated disequilibrium in a market economy.[3]

This last criticism can also be applied to the restriction of viticultural production through the practice of compulsory distilling. Although we have credited compulsory distilling (with some qualifications) as being the most effective measure introduced during the 1930–35 period, it did not, of course, reduce viticulture's capacity for excessive production. Such criticism, however, must be considered in the face of evidence that neither the government nor the winegrowing associations thought, in the main, that they were dealing from 1930 through 1935 with anything other than an exceptional situation brought on by a series of overabundant harvests. That this was the case is further suggested by the fact that the measures which offered the best possibility of reducing the production potential of the vineyard—i.e., prohibition of new vine plantings and granting exonerations from compulsory distilling and blockage for uprooting vines—were only intended to be in force for five and ten years, respectively.[4]

As we have pointed out in a previous chapter, it was not until 1950 that the government began to take public notice of the apparently chronic nature of viticultural overproduction. Thus the *Code du Vin* in 1953, while improving the mechanisms of blockage and compulsory distilling, emphasized uprooting and replacement crops as the proper remedy for overproduction. That this change of view should have taken more than twenty years plus another crisis does, of course, open the government to charges of short-sightedness and of being too late with too little, but the climate of opinion about the nature of the earlier crisis must, nevertheless, not be discounted.

Somewhat similar qualifications must be brought to bear on another major criticism of viticultural legislation. If it is assumed that restriction and valorization plans, although ineffective in correcting long-term market disequilibrium, can be helpful in short-term situations, then the great number of winegrowers that escaped blockage and compulsory distilling constituted one of viticultural legislation's most serious failings. That this was recognized is implied in the frequent *ad hoc* extension of blockage and compulsory-distilling production ranges during the crisis of 1930–35 and their further extension in 1953.

On the other hand, given the overwhelming majority of small growers, it is reasonable to assume that from 1930 through 1935 the government may have seen its immediate problem in terms of keeping the small grower in operation. Could the latter with his higher production costs carry the additional expense of compulsory distilling and the forced storage of part of his harvest? The recent difficulties of those smaller growers subject to the lowered ranges provided by the *Code du Vin* for blockage and distilling—ranges which still exempt roughly 45 percent of production—suggest that the earlier ranges were not as "demagogic" as might appear. Also, the recent exemptions brought to that part of the *Code* which required all growers to furnish the same percentage of their harvest in *alcool vinique* suggest the hardships that might have been involved for the small grower in controls that would have affected all alike.[5]

Thus, as we have presented the case, if the government felt during the 1930–35 period that a restriction rather than a permanent curtailment of production was called for, then the main burden of restriction had to fall on the big low-cost producers who could better afford it. Of course, penalizing the latter can be criticized as uneconomic and parasitical when, with locational and other factors being equal, their smaller neighbors could get the same yield of wine per hectare and still go free of all controls. But at this point our analysis must, as Professor Golob would phrase it, transcend purely economic considerations and raise the question of national attitudes.[6]

The French, for reasons and causes outside the scope of this summary, have seen fit, at an undeniable cost for the national collectivity, to maintain a large proportion of the population as peasant proprietors. Winegrowing has been an important element in the achievement of this aim because of its extent and the fact that it is often the mainstay of the small polycultural or mixed farm. A visitor to even a humble vineyard might also recognize a certain *mystique* about winegrowing which attaches men to the soil. Thus it is possible to conclude that government policy toward the winegrowers, for all its faults, responded to some deep-seated national attitudes, and that debate about it and the agricultural policy with which it was associated must at least consider, to borrow from Professor Golob again, "standards and value judgments, social philosophies, and ethics." [7] This is not to deny that winegrowing has enjoyed unusual solicitude on the part of the government, that the cost of viticultural support has run high, or that economic and social considerations which place the well-being of the whole nation first must have a part in the resolution of France's viticultural and agricultural problems. These points we hope we have made abundantly clear in our text.

Government solicitude and the economic consequences of support for winegrowing do, however, raise the question as to how far viticultural policy was shaped by the winegrowers themselves. Although we have gone into some detail in tracing the path of viticultural legislation through parliament and the various congresses of the winegrowing associations, we have produced no simple answer to this question. Two points may, however, be established. One is that even if a much greater percentage of the total number of winegrowers in Algeria came under blockage and compulsory distilling than in France, the government's failure otherwise to hobble Algerian wine production did not answer the wishes of the majority of metropolitan growers. The second point is that the complex of legislation which included the state alcohol regime, compulsory distilling, and quota purchases of wine alcohol was, in the main, the creature of winegrowing interests.

We have seen the part the winegrowers played in the establishment of the alcohol regime and then seen how they gradually dominated it until they obtained a regular quota of state alcohol purchases

in 1935. The high price of wine alcohol in comparison with that
of beet alcohol and the uses to which the state could put quota wine
alcohol made the purchase of such alcohol nothing less than an out-
right subsidy to the winegrowers. Compulsory distilling, it should
also be recalled, did not figure among the government's original
proposals for the *Statut de la Viticulture* but was included at the insistence of the C.G.V. After that the government had to concede
increases in the price paid for compulsorily distilled wine alcohol
until by 1935 the latter could be as high as three fourths the price
of quota wine alcohol. This development, along with invasion by
wine alcohol of the alcohol regime's regular operations, was instrumental in wrecking the regime's financing. There were other factors
that we have noted such as the decline in price of gasoline in relation to alcohol and the cutting off of the regime's tax revenues. But
on balance it is possible to say that the alcohol regime was increasingly sacrificed to winegrowing interests. The consequences, it is
reasonable to assume, were greater than the government might have
wished or foreseen.

About other aspects of viticultural legislation there was a closer
meeting of minds between the government and the winegrowers.
It is true that in 1931 and in 1953 government proposals met with
a certain amount of reserve from the winegrowing associations, but
differences were only ones of degree. There was recognition on
both sides that something along the lines proposed should be done.
And so such questions as the production ranges for blockage and
distilling, the limitation of new plantings, the uprooting of vines
and other measures were worked out by compromise and change.
A notable exception to this relative harmony of interests was the
government's failure to reapply viticultural legislation sooner after
World War II. Here the winegrowing associations seem to have
been ahead of the government. And particularly in the matter of
the control of new plantings, government policy during this period
may once again be charged with shortsightedness. The government,
however, had the interests of the consumer to consider in this question as long as wine was scarce and its price high, and these interests, especially in France, it would seem, have imperatives of their
own.

It remains, in closing, to ask what alternative policies the government could have followed in meeting the problem of viticultural overproduction. Although in this summary we have emphasized the determinants that helped shape the policies adopted, this need not preclude a final judgment on this question. We submit that the uprooting of vines accompanied by the payment of indemnities and the encouragement, financially and otherwise, of replacement crops, would have been the proper remedy to have adopted from the beginning. Such a policy was, of course, timidly recognized in the *Statut de la Viticulture* and is now the basis, in theory at least, of the *Code du Vin*.

The only alternative to this policy would, to our thinking, have been one of *laissez-faire*. But a climate of opinion has developed in our time that holds that where there is a profound disequilibrium between production and demand, the practice of *laissez-faire* can be unnecessarily wasteful of work and capital. Given only the natural if unpredictable fluctuations in agricultural production, governments in France and elsewhere have increasingly avoided leaving crops that are important for the national economy to a free market which can be crude and erratic. Even if the *Code du Vin* should succeed in bringing a closer correlation between the area of the French vineyard and the demand for wine, this would not necessarily mean the end of government intervention in the winegrower's market.

NOTES

LIST OF ABBREVIATIONS

ACDEB   Annales de la Chambre des Députés: Débats parlementaires.
ACDOC   Annales de la Chambre des Députés: Documents parlementaires.
ANCDOC   Journal officiel. Documents de l'Assemblée Nationale Constituante.
ANDEB   Journal officiel. Assemblée Nationale: Débats parlementaires.
ANDOC   Journal officiel. Assemblée Nationale: Documents parlementaires.
ARCE   Journal officiel. Avis et rapports du Conseil Économique.
AS   Ministère du commerce; Statistique générale de la France. Annuaire statistique.
ASCD   Annales du Sénat et de la Chambre des Députés.
BSL   Ministère des finances. *Bulletin de statistique et de législation comparée.*
CDEB   Journal officiel. Chambre des Députés: Débats parlementaires.
CDOC   Journal officiel. Chambre des Députés: Documents parlementaires.
JAP   *Journal d'agriculture pratique.*
JO   Journal officiel. Lois et décrets.
PAV   *Progrès agricole et viticole.*
RAF   *Revue des agriculteurs de France.*
RV   *Revue de viticulture.*
SDEB   Journal officiel. Sénat: Débats parlementaires.
SDOC   Journal officiel. Sénat: Documents parlementaires.

1. THE PHYLLOXERA EPIDEMIC

1. AS, 1890, pp. 504–5, (Tableaux rétrospectifs).

2. Henri Baudrillart writes of Narbonne and Béziers, the chief wine-marketing centers of the Midi, as "little Babylons," and Charles Gide

describes peasants still in their blouses coming to the stores of Nimes and Montpellier and asking for "whatever was most expensive." Baudrillart, *Populations agricoles,* III, 276; Gide, "La Question des vins au point de vue des traités de commerce," *Revue d'économie politique,* VII (1892), 818.

3. Figure from AS, 1912, Résumé rétrospectif, p. 44. It is based on estimates of the Contributions Indirectes. The *Statistique agricole* estimates a somewhat lower figure (78,202,088 hectolitres) which is still above the figure of 78,144,000 hectolitres registered for the harvest of 1935 when, after 1907, growers were obliged by law to declare the quantity of their harvest. In the literature of France's viticultural problem the harvest of 1875 survives as a record which it is claimed is not likely to be surpassed.

4. BSL, April, 1883, pp. 558–61.

5. Ministère des finances, *Tableau décennal,* 1888, *passim.*

6. There are five known varieties of the phylloxera insect. For a complete description see Viala, *Maladies de la vigne,* pp. 498–539.

7. Fisher, "Phylloxera," *Encyclopaedia Britannica,* eleventh ed., Vol. XXI.

8. JAP, July 11, 1867, p. 37.   9. *Ibid.,* July 16, 1867, p. 65.

10. *Ibid.*

11. *Ibid.,* March 19, 1874, p. 410.

12. *Ibid.* Italics added.

13. *L'Économiste français,* August 9, 1879, p. 153.

14. Planchon and Lichtenstein, "De l'identité spécifique du phylloxera des feuilles et du phylloxera des racines de la vigne," *Comptes rendus des séances de l'Académie des Sciences,* LXXI (1870), 298–301.

15. *L'Économiste français,* October 26, 1878, p. 517.

16. Philip Wagner has pointed out that "the degree of resistance is highly variable among the American species, in some the resistance being practically perfect, and in some the resistance being only slightly better than that of *V. vinifera,* the established French vine species." Wagner, *Wine-Grower's Guide,* p. 37.

17. There is an interesting and not too technical discussion of these experiments in Wagner, *Wine-Grower's Guide,* pp. 36–46.

18. JAP, January 2, 1873, pp. 29–46.

19. At the *Congrès Viticole de Montpellier* reported in *L'Économiste français,* October 26, 1878, p. 518.

20. ASCD, 1878, p. 100.   21. Law of August 3, 1891.

22. ASCD, 1879, p. 96.   23. Law of July 2, 1879.

24. These vine-defense syndicates should not be confused with the more famous *syndicats agricoles* authorized in 1884. They were limited by an earlier law (law of June 21, 1865) to specific projects contributing to agricultural welfare. Clapham makes the interesting observation that

the vine-defense syndicates marked the first use of the term "syndicate" in connection with an agricultural organization, and that they contributed much to the spirit of cooperation that led to the growth of the *syndicats agricoles.* See Clapham, *Economic Development of France and Germany,* pp. 184–85.

25. Law of December 2, 1887.

26. JAP, March 3, 1887, p. 294.

27. For example, in the year 1889, 681 syndicates were formed, representing 21,887 proprietors owning a total of 23,922 hectares of vines. Ministère de l'agriculture, *Bulletin,* IX (1890), 35.

28. Gide, "La Question des vins au point de vue des traités de commerce," *Revue d'économie politique,* VII (1892), 818, 830.

29. Cauwès, *Cours d'économie politique,* I, 530–31.

30. Ministère de l'agriculture, *Bulletin,* VII (1888), 21.

31. Law of December 1, 1887. 32. AS.

33. *Ibid.* 34. *Ibid.*

35. Fromont, "Splendeurs et misères de la vigne et du vin dans la France moderne," in *Le Vin de France dans l'histoire,* p. 41.

36. *Ibid.,* p. 42.

37. Gide, "La Crise du vin en France et les associations de vinification," *Revue d'économie politique,* XVI (1901), 218. This estimate may have a touch of polemic in it. Present-day authorities such as Professer Marres of the University of Montpellier speak of yields from the Aramon grape of "up to 150 hectolitres the hectare." See Marres, *Vigne et vin,* pp. 127–28.

38. The latter included propping up the branches of the overloaded vines with sticks or training them on wires.

39. In Hérault, the largest wine producer of the four departments, the area planted in wheat decreased from 61,900 hectares in 1882 to 13,928 hectares in 1892, and 8,389 hectares in 1902. The area planted in alfalfa dropped from 18,500 hectares in 1882 to 1,827 hectares in 1892. In France as a whole there was a general increase in wheat and fodder cultivation during the same period. AS; Ministère de l'agriculture, *Bulletin.*

40. *Vins de cru* are wines bearing regional or estate labels. They must be made from specified grapes according to fixed methods of viticulture, and come from certain limited areas. All of these requirements make impossible any real extension of their production and especially prevent any appreciable increase in their yield per hectare. An interesting example of the adherence of the growers of these wines to traditional viticulture is presented by the fact that several of the famous Burgundy vineyards kept their pre-phylloxera vines in production by elaborate and costly treatments until long after the epidemic ended.

41. This shift was inspired by the same motives as that of the Midi

growers. *Vins de cru* brought the top prices, but the extra cost, time, and care needed to bring their more delicate grapes back into production made *vins ordinaires* seem more profitable at the time. In many cases, the switch was a financial necessity. See Fromont, "Splendeurs et misères de la vigne et du vin dans la France moderne," in *Le Vin de France dans l'histoire,* p. 41.

42. ACDOC, June 9–July 10, 1900, p. 1288.

43. BSL, January, 1928, pp. 44–65.

44. The law forbade the sale of sugar wine but did not prohibit its manufacture. For a further description see p. 40.

45. ASDOC, June 9–July 10, 1900, p. 1288.

46. The Brussels Agreement, by removing export bounties and lowering domestic taxes on sugar, released large quantities for the home market, lowering the price, and by consequence making fraud more attractive for the winegrowers.

47. Degrully, *Essai sur la production et le marché des vins,* p. 360.

48. *Ibid.,* p. 353.

49. An idea of the speed of this development may be gained from the fact that whereas the vineyard area of Algeria stood at 30,482 hectares in 1881, it had increased to 103,407 hectares in 1888.

50. For example, French wines shipped by rail from Sète to Paris paid a freight of 27.30 francs per barrel, and Algerian wines shipped from the same port paid from 23.60 francs to 24.60. Moreover, French shippers had to pay 5 francs the barrel and other charges to have their containers returned, whereas the railroads returned the Algerian containers—including tank cars—free of charge.

51. Ministère de l'agriculture, *Statistique agricole,* 1904, p. 271.

52. De Romeuf, "La Crise viticole du Midi," *Revue politique et parlementaire,* LX (1909), 291.

2. THE CRISIS OF *1900–1907*

1. It is possible that both the pre- and post-phylloxera eras of prosperity appeared exaggerated because the secular trend for the period (1870–90) was downwards. By the same token after 1890, when wine production and the secular trend climbed upwards together, the price drops during 1900–1907 must have seemed all the greater. It is also interesting that parts of both prosperous periods fell within the time limits of what Henri Sée has called a predominantly agricultural depression from 1875 to 1896 in France.

2. AS, 1900, p. 169.   3. *Ibid.,* pp. 168–69.

4. Unless otherwise indicated, throughout this study prices quoted, including regional and national averages, refer to the price paid to the grower.

5. Caupert, *Essai sur la C.G.V.*, p. 20.

6. Price estimates for the Midi, unless otherwise indicated, are from a contemporary study by J. L. Gaston-Pastre, quoted in Meyrueis, *De la défense des intérêts de la viticulture méridionale,* p. 123. An alternative source would be the departmental price averages in the *Annuaire statistique,* which run slightly higher than the estimates quoted. A convenient rule of thumb puts the Midi (four departments) average ten to twelve francs below the national average during the period under discussion.

7. As with the subject of prices, the question of wine production costs involves a certain lack of precision. Degrully, *Essai sur la production et le marché des vins,* pp. 368 ff., estimates production costs in the Midi at about 8 francs the hectolitre on lowland vineyards, and as high as 15 francs the hectolitre on the more numerous hillside vineyards. Gide estimates production costs at 6 francs the hectolitre for alluvial vineyards planted in Aramon grapes, in "La Crise du vin en France et les associations de vinification," *Revue d'économie politique,* XVI (1901), 217.

8. Genieys, *La Crise viticole méridionale,* pp. 35–36.

9. Caupert, *Essai sur la C.G.V.*, p. 20.

10. Lafforgue, *Vignoble girondin,* p. 269.

11. Salavert, *Commerce des vins de Bordeaux,* pp. 203–4; Caziot, *Valeur de la terre,* pp. 430–34.

12. Mugnier, *Essai sur l'exportation des vins fins de Bourgogne,* pp. 103–4.

13. Although the production of quality wines was decreasing during this period, they still represented approximately 33 percent the value of a Bordeaux harvest as opposed to 6 percent for the Midi.

14. The Direction Générale des Contributions Directes estimated that the rental value of vineyards declined from 130 francs per hectare in 1879 to 76 francs per hectare in 1908. This represents a drop of about 40 percent as compared with an average drop of 25 percent for all categories of unbuilt property (orchards, pastures, etc.) during the same period. (Average figure weighted for area of each category.) Ministère des finances, *Evaluation des propriétés non bâties,* I, 264 ff. For an excellent analysis of these and related figures, see also Golob, *Méline Tariff,* pp. 223–26.

15. Caziot, *Valeur de la terre,* p. 434.

16. *Ibid.,* p. 437.　　　　　　17. *Ibid.,* pp. 436–37.

18. It must be remembered, however, that the *grands crus* represented a very small part of the Burgundy output. The famous *domaine de la Romanée-Conti* was (and is) only four and a half acres in size. It was sold in 1868 for 368,000 gold francs and again in 1912 for a reported 300,000 francs.

19. Caziot, *Valeur de la terre,* p. 387.

20. *Ibid.,* p. 395.   21. *Ibid.,* pp. 438–41.

22. Professor Marres describes even the intensively cultivated Bordeaux vineyards as being in a "preponderantly winegrowing but polycultural region." And Caziot notes that during the crisis the Bordeaux shippers began long-term advances (*abonnements*) to the growers to keep them from giving up vine growing. In lieu of any definite statistics, this action would suggest economic alternatives available to the Bordeaux region which the Midi did not have. See Marres, *Vigne et vin,* pp. 1–38, 91–100, and Caziot, *Valeur de la terre,* pp. 394, 432–34.

23. In 1905 the vineyard area of the four departments totaled 462,-025 hectares. By 1907 it had dropped to 431,271 hectares—a decrease of about 8 percent. In 1915 it totaled 427,856 hectares. These figures are significant only when compared with an increase of the same area from 325,014 hectares in 1890 to 462,502 hectares in 1900. Or for that matter the slight increase of 4,611 hectares registered the first three years of the crisis. (AS).

24. Caupert, *Essai sur la C.G.V.,* p. 22.

25. *Ibid.*

26. De Romeuf, "La Crise viticole du Midi," *Revue politique et parlementaire,* LX (1909), 291.

27. *Ibid.*   28. *Ibid.*

29. Caupert, *Essai sur la C.G.V.,* p. 23. It should be noted that agricultural credit was expanding rapidly throughout France at the same time. However, of 45 million francs in loans disbursed during 1907 by 88 *Caisses agricoles,* 13 million francs, nearly 30 percent of the total, were distributed by 5 *caisses* located in the Midi. Sagnier, *Crédit agricole,* pp. 90–91.

30. Caupert, *Essai sur la C.G.V.,* p. 23.

31. De Romeuf, "La Crise viticole du Midi," *Revue politique et parlementaire,* LX (1909), 291.

32. Nadal, "La Crise viticole dans le Midi de France," *Revue générale,* LXXVI (1907), 163.

33. Caupert, *Essai sur la C.G.V.,* p. 22.

34. Perrier, "La Crise viticole," *Revue politique et parlementaire,* LVII (1907), 55.

35. Caupert, *Essai sur la C.G.V.,* p. 23.

36. Ministère du travail, *Bulletin de l'office du travail,* XIV (1907), 848.

37. Caupert, *Essai sur la C.G.V.,* p. 23.

38. Hamelle, "La Crise viticole," *Annales des sciences politiques,* XXIII (1908), 626.

39. Augé-Laribé, *Problème agraire du socialisme,* p. 297.

40. Ministère du travail, *Bulletin de l'office du travail,* X (1903), XI (1904), *passim.*

41. Unemployment percentages and strike figures quoted in this paragraph have been compiled from the monthly bulletins of the Office du Travail for the years indicated.

42. Some estimates place the figure as high as 700,000. Exhibiting a baffling altruism, the government had supplied free trains and opened schools and *mairies* to lodge the demonstrators.

43. Albert was a curious figure. He was a sincere, if fanatic, regionalist with great oratorical gifts. He later went to prison voluntarily after "capitulating," in tears, to Clemenceau at Paris on June 23, 1907. For a biographical sketch, see Girou, *Vie des personnages célèbres de l'Aude,* pp. 237–40. For a journalist's detailed and documented account of the uprisings, see Le Blond, *La Crise du Midi.*

44. M. Tessere, President of the Committee of Baixas, quoted in *Le Figaro* (Paris), June 21, 1907.

45. Opinion of "Ceux d'Argelliers," quoted in *Le Gaulois,* (Paris) June 22, 1907. (Note: Low-grade wine is often sold by the hectolitre with the price based on the alcoholic content measured in degrees.)

46. Le Blond, *La Crise du Midi,* p. 28.

3. CAUSES OF THE CRISIS OF *1900–1907*

1. Gide, "La Crise du vin en France et les associations de vinification," *Revue d'économie politique,* XV (1901), 218–35.

2. *Ibid.,* p. 222.

3. It is hard to know how he arrived at these figures. One example: he writes off *all* children under fifteen as non-wine drinkers.

4. Gide, "La Crise du vin en France et les associations de vinification," *Revue d'économie politique,* XV (1901), 218. Italics added.

5. *Le Travail national,* November 17, 1901, p. 601.

6. *Journal des économistes,* May 15, 1903, p. 246.

7. *Le Temps* (Paris), quoted in Perrier, "La Crise viticole," *Revue politique et parlementaire,* LVIII (1907), 56.

8. ACDEB, October 22–November 26, 1901, p. 516.

9. Quoted *ibid.,* May 22–July 10, 1900, p. 554.

10. ACDEB, November 28–December 24, 1901, pp. 856–57.

11. *Ibid.,* May and June, 1905, *passim.*

12. *Ibid.,* June 1–July 13, 1906, p. 557.

13. "The problem [of fraud] is serious enough that one should guard against exaggerating it. . . . The rumours about fraud, and the resultant scare have done as much to lower prices as the sale of all fraudulently produced wine." ACDOC, March 6–April 22, 1905, p. 384. "One can

affirm that [this talk of] fraud does more harm by the motives it furnishes speculators on a falling market than by the quantity of fraudulent liquor actually put on sale." *Bulletin de la Société des viticulteurs et d'ampélographie,* March, 1905, quoted in ACDOC, March 6–April 22, 1905, p. 384.

14. Leroy-Beaulieu, "La Situation du Midi et la crise viticole," *L'Économiste français,* May 25, 1907, pp. 1–4.

15. *Ibid.,* p. 1.

16. Gide, "La Crise du vin dans le Midi de la France," *Revue d'économie politique,* XXI (1907), 481–512.

17. "It was not so long ago that one saw at harvest time in the villages of the Midi carts, barrels, tubs, and all sorts of other receptacles grouped around the public fountain while everybody waited to fill them with the wonder-working liquid so as to bring it back to the wine cellar. So much water was consumed in this process that there was none left to drink." *Ibid.,* p. 489.

18. This attitude is to some extent understandable. For some of the complications involved in regulating sugar and fraud in general, see Chapter V. For a full treatment of the historical and legal aspects of sugared wine, see Gourssies, *Le Sucrage des vins;* also Susplugas, *La Répression des fraudes.*

19. *Journal des économistes,* June 3, 1907, p. 466.

20. *Journal des débats,* May 24, 1907, p. 966.

21. For a discussion of this law, see pp. 41–42.

22. *Journal des économistes,* July 15, 1907, p. 151. Italics added.

23. *Ibid.,* October 15, 1907, p. 60.

24. Clough, *France: A History of National Economics,* pp. 227–28.

25. Ministère des finances, *Tableau général du commerce,* 1882–1907, *passim.* For a detailed description of the tariff war between the two countries and its effects see Eysoldt, *Der Zwollkreig.*

26. Herubel, *L'Exportation des vins,* p. 10.

27. AS, 1907, Résumé rétrospectif, p. 186.

28. *Ibid.,* Résumé rétrospectif, p. 186.

29. So called because the phylloxera epidemic took place chiefly during the 1880–89 decade, while the 1890–99 decade was a period of replanting.

30. Law of December 29, 1900.

31. *Le Travail national,* December 1, 1901, p. 632.

32. Gervais, *L'Exportation des vins,* p. 3.

33. ACDEB, May, 1901; July, 1906; June, 1907; *passim.*

34. Raynal, *Le Vignoble français,* p. 30.

35. Meyreuis, *De la défense des intérêts de la viticulture méridionale,* p. 128.

36. For a description of the anti-cooperative attitude, see Descamps,

"Les Populations viticoles, l'évolution du type du vigneron et la crise actuelle," *Annales sciences sociales,* XXII (1907), fasc. 37.

37. Gide, "La Crise du vin dans le Midi de la France," *Revue d'économie politique,* XXI (1907), 500. The example suffers somewhat by its political overtones. The members of the cooperative represented themselves to the Paris workers as "blood brothers" engaged in a "common struggle."

38. For a discussion of this point, see Augé-Laribé, *Problème agraire du socialisme,* pp. 348–49, 353.

39. BSL, July, 1913, p. 34.

40. One hectolitre (100 litres) of wine yielded from 7 to 10 litres of distillate.

41. BSL, July, 1913, p. 35.

42. Law of December 29, 1900; law of March 31, 1903. The *privilège* permitted the landowner to distill his produce tax free on his own property provided the resulting alcohol was consumed there. Since alcohol taxes were high, this practice encouraged a good deal of illicit trading. The *privilège* was bitterly attacked by the commercial distillers, but it was just as heavily defended by a solid peasant vote.

43. Law of February 27, 1906.

44. Official estimates of the annual production of the *bouilleurs de cru* during the period average around 235,000 hectolitres a year. It must be remembered that this figure includes alcohol distilled from fruits, grains, and vegetables, as well as wine. Opponents of the *privilège* claimed the figure was much higher. See BSL, July, 1913, p. 35.

45. The number of commercial distillers doubled between 1900 and 1907. Almost all the distilleries producing more than 50,000 hectolitres annually were in the North. During the same period alcohol produced on individual farms accounted for only 10 percent of production. Moinvoisin, *Alcool et distillerie,* pp. 11–13.

46. *Le Travail national,* December 1, 1901, pp. 632–34.

47. ACDOC, January 8–July 11, 1907, pp. 1018–19.

48. This claim answered to a popular French prejudice. See Note 72, Chapter Five.

49. Law of March 31, 1903.

50. Weill, *Monopole de l'alcool,* p. 190.

51. Law of December 29, 1900.

52. Zola's *L'Assomoir* gives a graphic description of the prevalence of this consumption.

53. ACDEB, May 15–June 16, 1905, p. 258.

54. ACDOC, January 10–July 5, 1905, p. 384.

55. De Romeuf, "La Crise viticole du Midi," *Revue politique et parlementaire,* LX (1909), 297.

56. Degrully, *Essai sur la production et le marché des vins,* p. 359.

57. Gide, "La Crise du vin dans le Midi de la France," *Revue d'économie politique,* XXI (1907), 490.

58. Although *octroi* duties on wine were suppressed in 1901, wine still had to pass through the *octrois* to determine a city's share of part of the compensatory alcohol surtax collected by the state.

59. Quoted in De Romeuf, "La Crise viticole du Midi," *Revue politique et parlementaire,* LX (1909), 297.

60. In 1900 there were 435,379 shops selling wine in France. By 1907 this figure had increased to 477,323. AS, 1901, p. 215; 1907, p. 161.

4. THE GOVERNMENT AND THE CRISIS OF *1900–1907*

1. Law of August 14, 1889.   2. Law of July 24, 1894.

3. Gide, "La Crise du vin dans le Midi de la France," *Revue d'économie politique,* XXI (1907), 490.

4. Law of December 29, 1900.   5. Law of July 11, 1891.

6. Law of April 6, 1897.

7. ACDEB, May 22–July 10, 1900, p. 52.

8. Law of December 29, 1900.   9. Law of January 28, 1903.

10. Law of July 18, 1904; Commission sur la réforme des boissons, 1905; Enquête parlementaire sur la viticulture, 1907.

11. Law of August 6, 1905; law of June 29, 1907.

12. ACDOC, January 8–July 11, 1907, p. 1020.

13. The "legal" use of sugar in fermenting wine improves its strength and not its quantity. Burgundies, while strong in flavor and other qualities, are weak in alcohol. Thus in 1906 the single department of Côte-d'Or used almost four times as much sugar as the four departments of the Midi.

14. Susplugas, *La Répression des fraudes,* pp. 10–11.

15. Caupert, *Essai sur la C.G.V.,* p. 44.

16. For example, it was possible to bring wine through an *octroi,* get a permit, and later pass through the same *octroi* with the same wine and get another permit. This way one could double the original quantity of wine and still have papers covering the increased amount. With the declaration system a dishonest wine shipper could go to a *mairie* and, unknown to the proprietor, say that he had bought so much wine from a local vineyard. He could than get a receipt from the *mairie* if it was not disposed to investigate—and use the receipt to declare his stocks of watered wine.

17. ACDOC, June 9–July 10, 1900, p. 1288.

18. Under the law of August 1, 1905, samples of fraudulent wine were to be submitted to municipal laboratories (which had neither a uniform organization nor existence), and the laboratories were to initiate

charges if they were justified. Irritated over what it claimed was an imposition and cautious over the new tie-up with the government, the laboratory in Paris finally concluded in its first case that since "official methods of analysis have not been set up, nor the composition-type of the product determined, it is impossible to conclude that the product has or has not been adulterated or falsified." ACDEB, May 7–June 18, 1907, p. 375.

19. Law of August 1, 1905.

20. ACDEB, June 20–July 11, 1907, p. 713.

21. JAP, January 31, 1907, p. 131.

22. *Le Tocsin,* June 23, 1907, quoted in Meyrueis, *De la défense des intérêts de la viticulture méridionale,* p. 52.

23. Quoted in Caupert, *Essai sur la C.G.V.,* p. 75.

24. This was because of its origins and the fact that Dr. Ferroul, mayor of Narbonne, who had succeeded Albert as leader of the revolt, became the first president. See Le Blond, *La Crise du Midi,* pp. 181–84.

25. These included pulling up of vines and other acts of vandalism against proprietors who were rumored to have made sales below 15 francs the hectolitre.

26. Quoted in Caupert, *Essai sur la C.G.V.,* p. 79.

27. See p. 40.

28. The syndicates themselves had only been given a legal personality in 1884, and the cases they initiated were subject to certain prejudices (in the legal sense of the word). Thus M. Ruau, the Minister of Agriculture, when confronted with the Confederation's request, answered: "No matter how good the faith of the members of the syndicates, there would be inconveniences in commissioning an agent from a syndicate, as he could be charged with bias."

29. Article 56, *Lois des Finances,* February 27, 1912. For the historian, the similarity between these agents and the professional police of the old guilds is worth noting.

30. The plural vote based on production and acreage was deemed necessary as protection against polycultural communes where, under the single-vote system, a fruit grower with a few vines might have the same vote as a grower who concentrated in vines. This was especially necessary as the councils of the C.G.V. were organized on the basis of representation from the communes.

31. Meyrueis, *De la défense des intérêts de la viticulture méridionale,* p. 62.

32. *Ibid.,* p. 94.   33. *Ibid.,* p. 95.

34. An exception was the vineyard of upper Burgundy where, starting in 1909 and extending through 1912, a series of exceptionally light harvests brought a serious local depression. In 1910 the harvests did not even take place. Caziot, *Valeur de la terre,* p. 380.

35. *Ibid.*, p. 410.
36. Augé-Laribé, *Politique agricole de la France*, p. 173.
37. The Méline Tariff (law of January 12, 1892) raised the duty on foreign wines from 4.50 francs to 12 to 7 francs the hectolitre of 10° wine. There were further raises in 1899, 1900, and 1906.
38. Golob, *The Méline Tariff*, pp. 147 ff.
39. Augé-Laribé, *Politique agricole de la France*, p. 173.
40. Clough, *France: A History of National Economics*, pp. 250–53.

5. THE GOVERNMENT AND THE WINE INDUSTRY DURING WORLD WAR I

1. Augé-Laribé, *L'Agriculture pendant la guerre*, p. 53.
2. JO, August 3, 1914.
3. Augé-Laribé, *L'Agriculture pendant la guerre*, p. 52.   March, *Mouvement des prix*, p. 52.
4. March, *Mouvement des prix*, p. 52.
5. Augé-Laribé, *L'Agriculture pendant la guerre*, p. 127.
6. Pinot, *Contrôle du ravitaillement*, p. 52.
7. CDEB, 1916, p. 1619.   For a description of the difficulties and problems of commercial transport during the war, see Peschaud, *Politique et fonctionnement des transports*, pp. 103–12, and Olphe-Gaillard, *Histoire économique et financière de la guerre*, pp. 41–59.
8. RV, April 10, 1917, p. 252.   It is interesting to note that Gaston Doumergue, complaining in the Senate about transportation, said that "wheat and wine should have a right of priority in the social interest." *Ibid.*, October 16, 1919, p. 255.
9. Pinot, *Contrôle du ravitaillement*, p. 136.
10. CDEB, 1918, p. 988.
11. CDOC, 1918, pp. 225–32 (Annexes 4348, 4349).
12. Pinot, *Contrôle du ravitaillement*, p. 136.
13. Pinot points out that the Vilgrain measures were responsible for lowering wine prices in Paris in 1919.   Since the national price average increased, however, this was of limited significance.   *Ibid.*, p. 133.
14. Peschaud, *Politique et fonctionnement des transports*, p. 107.
15. Augé-Laribé, *L'Agriculture pendant la guerre*, p. 110.
16. *Ibid.*, pp. 67–68; Ricard, "La Vie paysanne d'août 1914 à octobre 1915," *Revue politique et parlementaire*, LXVI (1915), 358–59.
17. Augé-Laribé, *L'Agriculture pendant la guerre*, pp. 71–72.
18. Ricard, "La Vie paysanne d'août 1914 à octobre 1915," *Revue politique et parlementaire*, LXVI (1915), 367.
19. Augé-Laribé, *L'Agriculture pendant la guerre*, p. 71.
20. RV, 1915, *passim*.
21. JAP, March 23, 1916, pp. 110–11.
22. CDOC, 1916, p. 579 (Annex 1985).

23. Augé-Laribé, *L'Agriculture pendant la guerre,* p. 73, states that 146,446 Spanish and Portuguese workers were imported for agricultural labor purposes during the war.

24. CDOC, 1916, p. 579 (Annex 1918).

25. Nogaro and Weil, *La main-d'oeuvre étrangère,* p. 55.

26. CDOC, 1917, p. 1063 (Annex 3601).

27. *Ibid.,* p. 1151 (Annex 3698).

28. CDEB, 1916, p. 1507.

29. RV, September 2, 1915, p. 187. It should be noted that, according to the circular issued by the Ministry of War, the leaves were to be independent of those regularly given for haying and wheat harvesting.

30. Augé-Laribé, *L'Agriculture pendant la guerre,* p. 76.

31. Ricard, "La Vie paysanne d'août 1914 à octobre 1915," *Revue politique et parlementaire,* LXVI (1915), 367.

32. CDOC, 1917, p. 1063 (Annex 3601).

33. Augé-Laribé stresses the failure of all government attempts to recruit military or civilian labor for the farms and emphasizes the role played by some three million women and children. Augé-Laribé, *L'Agriculture pendant la guerre, passim.*

34. RV, August 13–December 25, 1914, p. 171.

35. *Ibid.*

36. Augé-Laribé, *L'Agriculture pendant la guerre,* p. 126.

37. RV, January 7, 1915, p. 198.

38. Augé-Laribé, *L'Agriculture pendant la guerre,* p. 126.

39. SDOC, 1919, p. 256 (Annex 413).

40. *Ibid.*

41. Augé-Laribé, *L'Agriculture pendant la guerre,* p. 127.

42. In two instances where the supply services bought wine and paid for it several months later, local courts at Valence and Perpignan made them pay at the current price instead of the requisition price. RV, January 20, 1916, p. 63.

43. RV, December 2, 1915, p. 484; January 20, 1916, p. 96; April 10, 1917, p. 252; August 30, 1917, p. 177; 1918, *passim.* JAP, September 6, 1917, p. 335; 1918, *passim.*

44. AS.

45. There is an interesting letter from Herriot, then Minister of Public Works, Transport, and Supply, to a deputy from Vienne, showing the close cooperation of the winegrowing associations and especially the C.G.V. with the government in these matters (quoted in RV, March 15, 1917, p. 171). The associations seem to have been ahead of their membership in this respect. A footnote to this consideration is provided by the fact that in spite of strong opposition by the associations a bill was passed in 1917 to legalize the sale of *piquettes* or "second" wines (forbidden in 1905; see p. 41) as a wartime emergency measure. The

bill was proposed by a deputy from the Gironde. It had as its purpose "on one hand, to permit the winegrowers to draw, in addition to the profit resulting from the sale of their wine, a supplementary resource from the sale of *piquettes;* on the other hand, to offer to consumers of limited circumstances a drink at bargain prices in place of the wine beyond the reach of their small purses." Quoted in RV, October 18, 1917, p. 248.

46. SDOC, 1919, p. 537 (Annex 413).

47. There were cases where wine requisitioned in 1914 had not been paid for in 1917. RV, October 10, 1918, p. 228.

48. Augé-Laribé feels that the government should have made more use of specialists from the trade than it did (*L'Agriculture pendant la guerre,* p. 127). A government spokesman admitted in the Chamber of Deputies (session of January 28, 1916) that "perhaps the professional background [of the officers of the supply services] did not fit them for the immensity of the actual task." Reported in RV, February 3, 1916, p. 96.

49. JAP, October 17, 1918, p. 404.

50. *Ibid.,* February 7, 1918, p. 44.

51. RV, February 3, 1916, p. 96.

52. SDOC, 1919, p. 532 (Annex 413).

53. Augé-Laribé, *L'Agriculture pendant la guerre,* p. 132.

54. The court decided that "the indemnity representative of the value of goods requisitioned should be fixed in accordance with commercial prices at the time of requisition." Reported in RV, March 15, 1917, p. 168.

55. The court decided that "Military requisitions in time of mobilization or war are acts of the public power consisting of seizure by the State, independent of all consent or agreement on prices and without previous indemnity, of things necessary to the needs of the army in order to make up for the insufficiency of ordinary means of provisioning.

"They do not have the character of a commercial purchase or sale of goods nor of any contract of common law.

"It is understood, on the other hand, that the indemnity has to be calculated on the basis of loss to the requisitionee exclusively, abstraction being made of the gain which might be procured for him by the rise in prices distorted by speculation, hoarding, or any other conditions resulting from the war, including the act of requisition itself. The State is not an ordinary buyer and in making of the current price not just a simple element of evaluation, but the exclusive and necessary basis of indemnity, the decree [of the Rennes court] is wrong. We therefore set it aside." Reported in RV, March 15, 1917, pp. 169–70.

56. RV, February 3, 1916, p. 96.

57. SDOC, 1919, p. 537 (Annex 413).

58. *Ibid.*
59. Augé-Laribé, *L'Agriculture pendant la guerre,* p. 229.
60. *Ibid.,* pp. 115, 176.   61. JO, November 4, 1915.
62. Pinot, *Contrôle du ravitaillement,* p. 188, says that the compromise bill was adopted by both houses without amendment. For a contradictory view see CDOC, 1916, p. 665 (Annex 2105).
63. CDEB, 1916, p. 1131.
64. CDOC, 1916, p. 1630 (Annex 2670).
65. JO, September 3, 1917.   66. *Ibid.,* February 11, 1918.
67. CDEB, 1918, p. 1406.   68. RV, June 1, 1916, p. 389.
69. Because wine had been exempted from the *octroi* in 1900 (a crisis measure which had never been repealed), the growers felt that they were being discriminated against by the new tax. RV, February, 21, 1918, p. 122.
70. These were potatoes and cheese whose prices rose between 10 to 20 percent more than wine. Fish was the only uncontrolled major food to approximate wine's price rise. Fishing was of course severely curtailed by wartime conditions. See March, *Mouvement des prix,* pp. 52–53, 57–59, 65.
71. SDOC, 1919, p. 537 (Annex 413).
72. The French make a distinction between *boissons alcooliques* or *alcool,* and wines, beer, and cider. A further distinction is made between *alcools de bouche,* which are derived exclusively from fruits, and *alcools d'industrie,* which are distilled from grains and vegetables. Although the latter are of course drunk, there is a popular prejudice in favor of the former which are reputedly more "hygienic." Beginning in 1916 this distinction has been incorporated in much legislation directly affecting the alcoholic beverage industry and indirectly affecting the wine industry.
73. On July 3, 1915, General Gallieni forbade the consumption of all alcohols including vermouths and *apéritifs* in the military district of Paris.
74. Quoted in *L'Économiste français,* July 24, 1915, p. 117.
75. Quoted in RV, July 1, 1915, p. 15. The *privilège,* it will be remembered, permitted the landowner to distill his produce tax free on his own property provided the resulting alcohol was consumed there. When the *privilège* had been temporarily suppressed in 1900 it was purely a fiscal problem; now the emphasis was on the social aspect of the question.
76. *Le Temps* (Paris), May 10, 1915.
77. RV, June 17, 1915, p. 512.
78. One suggestion widely quoted in the press in 1915 maintained that since the Germans poisoned wells it would be better if the soldiers drank nothing but wine.

79. *Pinard* was a colloquial word whose usage became widespread during the war to describe the cheap red wine that comprised the bulk of the army wine ration.

80. CDOC, 1916, p. 1063 (Annex 3601).

81. In 1915 the distillers of the department of Charente gave 6,935 litres of brandy to the army, and the anti-alcohol campaign notwithstanding, there was even talk of a regular ration. The winegrowers met objections to the sale of *eaux-de-vie* to the troops by pointing out that it was nothing but "concentrated wine" and consequently "hygienic" and incidentally "easier to transport." See RV, February 11, 1915, p. 258.

82. CDOC, 1916, p. 795 (Annex 2034).

83. Although relatively little distilling of this sort was being done by the winegrowers, they objected as strongly to the suppression as they had in 1900 and claimed it would ruin distillation to the "great detriment of national [agricultural] production." RV, June 1, 1916, p. 392.

84. JO, December 15, 1916.

85. In an editorial on Briand's request, as distinguished an economist as Yves Guyot wrote that the anti-alcohol campaign would lead to the "physical and moral weakening" of the soldier and called it a "national danger." *Journal des économistes,* February 15, 1917, p. 184.

86. CDEB, 1918, p. 1627.   87. *Ibid.*

88. RV, February 1, 1917, pp. 77–78.

89. *Ibid.,* June 1, 1916, pp. 389–90.

90. In 1917 at the same time the government raised the *droits de circulation* on wine, mineral waters previously exempted were taxed one centime the half litre (law of January 1, 1917). The winegrowing associations had asked for a tax of ten centimes.

6. BETWEEN TWO WARS: CHRONIC OVERPRODUCTION

1. RV, July 1, 1920, p. 10.

2. The only previous example of such a negative relationship between price and supply occurred during the crisis of 1900–1907. See p. 18.

3. CDEB, 1925, p. 3434. A more detailed study places the cost price in 1922 at 66.59 francs the hectolitre on a *domaine* in Hérault, 30 hectares in area with a yield of 70 hectolitres the hectare. This would suggest a higher national average cost price, since the national average yield in 1922 was 50.29 hectolitres the hectare. As has been pointed out, with production costs varying so much even within the same region and from season to season, the study of "average" costs is a difficult and relatively untouched subject. In the period under discussion it is made even more difficult by strong and sudden inflationary movements. For

a study of the property described above, see M. Ferrouillet, "Prix de revient de l'hectolitre de vin dans un domaine moyen de l'Hérault," *Comptes rendus des séances de l'Académie d'Agriculture de France,* VII (1922), 631–35.

4. RV, August, 12, 1920, p. 122. The government was actually asked to intervene against this campaign. See CDEB, 1920, p. 122.

5. The long-term trend was down, however. See Table 16.

6. Augé-Laribé, *L'Agriculture pendant la guerre,* p. 196. Caziot claims that by 1929 the prices of vineyard properties had multiplied to 8 to 10 times those of 1914. The coefficient for the most valuable of other types of farm land was only 5. Caziot, "La Chute de la valeur de la terre," RAF, March, 1935, p. 68.

7. Augé-Laribé, *L'Agriculture pendant la guerre,* p. 196; Caziot, "La Chute de la valeur de la terre," RAF, March, 1935, p. 70.

8. These included regional and departmental offices "in view of intensifying agricultural production and assuring its development." JO, January 9, 1919.

9. Law of June 25, 1920; law of July 15, 1921.

10. See p. 89.

11. The most important of the organizations favoring the export of French wines was the Association Nationale d'Expansion Économique. See also *Comptes rendus des séances de l'Académie d'Agriculture de France,* VII (1922), 169–83.

12. See: Semaine nationale du vin, *Compte rendu des travaux* (Paris: Association Nationale d'Expansion Économique, 1922).

13. CDEB, 1925, p. 3434.

14. *Bulletin de la Société des Agriculteurs de la France,* May, 1925, p. 173.

15. CDEB, 1925, p. 3434.

16. Chiefly at meetings in Béziers, inspired by the example of Spain in this matter. Reported in PAV, March 29, 1925, p. 294.

17. Prices as high as 300 francs the hectolitre were registered in the Midi. Production costs were estimated at 60 francs the hectolitre or, at the most, 80 francs. Brault, *Problème du vin,* p. 55.

18. SDEB, 1927, pp. 583–600; CDEB, 1927, pp. 1557–74.

19. They were now estimated in the Midi at an average of 100 francs the hectolitre. Brault, *Problème du vin,* p. 59.

20. CDEB, 1929, p. 4296.   21. JO, June 4, 1930.

22. RV, June 12, 1930, pp. 493–94; *ibid.,* July 31, 1930, pp. 45–96; PAV, November 30, 1930, p. 514.

23. RV, October 23, 1930, p. 292; Marsais, "Comment se résoudra la crise viticole," RAF, May, 1930, pp. 148–49.

24. Law of December 24, 1934. See p. 113.

25. RV, September 20, 1934, p. 187.

26. Roger, "La Viticulture et ses destinées," RAF, February, 1935, p. 36.

27. Pierre Viala, member of the Academy of Agriculture, in RV, October 25, 1934, p. 261. See also Caziot, "La Chute de la valeur de la terre," RAF, March, 1935, p. 70.

28. Roger, "La Viticulture et ses destinées," RAF, February, 1935, p. 36.

29. RV, November 15, 1934, p. 322.

30. *Ibid.,* May 16, 1935, pp. 321–22.

31. *Ibid.,* June 13, 1935, p. 275.

32. CDOC, 1931, pp. 37, 67, 71 (Annex 3156).

33. Caziot, "La Chute de la valeur de la terre," RAF, March, 1935, p. 70.

34. *Ibid.*

35. Statistics only give the amount of wine alcohol produced. It is possible however to make an estimate of the amount of wine distilled by figuring from the fact that 10 hectolitres of 10° wine give one hectolitre of distillate. Some wines, of course, are stronger or weaker than 10°, but the latter figure is probably closest to average.

36. The impetus given to distillation by extraordinary government purchases of wine alcohol in 1935 would have thrown this comparison out of perspective had the latter year been included.

37. Figured on a per capita basis, this increase comes to only 5.1 percent.

38. Professor Marres estimates that under normal conditions 10 to 12 percent of total national production is reserved for family consumption. The remaining portion of non-taxed wine presumably goes to laborers, who are given 2 litres per day worked. During harvest men receive 3 litres and women 2 litres per day. Of course a certain amount of non-taxed wine circulates (i.e., is sold) locally. Marres, *Vigne et vin,* p. 195.

39. Milhau, *Étude économetrique du prix du vin.*

40. *Ibid.,* p. 49. This assertion is preceded by an interesting demonstration showing that a closer correlation exists between wine prices and total metropolitan production than exists between wine prices and Algerian production and (although the correlation is closer) Midi production. Milhau thus makes total metropolitan production the price determinant (pp. 19–25).

41. Marres, *Vigne et vin,* p. 129.

42. In the department of Bouches-du-Rhône, where this vineyard was located, the area planted in vines increased from 21,214 hectares in 1919 to 30,230 hectares in 1930.

43. Marres, *Vigne et vin,* p. 129.

44. *Ibid.*, p. 28.   45. See p. 5.
46. JAP, August 6, 1914, p. 174.
47. RV, January 2, 1919, p. 5.
48. JAP, September 19, 1918, pp. 371–72.
49. On March 2, 1925, the Ligue des Viticulteurs, a professional group, meeting at Bordeaux, asked for a "program of action" against the hybrids. For this and further discussion of the hybrid problem, see RV, May 14, 1925, pp. 367–68; 372; also PAV, September 21, 1930, pp. 286–87.
50. RV, May 14, 1925, p. 367.
51. Ministère de l'agriculture, *Résultats généraux de l'enquête de 1929*.
52. If these figures seem a reflection on the high-yielding qualities of the hybrids, it should be pointed out that higher-yielding non-hybrid varieties such as the Aramon, are pretty much confined to the Midi, and do not do well elsewhere.
53. From 1921 to 1930 the vineyard area of the primarily viticultural department of Gironde (in which the Bordeaux vineyard is entirely situated) increased by 2 percent. During the same period the vineyard area in three neighboring departments primarily polycultural (Lot-et-Garonne, Dordogne, and Landes) increased by 12 percent.
54. The greatest percentage of increase in vineyard area registered by any department was 25.4 percent. The department was Hautes-Alpes.
55. Marres, *Vigne et vin*, p. 10.
56. Sabadie, *Nouveau Statut de la viticulture*, p. 28.
57. Marres, *Vigne et vin*, p. 28.
58. For an analysis of the debate see Volck, *Problème viticole franco-algérien*, pp. 34–55.

Algerian advantages, besides the preferential freight rates, included lighter taxes on wages and salaries, noncommercial, commercial, and industrial profits, securities and capital, and real property. On the Algerian side it was pointed out that although the tax rate on landed property was lower in Algeria than in France, the basis of valuation was so much higher that when the tax on profits was added to the land tax of the Algerian winegrower, the two taxes averaged out to 152.63 francs the hectare as opposed to 123.10 francs in France (1932). It was also noted that exemptions were greater in France than in Algeria because of the preponderance of small property in the mother country.

In the matter of transportation costs Volck estimates that even with the preferential freight rates in France, the cost of transporting a hectolitre of wine from Algeria to Paris was 6 to 10 francs greater than the cost of transporting the same amount of wine from the Midi to Paris. Volck also mentions that interest rates charged by the Crédit Agricole Mutuel were higher in Algeria than in France (they averaged 2 percent more for all types of loans). He does not mention commercial banks. However, Isnard, "Vigne et colonisation en Algérie, 1880–1947," *Annales: économies, sociétés, civilisations,* II (1947), 296, points out that the easy-credit policies of the Algerian banks were an important cause of the development of the Algerian vineyard.

Nonfiscal advantages enjoyed by Algeria were cheaper labor costs and a longer growing season, but the Algerians maintained that the former were canceled by the inefficiency and unreliability of the labor, while special weather conditions, aridity of the soil, and prevalence of vine diseases negated the latter.

59. A law of Dec. 9, 1900, gave Algeria separate legal status and a special budget. The government claimed the law was necessary for the most efficient development of the colony and in the best interests of the metropolitan budget, and did not mean an end to the policy of assimilation begun in 1881. The C.G.V., on the other hand, claimed it did, and protested the unfairness of Algeria's "fiscal autonomy," while her products competed on the metropolitan market on a basis of equality with French products (Volck, *Problème viticole franco-algérien,* pp. 34–37). A resolution adopted by the C.G.V. at Narbonne in 1933 read in part as follows: ". . . Let us tell the government clearly that we will never consent to the economic equality imposed on us with a population which the public authorities themselves have placed under a different social, administrative, and financial regime than ours, and which, for the most part, is not even made up of French citizens" (RV, June 8, 1933, p. 368).

60. Volck, *Problème viticole franco-algérien,* p. 67.

61. RV, July 1, 1920, p. 10.

62. One of the more interesting of these was to have the Algerians grow oranges. "Give them protection from Spanish oranges," the author of the proposal wrote, "and they will do it." *Le Petit Méridionale* (Montpellier), June 5, 1926.

63. One concrete result stemming from a resolution adopted at the conference was the fixing of a quota of 500,000 hectolitres a year for Tunisian wines (decree of June 5, 1926).

64. Courtin, "La Viticulture devant les pouvoirs publiques," *Revue politique et parlementaire,* CXLVII (1931), 462.

65. RV, December 18, 1930, p. 430.

66. The profits of the Algerian winegrowers were denounced as "large and scandalous." It was considered shocking that the vineyards were organized as capitalist concerns which paid dividends to their shareholders. See CDEB, p. 2883.

67. Quoted in Brault, *Problème du vin,* p. 106. David was succeeded in January of 1931 by Tardieu, who was responsible for putting through the *Statut* and who declared himself unfavorable to any discrimination against Algeria.

68. The C.G.V. seems to have been confident that the government would sponsor the Commission's proposal or an earlier *projet de loi* along similar lines. See RV, June 8, 1933, p. 367.

69. Quoted in RV, July 6, 1933, p. 367.

70. Quoted in Augé-Laribé, *Politique agricole,* p. 428.

71. Quoted in Gaston-Pastre, "Le Problème du vin," *Revue des deux mondes,* XXX (1935), 361.

72. *Ibid.,* p. 367.

73. *Comptes rendus des séances de l'Académie d'Agriculture de France,* VII (1922), 182.

74. RV, May 16, 1935, p. 321.

75. *The Treaty of Peace between the Allied and Associated Powers and Germany and Other Treaty Engagements Signed at Versailles, June 28, 1919* (London, H. M. Stationery Office), Article 269, Part X, Section I, p. 125.

76. Muglioni, *Accords commerciaux sur les vins,* pp. 184–85.

77. The quota system was abandoned after this period by the United States and wine imports from France dropped behind those from Italy.

78. *Annales des douanes, passim.* The balance of trade in wine was in favor of these countries, however.

79. Conseil National Économique, *Politique agricole destinée à réduire,* pp. 67–68.

80. The Council actually proposed doing this in the French colonies but was opposed on technical grounds by the Administration des Contributions Indirectes. Conseil National Économique, *Politique agricole destinée à réduire,* pp. 70–71.

81. *Bulletin international du vin,* 1931, p. 55.

82. Conseil National Économique, *Politique agricole destinée à réduire,* p. 68; Volck, *Problème viticole franco-algérien,* p. 26.

83. It is interesting to note that France was able to force a breach in Norway's prohibition law by pointing out the existence of a commercial treaty by which Norwegian fish received preferential treatment in return for preferential treatment of French wines. In 1921 Norway amended her prohibition law and admitted French wines of less than 14 percent alcoholic content. McConnell, "Liquor Traffic," *Encyclopaedia of the Social Sciences,* Vol. IX.

84. *Ibid.*

85. Conseil National Économique, *Politique agricole destinée à réduire,* p. 68.

86. *Ibid.* 87. *Ibid.* 88. *Ibid.* 89. AS.

90. A contemporary observer described it as being "like the Comité des Forges, one of the most powerful economic groups [in the nation]" ((Gaston-Pastre, "Le Problème du vin," *Revue de deux mondes,* XXX (1935), 361). As the largest group in the Fédération des Associations Viticoles, the C.G.V. supplied the majority of that organization's officers,

and the adherence of nearly all the Midi deputies gave the C.G.V. an overwhelming voice in the *groupe viticole* of the Chamber of Deputies.

91. PAV, November 30, 1930, p. 514.

92. RV, December 18, 1930, p. 430.

93. Decree of March 31, 1951 ("Protocol additionel à l'accord commerciel franco-italien du 7 mars 1928"), JO, April 1, 1931; *Annales des douanes,* April 9, 1931, p. 146.

94. Muglioni, *Accords commerciaux sur les vins,* p. 24.

95. *Ibid.*

96. Ministère des finances, *Statistique mensuelle du commerce extérieur de la France,* 1931.

97. RV, September 10, 1931, p. 177. It should be pointed out that the prospect of a harvest which totaled nearly 60,000,000 hectolitres cannot be discounted as the major cause of the price drop.

98. *Ibid.*

99. Article 17 of the decree stated: "The government by decrees rendered in the Council of Ministers can take in an emergency all the dispositions appropriate to the circumstances in the case where measures decreed by foreign countries are of a nature to impede French commerce." The decree was a recodification of an earlier law (1910), phrased in similar language. For a description of the law and its uses, see Haight, *French Commercial Policies,* pp. 56, 163.

100. *Arrêté* of August 27, 1931, in JO, August 28, 1931; *Annales des douanes,* September 3, 1931, p. 435.

101. "Protocole additionel à l'accord commercial franco-italien du 7 mars 1928, modifié par le protocole additionel du 16 mars 1931," Article 1, in JO, November 26, 1931; *Annales des douanes,* December 3, 1931, p. 591.

102. The French government tried to have the quantities in excess of the March 16 quota applied against the new one. Italy rejected this or any plan that would have applied the excess to subsequent quotas. The best the French were able to do was to have Italy agree that her supplementary quota at the 84 franc rate would be 10 percent less than that of Greece. Muglioni, *Accords commerciaux sur les vins,* p. 25.

103. Article 4 of the agreement stated: "The limitations on importation referred to in the present protocol are of a provisional and exceptional character and they will be abolished as soon as circumstances permit" (*Annales des douanes,* December 3, 1931, p. 591). Brault, *Problème du vin,* p. 52, says the agreement was not intended to run more than a year.

104. Although dating from the summer of 1931, when Italian imports were at their height, the following is typical of a type of sentiment aroused by the whole question of wine imports at this time:

"We know winegrowers who do not accept this situation with a light heart. One of them who is anything but an anarchist said to me recently, perhaps unconsciously remembering the gallant cry of Pétain at Verdun, 'They [imports] will not pass!' They will not pass because we will wreck the trains that bring them. It is not to be wished and not very likely that this menace will ever be put into execution, but if, in spite of controls, the price of wine remains insufficient, one may expect violent protests from the disappointed winegrowers when they see our market invaded by foreign wines." Editorial in PAV, July 10, 1931, p. 53.

105. Brault, *Problème du vin,* p. 52.

106. Decree of March 25, 1932 ("Publication et mise en application provisoire du 'modus vivendi' commercial franco-italien signé à Rome le 4 mars 1932"), in JO, April 3, 1932; *Annales des douanes,* April 17, 1932, pp. 338–45.

107. Muglioni, *Accords commerciaux sur les vins,* p. 29.

108. France was presumably justified in doing this because at the time of the November 16 agreement, both nations had pledged themselves to make "new efforts" to settle the question of wine imports. Muglioni, *Accords commerciaux sur les vins,* p. 29.

109. Decree of May 8, 1933 ("Avenant au 'modus vivendi' commercial entre la France et l'Italie signé à Paris le 10 mai 1933"), in JO, May 12, 1933; *Annales des douanes,* May 18, 1933, pp. 272–74.

110. Pinot, *Contrôle du ravitaillement,* p. 129.

111. JAP, April 13, 1919, p. 210; and September 2, 1920, p. 186.

112. Decree of December 8, 1921. In JO, December 9, 1921. For a description of the theory and workings of the coefficient system, see Haight, *French Commercial Policies,* pp. 110–12, 114–17.

113. PAV, December 11, 1921, p. 585.

114. *Annuario Estadisco de Espana,* 1920, 1921.

115. Muglioni, *Accords commerciaux sur les vins,* p. 47.

116. Decree of July 11, 1922 ("Convention franco-espagnol du 8 juillet 1922"), in JO, July 12, 1922.

117. This meant a reduction of 20 percent in the total duty.

118. CDEB, 1923, p. 860.

119. CDOC, 1923, p. 447 (Annex 5671).

120. See Table 18.

121. Before World War I France had always had a deficit in her trade balance with Spain. In 1922 the value of French exports to Spain totaled approximately 518 million francs while the value of Spanish exports to France totaled approximately 349 million francs. In 1925 these two figures stood at 1,421 million francs and 835 million francs respectively. Ministère des finances, *Statistique mensuelle du commerce extérieur de la France.*

122. *Avenant* of August 14, 1926; JO, August 15, 1926. The chief

difference between the new agreement and the old was that through it Spain recovered her liberty of tariff action against other countries. The real motivation behind the denunciation of the older agreement was apparently protectionist sentiment on the part of Spanish metallurgical and textile interests. Muglioni, *Accords commerciaux sur les vins,* p. 50.

123. RV, January 16, 1930, p. 52.

124. JO, January 12, 1930. *Annales des douanes,* January 16, 1930, pp. 26–27.

125. Resolution adopted January 10, 1930, by the Comité International du Commerce des Vins, Cidres, Spiriteux et Liqueurs. Reported in RV, February 6, 1930, p. 116.

126. *Le Matin* in an editorial described the law as good "in principle . . . but not enough thought has been given, it seems, to the fact that the question affects interests other than those of viticulture" (January 13, 1930). Resolutions against the law were passed by the chambers of commerce of Roubaix, Nantes, Saint-Nazaire and Dunkerque. Shipping interests in Bordeaux were also opposed in many cases. A good deal of the Spanish wine used in blending was of course reexported from France. The law brought reprisals from Greece and protests from Portugal as well as Spain.

127. RV, January 22, 1931, pp. 62–63.

128. Muglioni, *Accords commerciaux sur les vins,* p. 55. In 1930 the deficit of the French commercial balance with Spain was 379,848 francs; in 1931, 716,901 francs. Ministère des finances, *Statistique mensuelle du commerce extérieur de la France.*

129. Augé-Laribé claims that although manufacture benefited from and abused the system of quotas, the wine industry was the biggest practitioner of this method of limiting imports. Augé-Laribé, *Politique agricole,* pp. 418–19.

130. Decree of November 7, 1931 ("Arrangement complémentaire à la convention franco-espagnol du 8 juillet 1922 et à l'avenant du 14 août 1926 signé à Paris le 23 octobre 1931"), in JO, November 10, 1931; *Annales des douanes,* November 12, 1931, p. 537.

131. RV, April 16, 1931, p. 246.

132. Conseil National Économique, *Politique agricole de la France,* pp. 29–30.

7. GOVERNMENT EFFORTS TO LIMIT PRODUCTION AND
STABILIZE THE MARKET, *1928–38*

1. The committee's report is published in CDOC, 1933, pp. 99–136 (Annex 1270); 1934, pp. 420–44 (Annex 1270); 1935, pp. 425–39 (Annex 1270).

2. Law of April 19, 1930. It was suspended in December, 1930, and reapplied December, 1931. For a further description, see p. 110.

3. CDOC, 1930, pp. 827–29 (Annex 3365).

4. *Ibid.,* p. 829.

5. This would have made new planting prohibitive in marginal wine-growing regions, a factor that was instrumental in the defeat of this article during the subsequent parliamentary debate. A particularly strong opposition was registered by deputies from central France.

6. CDOC, 1931, p. 867 (Annex 5043).

7. Law of August 4, 1929.   8. RV, June 12, 1930, p. 494.

9. Law of January 1, 1930.

10. Law of April 19, 1930.   11. Law of January 1, 1930.

12. Quoted in Sabadie, *Nouveau Statut de la viticulture,* p. 107.

13. CDOC, 1931, p. 886 (Annex 5068).

14. CDOC, 1930, pp. 1355 ff. (Annex 3765).

15. CDEB, 1931, pp. 3262–65, 3297–98. The first addition was proposed by Léon Blum; the second by Daladier.

16. Law of July 4, 1931, Article 1, paragraph seven.

17. Quoted in Courtin, "La Viticulture devant les pouvoirs publiques," *Revue politique et parlementaire,* CXLVII (1931), 477.

18. RV, February 25, 1932, p. 128.

19. By contrast, interest shown in the daily press and by the public at large was negligible. For comment on this point see Liesse, "Le Statut du vin," *L'Économiste français,* June 27, 1931, p. 801.

For the researcher, the disparity between the great amount of attention given the crisis of 1900–1907 in the economic weeklies and the economic and political journals, and the relative neglect of the later crisis by the same publications, is striking. Certain obvious answers suggest themselves, such as the growth of state intervention in many sectors of the national economy and the technical nature of later viticultural legislation.

20. Courtin, "La Viticulture devant les pouvoirs publiques," *Revue politique et parlementaire,* VXLVII (1931), 460.

21. RV, July 31, 1931, p. 96.

22. These included the Syndicat Régional des Vignerons du Sud-Est and the Chambre d'Agriculture de Vaucluse. The former represented growers in the Rhone delta where new plantings were being made in the Camargue and neighboring areas. See pp. 76–77. In Vaucluse improved irrigation practices were responsible for a recent growth of the vineyard area. These regions and others on the Mediterranean littoral where vines were being planted in marshy and sandy areas objected particularly to the proposed limitation of plantings.

23. RV, July 31, 1930, p. 96 and *passim;* and PAV, 1930, *passim.*

24. Courtin, "La Viticulture devant les pouvoirs publiques," *Revue politique et parlementaire,* CXLVII (1931), 460.

25. "Les Correctifs apportés au projet de loi no. 3365 sur la viticulture et les positions respectifs des grandes associations agricoles ou viticoles," RAF, September, 1931, p. 282.

26. CDOC, 1930, p. 827 (Annex 3365).

27. *Ibid.*

28. CDOC, 1930, pp. 1355–67 (Annex 3765).

29. *Ibid.,* p. 1356.   30. *Ibid.*   31. *Ibid.*

32. *Ibid.,* p. 1357. Justifying this suggestion, the Commission said: "In a social as much as an economic interest we have wished by this to protect the little, the medium, and *even the big producers* against viticultural feudalism." (Italics added.)

33. In a later report the Commission suggested lowering the blockage limit to include a production of 200 hectolitres, "a figure low enough to produce an imposing mass of blocked wines and also high enough not to disperse the blockage effort on a scattering of growers, who in any case are not responsible for overproduction." CDOC, 1931, p. 867 (Annex 5043).

34. CDOC, 1931, pp. 957–58 (Annex 5120). It was specified in the proposed law, however, that the revenue from the tax on yields and from fines for failure to comply with other provisions would be spent on propaganda to encourage the consumption of wine at home and abroad. After passage of the bill a government agency was set up which until 1941 carried on an ambitious advertising program in favor of wine.

35. CDOC, 1931, pp. 885–87 (Annex 5068).

36. *Ibid.,* p. 886.   37. CDEB, 1931, p. 3078.

38. There was a considerable development in the debate of the concept of an *artisanat viticole* passing from father to son, rooting men to the soil, and strengthening the social bases of the nation.

39. CDOC, 1931, p. 867 (Annex 5043).

40. *Ibid.,* pp. 867–68.

41. CDEB, 1931, p. 2881.   42. *Ibid.,* p. 3087.   43. *Ibid.,* p. 2933.

44. *Ibid.,* p. 2948. It was claimed that a 50 percent drop in the price paid to the grower brought a drop of only 20 centimes the litre in Paris.

45. For a mention of the traditional Socialist affiliation of the agricultural Midi, see Siegfried, *France: A Study in Nationality,* pp. 80–82.

46. CDEB, 1931, p. 2956.

47. *Ibid.,* p. 2957. These reflections led to proposals to have the law operate on a regional basis. The government simply replied that this would make the law "inoperative"—"the territorial formula corresponds to nothing" (*ibid.*). Tact and the bias of the debate probably prevented

the government from mentioning the advantages of a territorial formula for the Midi and Algeria.

48. The dilemma involved in this question is well summarized by the witty remarks in the Chamber of M. Jean Hennessy, a former Minister of Agriculture. Although declaring himself in favor of limiting planting, he had this to say to the government about the tax on yields: "You are proposing nothing less than to say to the winegrower who cultivates well: 'You have been to the school of Montpellier, that excellent agricultural academy for which the whole world envies us. You have known how to choose your plants and select your grafts. You have planted with care. You have cultivated your land in a way so as to develop its fertility. You have given to this land supplementary fertilizers. You have sulfured your vine, you have protected it against all maladies. For your harvest you will perhaps be crowned by your *comice agricole*. You will receive the rewards of your efforts; you will be named to the Order of Agricultural Merit. But at the very same moment a law which has been proposed by an imposing number of ministers will make you pay a tax.' . . . This principle I do not admit, it is unfavorable to good agriculture. Will you come next to ask us to afflict the most 'lactiferous' cows with a tax?" CDEB, 1931, p. 3175.

49. *Ibid.*, p. 2951.   50. *Ibid.*   51. *Ibid.*, pp. 3094–95.
52. *Ibid.*, p. 3078   53. *Ibid.*, pp. 3278–79.   54. *Ibid.*, pp. 2876–77.
55. *Ibid.*, pp. 2879, 3281.

56. This privilege was somewhat restricted by the fact that if new plantings brought production to more than 500 hectolitres, the additional wine was taxed at the relatively heavy rate of 50 francs the hectolitre.

57. The average was to be furnished the government by the Chambers of Agriculture and of Commerce of these cities.

In the light of earlier discussions, in this study, of Midi prices, the government's action makes an interesting and official confirmation of the preponderant effect of Midi prices on the whole wine market.

58. One reason may have been that the law of April 19, 1930, although suspended at the end of that year, was still on the books with provisions to put it in operation again if the total stock of wine should come to more than 75 million hectolitres. The law was supposed to effect voluntary distillation, but provided for compulsory distilling if a certain quota of alcohol was not met—a measure which in fact had to be enforced after June 20, 1930.

59. The grounds for rejection are interesting in that they show what turned out to be an unjustified belief in a fat-year, lean-year cycle. In the words of the Commission: "As seductive as it [compulsory distilling] appears from certain points of view, we have thrust it aside, given notably the practical difficulty of so generalized a distillation and the

danger there would be in destroying once and for all an asset when a reserve of wine is essential to guard against an eventual deficit the following year and a resulting excessive rise in the price of wine." CDOC, 1931, p. 867 (Annex 5043).

60. For a further discussion of the *carburant national,* see pp. 125–28.

61. One observer called it "a requisition almost without indemnification." Sabadie, *Nouveau Statut de la viticulture,* p. 122.

The prices paid for compulsorily distilled wine alcohol in 1931 ranged from 250 francs (100° rectified) to 200 francs (60° to 70°, raw alcohol). These prices were roughly equal to beet-alcohol prices, and about two times less than the price of wine alcohol on the open market.

Since ten hectolitres of wine (10°) when completely distilled produce one hectolitre of alcohol (100°), the first price represented a return of 25 francs for each hectolitre of wine, distilled. Distilling costs took up about half this sum, leaving a net return of 12.50 francs. In December, 1931, when compulsory distilling went into effect, the average price of a hectolitre of wine on the five markets of the Midi was about 100 francs.

62. In the compulsory-distilling provisions of the earlier law of April 19, 1930, the percentages had ranged from 10 to 33 percent. They were reduced somewhat by a complicated schedule of exemptions and abatements. Also, the price paid for the alcohol distilled was higher, being roughly equivalent to the open-market price.

63. CDEB, 1931, p. 3320.

64. My source is Ministère de l'agriculture, *Résultats généraux de l'enquête de 1929.* The percentages abstracted from the *enquête* are not exact because production and yield groupings in the *enquête* tables do not correspond with those of the law of July 4, 1931. Also, there is no table combining yield and production such as would be necessary for a correct accounting. If inexact, the percentages quoted probably err on the conservative side. Estimates that indicate even greater gaps in the law have been observed in some of the primary and secondary source material consulted.

65. *Ibid.,* pp. 482, 493, 497.

66. PAV, September 20, 1931, p. 274.

67. Decree of December 19, 1931. The percentages to be blocked were fixed from 7 percent for productions of 400 to 1000 hectolitres up to 17 percent for productions of 50,000 or more hectolitres. The amounts blocked in this manner were to be increased by 10 percent if yield per hectare was 60 to 80 hectolitres and up to 50 percent if it was 150 hectolitres or more.

68. The *Statut* had nothing to say about such a contingency, but subsequent interpretations by the Service des Contributions Indirectes ruled that the last-named wines were blocked in their entirety.

69. Decree of December 24, 1931.

70. Decree of December 22, 1931. This "double distilling" was criti-cized, but it should be pointed out that the price paid for wine alcohol under the law of April 19, 1930, was exactly twice that paid under the law of July 4, 1931. The law of April 19, 1930, does not appear to have been abrogated, but after 1931 all compulsory distilling was carried out under the provisions of the law of July 4, 1931, and its subsequent versions.

71. Decree of December 19, 1931. It was stated, however, that in no case could the quantities blocked exceed 50 percent of a grower's harvest.

72. Both the double-blockage and the late-blockage decree were attacked on legal grounds. The language of the *Statut* indicated that blockage should be decreed *before* the harvest and there were no specific provisions saying it could be decreed after the harvest. Double blockage had absolutely no foundation in either the *Statut* or the law of April 19, 1930, and appears to have been quite arbitrary. Objections were raised against it in the Council of State. Dalloz, *Recueil périodique et critique,* 1932, p. 73.

73. The winegrowers of the department of Haut-Garonne offered to "give" their wines to the government in view of the impossibility of distilling them in their region. PAV, February 7, 1932, p. 130.

74. Sabadie, *Nouveau Statut de la viticulture,* p. 163.

75. This inspired a lawsuit, the subject of much comment, between a grower and dealer to determine where the responsibility for blockage lay in sales effected before December 19, 1931. The Appeals Court of Montpellier decided that the dealer was subject to blockage. The case was not decided until June 15, 1932, but there does not seem to have been any organized move on the part of the government to follow up on the precedent set by the decision. Subsequent legislation, made a repetition of the situation created by the late-blockage decree impossible. The chief significance of the case, therefore, was that it added a large element of uncertainty to sales in the first half of 1932. For a text of the decision, see Dalloz, *Recueil hebdomadaire de jurisprudence,* 1932, pp. 501–2.

76. The *Progrès agricole et viticole* spoke indiscriminately of the "ruin" of the winegrowers and the "bullying" of the law, but the *Revue de viticulture* gave some detailed figures showing a loss of over 1,300,000 francs for a large *domaine* in Algeria producing over 50,000 hectolitres. The loss was attributed to double blockage and compulsory distilling. At the very least double blockage and the confusion surrounding the various decrees created more ill will than necessary for the *Statut* in its first year of operation. PAV, December 13, 1931, p. 561; RV, June 2, 1932, p. 369.

77. Estimate based on weekly market quotations, JAP, 1931, 1932.

78. Decree of July 22, 1932.

79. Decree of February 14, 1933. The simultaneous release of the blocked portions of the 1931 harvest and the lifting of the provisional blockage probably helped drive prices down. On February 1, 1933, they averaged 135 francs the hectolitre on the five markets of the Midi; on March 3, 108 francs; on April 1, 126 francs.

80. RV, December 6, 1934, p. 366.

81. The law assured the grower, however, that distillation could not exceed 33 percent of his harvest if production was equal or inferior to 5,000 hectolitres, or 50 percent if it was greater.

82. These were the Noah, Othello, Isabella, Jacquez, Clinton, and Herbmont. All were American hybrids introduced during the phylloxera epidemic. According to the new law, wines coming from vineyards already planted in these grapes could not be put on the regular market but could, until July 31, 1942, be sold directly to consumers or shops within the *arrondissement* where they were produced.

83. The law read: "Whoever will have been convicted of having knowingly and with the end of procuring an illegitimate profit practiced, tried to practice, or provoked a rise in prices not justified by the conditions of the market and the usages of commerce, will be punished by a fine of 50 to 5,000 francs and, in the case of a repetition, to imprisonment for one to six months."

84. RV, July 4, 1935, p. 13.

85. The previous limits (law of July 4, 1931) had been 400 hectolitres for blockage and the tax on yields, and 500 hectolitres for compulsory distilling.

86. The producers of 100 hectolitres or less were exonerated from all but one period of detention.

87. For a further description of this development, see pp. 146–50.

88. Marc is made by distilling stems and pulp left in the vats after the grapes have been pressed. It will be remembered that "second wines" or *piquettes* were made by passing hot water over this fermenting mash. Thus by encouraging distillation of marc the government discouraged the making of *piquettes*. A further step in this direction was the compulsory distilling of marc up to three quarters the amount of compulsorily distilled wine alcohol (law of July 12, 1937).

89. See p. 148.

90. RV, December 26, 1935, p. 410.

91. *Ibid.*   92. *Ibid.*   93. CDEB, 1936, pp. 66–69.

94. Cellier, *Projets d'office national du vin,* p. 111.

95. RV, September 30, 1937, p. 239.

96. *Ibid.,* January 7, 1939, p. 21.

97. For bringing blockage into play these had been 70 million hectolitres for a production of 400 hectolitres, 78 million hectolitres for a

production of 300 hectolitres, and 84 million hectolitres for a production of 200 hectolitres. The new quantities were 76, 84, and 90 million hectolitres respectively. They were the same for compulsory distilling except that the lowest quantity affecting compulsory distillation, which had been 72 million hectolitres, became 78 million.

98. Law of December 15, 1937.

99. Decree-law of May 31, 1938. The schedule was also made tighter by including productions of 250 and 350 hectolitres when the total of wine available was 81 to 84 million hectolitres and 75 to 78 million hectolitres respectively. The new law also forged blockage and the staggered-release system into one instrument, making the percentages of the latter operative on the entire harvest rather than on the unblocked portions of it.

100. RV, November 24, 1938, p. 517.

101. An interesting footnote to this consideration was offered by an editorial in the *Revue de viticulture,* which read in part: "We know well that compulsory pulling up [of vines] would be the heroic method for making permanent overproduction disappear, but where could be found a parliament or a government to vote and impose such a measure and triumph over the economic, political, and sentimental objections which would be offered against it?" RV, January 24, 1935, p. 65.

102. Some of these were the exemption of *vins d'appellations d'origine* and wines destined for export from blockage and distillation. It was claimed that a lot of ordinary wine was appearing as *vin d'appellation.* Wines presumably destined for export sometimes turned up on the domestic market. PAV, February 9, 1936, p. 129.

103. Augé-Laribé speaks of the general practice of dividing up a property between members of the same family to escape the blockage and distillation limits (*Politique agricole,* p. 439). Edouard Barthe, long-time head of the Commission des Boissons in the Chamber, reported clandestine plantings in some regions.

104. I am here following the general custom of referring to all viticultural legislation enacted from 1931 through 1938 as the *Statut.*

105. Milhau, "Sur l'économétrie et ses applications," *Revue d'économie politique,* LII (1938), 124–25.

106. Augé-Laribé, *Politique agricole,* p. 440.

107. Milhau, "Sur l'économétrie et ses applications," *Revue d'économie politique,* LII (1938), 124. This he attributes to the fact that the last three tenths were "subtracted" from the 1935–36 season and "carried over" to the next with the new harvest, rather than to any *"pouvoir interne de hausse"* of the staggered-release system. Without substraction the best the latter can do, acording to Milhau, is "regularize prices around the average."

108. *Ibid.,* p. 123.

109. See Porcher, *Le Marché des vins,* p. 24.

110. According to one observer, "the paradoxical result" of the law was a "frenzy of planting" (Roger, "La Viticulture et ses destinées," RAF, February, 1935, p. 38). Gaëtan Pirou suggests that the rush was encouraged by the belief of the small growers that the government's program would permanently raise prices. Pirou is also among those who gave a negative opinion on the efficacy of blockage and the staggered release. Pirou, *La Valeur et les prix,* pp. 454–55.

8. THE WINEGROWERS AND THE STATE ALCOHOL MONOPOLY

1. See p. 36.   2. JO, July 1, 1916.

3. CDOC, 1915, pp. 556–64 (Annex 964).

4. By 1923 Barthe was head of the Chamber's powerful Commission des Boissons, which initiated all viticultural legislation, and its less official *groupe viticole,* an important gathering of deputies from the wine-growing regions. He held these posts until 1940, and continued to exercise an important influence in the Fédération des Associations Viticoles after World War II.

5. See CDOC, 1915, pp. 571–72 (Annex 992) ; pp. 913–20 (Annex 1241) ; 1916, pp. 795–857 (Annex 2034) ; pp. 960–66 (Annex 2165) ; pp. 891–93 (Annex 2210) ; pp. 1066–68 (Annex 2310) ; 1917, pp. 558–68 (Annex 2943) ; pp. 796–98 (Annex 3387) ; pp. 1642–45 (Annex 3736) ; 1918, pp. 284–87 (Annex 4387) ; p. 372 (Annex 4430).

6. Marbeau, *Régime des alcools,* p. 140.

7. For the summary of the alcohol situation in 1919, I am in large part indebted to Weill, *Monopole de l'alcool,* pp. 45–52.

8. *Ibid.,* p. 47.

9. Laws of December 31, 1919; July 31, 1920; December 31, 1920; September 30, 1921; June 30, 1922; August 1, 1924.

10. RV, April 28, 1921, p. 320.   11. *Ibid.,* May 26, 1921, p. 396.

12. CDOC, 1921, pp. 1885–86 (Annex 2797).

13. PAV, July 3, 1921, p. 14.

14. Weill, *Monopole de l'alcool,* p. 197.

15. PAV, July 16, 1921, pp. 371–72.

16. *Bulletin de la Société des Agriculteurs de France,* May, 1922, p. 133.

17. CDOC, 1922, pp. 317–20 (Annex 5092).

18. CDEB, 1923, p. 413.   19. *Ibid.,* p. 415.

20. *Ibid.* This view was based on the fact that the beet is a rotation crop which enriches the soil. But when one considers that in 1923 approximately 275,000 hectares were planted in beets and more than 5 million hectares in wheat, the argument appears somewhat demagogic.

21. *Ibid.,* p. 416.   22. *Ibid.*   23. JO, March 1, 1923.

24. Rooy, *Le Carburant national,* p. 21. Weill, *Monopole de l'alcool.* pp. 209, 224–25.

25. Quoted in Weill, *Monopole de l'alcool,* p. 199.

26. Rooy, *Le Carburant national,* p. 49. Weill, *Monopole de l'alcool,* p. 209. This was also realized in government circles and probably by some members of the Chamber. Weill states that this consideration was the reason for a three-month delay in the introduction of Barthe's bill.

27. In 1923 alcohol sold for the *carburant national* equaled 1.45 percent of the quantity of motor fuel imported into France. In 1930, it equaled 1.3 percent.

28. Marbeau, *Régime des alcools,* pp. 155–63. For a dissenting opinion see Rooy, *Le Carburant national,* pp. 30–44. For a summary of opinions on the merits and disadvantages of the *carburant national,* see Weill, *Monopole de l'alcool,* pp. 219–24.

29. Weill, *Monopole de l'alcool,* Appendix B, Tables VI and XVI.

30. Figures from Rooy, *Le Carburant national,* p. 48.

31. *Ibid.,* p. 11.

32. Weill, *Monopole de l'alcool,* p. 160.

33. BSL.   34. *Ibid.*   35. Weill, *Monopole de l'alcool,* p. 160.

36. BSL.

37. Henri Hitier, "La Betterave industrielle," *L'Expansion économique,* January, 1920, quoted in Rooy, *Le Carburant national,* p. 61.

38. Rooy, *Le Carburant national,* p. 60.

39. BSL.   40. *Ibid.*   41. CDOC, 1934, p. 421 (Annex 1270).

42. *Ibid.,* p. 421.   43. *Ibid.*   44. BSL.

45. Law of April 30, 1921.   46. BSL.

47. PAV, August 25, 1929, pp. 174–75. See also *ibid.,* January 8, 1928, p. 33; March 11, 1928, p. 281.

48. Ministère des finances, *Tableau général du commerce,* 1910–1914.

49. Rectification is the process whereby alcohol is purified by successive distillations until a "neutral," or pure, spirit (i.e., containing no acid or alkaline properties) is obtained.

50. Marbeau, *Régime des alcools,* p. 227.

51. Law of December 25, 1923; law of August 26, 1925.

52. CDOC, 1934, p. 421 (Annex 1270).

53. *Vinage* is a term used to describe fortifying wine by adding alcohol. This process is used in the manufacture of sherry, port, and similar wines which the French call *vins de liqueur,* to distinguish them from true wines. The best fortified wines, such as native sherries and ports, have wine alcohol added to them, but the availability of cheaper "industrial" alcohols in France made the use of the latter for *vinage* widespread. Their use was also encouraged, from the point of view of ex-

port, by the high cost of French wine alcohol in comparison with the cost of wine alcohol in Portugal and Spain.

Mutage is a term used to describe the process whereby the fermentation of the must (grape juice drawn off or pressed from the leavings in the vats) is stopped by the addition of alcohol. This gives a product called *mistelle,* which is the basis of the numerous wine *apéritifs* manufactured in France.

54. BSL.

55. Law of June 25, 1920. This was the highest-priced alcohol sold by the Service, but sales averaged only around 6,000 hectolitres a year until wine alcohol captured this outlet.

56. Weill, *Monopole de l'alcool,* Appendix B, Table XVI. PAV, March 11, 1928, p. 281; August 25, 1929, p. 175.

57. RV, January 30, 1930, pp. 94–95.

58. Weill, *Monopole de l'alcool,* Appendix B, Table XVI.

59. *Ibid.,* p. 129. See also pp. 177, 229–30.

60. Sales to this source show the following fluctuations during the same period (Weill, *Monopole de l'alcool,* Appendix B, Table XVI):

Year	Hectolitres	Year	Hectolitres
1921	6,521	1926	no sales
1922	10,634	1927	no sales
1923	2,549	1928	10,563
1924	6,731	1929	9,714
1925	5,615	1930	60

61. BSL.

62. Weill, *Monopole de l'alcool,* Appendix B, Table XII.

63. Resolutions of the Confédération Générale des Planteurs de Betteraves, quoted in PAV, March 11, 1928, p. 279.

64. Weill, *Monopole de l'alcool,* pp. 245–46.

65. CDEB, 1930, pp. 1629–30. Barthe, in presenting the bill to the Chamber, gave a long summary of the positions taken and the compromises effected at these meetings, with the hope, no doubt, of preventing debate.

66. *Ibid.,* p. 1630. The production of synthetic alcohol in 1930 amounted to only 17,700 hectolitres or one half of one percent of toal alcohol production. Synthetic alcohol was classified as a "natural" alcohol.

67. *Ibid.,* p. 1632.   68. *Ibid.,* p. 1687.

69. There were in France prior to 1931 three grades of gasoline in popular use: the *carburant tourisme* for automobiles, the *carburant poids lourds,* a cheaper gasoline for trucking, transport, and the less sensitive automobile engines, and the *carburant national.* The latter was sold from pumps decorated with the national colors. The cost of installing a third pump for a gas that had to sell for less than the *poids lourds* and

which was never available in sufficient amounts for quantity sales has been cited to explain the reluctance of gasoline retailers to accept the *carburant national*. Numile, "L'Alcool et l'essence français carburant national," *L'Économiste français,* August 31, 1935, pp. 260–61.

70. A Decree of March 23, 1933, subsequently required 10 to 15 percent of alcohol to be mixed with the *carburant tourisme* so that theoretically every motor vehicle in France should have consumed some alcohol along with gasoline. Gasoline refiners and distributors, however, created a new grade of carburant, the *carburant tourisme sans alcool*. A decree of August 8, 1935, forbade the description *sans alcool* to be used in connection with the sale of gasoline, and a decree of September 28, 1935, raised the percentage of alcohol that importers of motor fuel were obliged to buy from 10 to 15 percent. Still, in 1936, when a record 3,835,361 hectolitres of alcohol were sold for carburation, this quantity equaled only about 5.6 percent of motor-fuel imports. This was a real gain over the percentage of 1.3 registered in 1930, but it shows that the *carburant national* was a failure in terms of the fulsome hopes held for it in 1923.

71. Weill, *Monopole de l'alcool,* p. 71.

72. BSL.

73. *Bulletin de la Chambre Syndicale des Distillateurs en gros de Paris et de la région parisienne.* Prices quoted are for the Paris market.

74. Sales for *vinage* and *mutage* were 118,251 hectolitres in 1931; 56,294 hectolitres in 1932; 10,896 hectolitres in 1933. Figures are from Aumage, *Régime économique de l'alcool.*

75. Banque Nationale pour le Commerce et l'Industrie, *Bulletin d'information économique,* May, 1936.

76. "Le Marché de l'alcool en France," RAF, June, 1936, p. 312. Figures quoted are for the end of July, 1934. The BSL gives a total stock of 3,225,459 hectolitres for 1934 but does not contain the interesting breakdown between natural and industrial alcohol.

77. *Bulletin de la Chambre Syndicale des Distillateurs en gros de Paris et de la région parisienne.*

78. BSL.

79. Aumage, *Régime économique de l'alcool,* p. 39.

80. CDEB, 1934, p. 3241.   81. *Ibid.*   82. *Ibid.*

83. *Ibid.,* p. 3233.   84. *Ibid.,*   85. *Ibid.,* p. 3234.

86. *Ibid.,* p. 3237

87. This was to prevent *eaux-de-vie* bought for blending from being used for *vinage* and *mutage.*

88. AS.   89. BSL.

90. Aumage, *Régime économique de l'alcool,* p. 103.

91. From 1933 through 1935 annual beet-alcohol production averaged 16 percent more than the quota figure.

92. CDEB, 1934, p. 3233.
93. "Le Marché de l'alcool en France," RAF, June, 1936, p. 313.
94. RV, August 1, 1935, p. 82.   95. *Ibid.*
96. JO, March 21, 1939.
97. Augé-Laribé, *Politique agricole,* p. 426.
98. These were popularly known as the *décrets-lois de la vie chère* because they brought among other things increased taxes on wine, a one percent sales tax for rearmanent, and the possibility of an increase in the price of bread due to the stopping of subsidies to the Office des Blés. They caused sporadic demonstrations by workers and peasants, chiefly Communist-inspired, of short duration and little impact, although there was much grumbling.
99. Unlike the Service des Alcools, the Office des Blés was almost entirely dependent on government subsidies. In the less than two years since its organization it had accumulated a deficit of 2,800,000,000 francs.
100. JO, April 22, 1939.
101. Weill, *Monopole de l'alcool,* Appendix B, Table XVI.
102. *Ibid.*
103. Aumage, *Régime économique de l'alcool,* p. 28. This sum was less, however, than any two years' profits (revenue from the motor-fuel import surtax included) during the regime in force from 1923 through 1931.
104. *Ibid.,* p. 38.
105. In 1937, for example, a net deficit of 240,040,200 francs (losses of 520,764,000 francs in 1936 and profits of 280,723,800 francs in 1937) in the *caisse annexe de la viticulture* was wiped out by a decree-law of August 25, 1937, which permitted the *caisse annexe* to credit the value (375,238,200 francs) of the amount by which the purchases of wine alcohol by the *caisse générale* fell short of quotas in 1936 and 1937. *Bilan fourni par le directeur de la régie commerciale à la réunion du Comité des Alcools tenue à Paris le 16 novembre 1937,* quoted in Sabadie, "La Dernière Réunion du Comité Supérieur des Alcools," *Bulletin mensuel: Société Centrale d'Agriculture de l'Aude,* January 1938, p. 44.
106. BSL. These figures raise the question of the government's concern in 1939 with granting no more subsidies to the Service. Perhaps the best available answer is Aumage's characterization of the Service as a *compte occulte* which did not figure in the series of extra-budgetary accounts (Aumage, *Régime économique de l'alcool,* p. 14).
There are two entries allotted to the Service in the *Compte Générale de l'Administration des Finances, Compte de Trésorie,* but they show financial transactions of a much greater magnitude than those recorded in the summaries of the Service's operations quoted by the authorities cited in this chapter. The BSL in its abstract of the entries in the *Compte Générale* points out that only the relations of the Service with

the Treasury are involved, not the operations of the Service itself. But because of the favorable balance indicated for the Treasury, the figures throw no light on the problem of subsidies.

In 1950 it was revealed that nonrepayable advances to the Service were hidden under the rubric of advances for the current operations of the Treasury. There would appear to be a need for a study of the unusual financing of the Service.

107. Radio speech delivered April 21, 1939, to defend the economy measures adopted by the government that day. Quoted in "Chronique financière," *Revue politique et parlementaire*, XLVI (1939), 333.

108. Reynaud did not give a breakdown; this is a projection from motor-fuel and alcholic-beverage import figures (Ministère des finances, *Statistique mensuelle du commerce extérieur*) and wine and cider production figures (AS) which indicate that Reynaud's estimate only included surtaxes on these items which went directly to the Service less returns to the Treasury from surpluses in the Service's general account and the reimbursement from the viticultural account of domestic taxes lost through mixing wine alcohol with gasoline.

109. Aumage, *Régime économique de l'alcool*, p. 83.

110. A very rough projection of the revenue actually lost on this account would be 630 million francs.

111. BSL.   112. SDEB, 1936, p. 167.

113. CDEB, 1933, p. 3345.

114. In 1937 taxes represented 56 percent of the purchase price of a hectolitre of gasoline.

115. CDOC, 1937, p. 514 (Annex 3396).

116. The interesting observation has been made that delegates from consumer organizations were present at meetings of the Interministerial Commission on Viticulture and while asking for guarantees against an exaggerated rise in the retail price of wine, they put themselves on record as favoring a stable price for the growers. They "constantly" approved viticultural legislation from July 4, 1931, on, proposed to help the winegrowers out of their production difficulties. See Défossé, *La Place du consommateur*, pp. 94–96.

117. Clough, *France: A History of National Economics*, p. 367.

118. Grinberg, "Le Régime des alcools et les branches organisées de l'économie agricole française," *Revue d'économie politique*, LII (1938), 428.

119. Commentary by M. Jean-Charles Leroy, Chef du Contentieux des appellations d'origine au Ministère de l'agriculture, *Annuaire de législation française*, 1932, p. 77.

120. Courtin, "La Viticulture devant les pouvoirs publiques," *Revue politique et parlementaire*, CXLVII (1931), 460.

9. THE WINEGROWERS AND THE GOVERNMENT, *1939–53*

1. Quoted in RV, September 7, 1939, p. 227.

2. Reported in PAV, September 10, 1939, p. 206.

3. This was the decree-law of July 29, 1939, "*relatif à la famille et à la natalité française.*" One section was entitled "Lutte contre l'alcoolisme." Among other things the law raised the *droits de consommation* on alcoholic beverages including *apéritifs* and forbade the opening of any new cafés, cabarets, or *débits de boissons* in places where there already existed one for each 300 people.

4. PAV, September 10, 1939, p. 206.

5. Since 1931 the revenue from the tax on excessive yields of wines had been used to finance a propaganda campaign to increase wine drinking. The role of this campaign insofar as it affected the military wine ration has been criticized as "government-inspired *consommation à outrance* . . . by which the French infantryman, like his father as Verdun, would win the '*drôle de guerre*' while promoting the disposal of [wine] stocks in danger [of nonconsumption]." Dérobert, *L'Économie de l'alcoolisme,* p. 43.

6. PAV, September 19, 1929, p. 207.

7. RV, February 29, 1940, p. 110.

8. "Les Récoltes viticoles de 1939 à 1944," RV, November, 1945, p. 6. This phenomenon was attributed to the fact that wine tended to reach metropolitan centers more slowly, keeping demand up in these regions while in other regions closer to the vineyards there was an immediate demand because of the concentration of troops. Mobilization was also believed to have created a general increase in consumption over the previous years.

9. "Les Récoltes viticoles de 1939 à 1944," RV, November, 1945, pp. 6–8.

10. Combes, *Dix Ans d'histoire viticole,* p. 25.

11. See Table 13.   12. Law of July 30, 1940.

13. During World War I only bread and sugar had their price fixed at all levels of production and distribution. The price of meat was fixed at the retail level and partially controlled at wholesale by government purchases. The prices of other foods and goods were fixed at the wholesale level. Wine, as has been noted, escaped price fixing. See Pinot, *Contrôle du ravitaillement,* pp. 193–206.

14. Law of December 2, 1940.

15. It has been suggested that the reason for this was that in the disorganization immediately following the armistice prefects had fixed excessively high prices to attract food and foodstuffs to their departments. Combes, *Dix Ans d'histoire viticole,* p. 38.

16. *Ibid.,* pp. 82–85.

17. It is almost superfluous to point out that a great deal of wine was sold on the black market, but this was done chiefly and most successfully in polycultural regions close to important consumption centers. The Midi growers with their large production found it difficult to escape price controls, although barter offered some relief.

18. Combes, *Dix Ans d'histoire viticole,* p. 82.

19. Douarche, *Le Vin et la vigne,* p. 67.

20. This criticism is perhaps unfair. The Vichy government could not very well have announced a large-scale program for pulling up vines in the face of wartime wine shortages.

21. Law of October 10, 1941.

22. Ministerial order of October 6, 1941. The minimum alcoholic content was fixed at 6.5 percent. Good wines usually contain from 10 to 12 percent alcohol. For a description of earlier legislation on alcoholic content, see p. 95.

23. Law of October 13, 1941. For a descripton of *piquettes,* see p. 13.

24. Ministerial order of August 13, 1942.

25. Law of November 16, 1942. The law of December 24, 1934, had prohibited any new planting of these varieties but permitted wine from already existing vines to be sold under certain conditons until July 31, 1942. (See p. 245, note 82.)

26. Contributions Indirectes, letter of June 30, 1942.

27. Compulsory distilling had been carried out after the harvest of 1940. This harvest was light in France and moderate in Algeria, but there were substantial stocks left from the bumper harvest of 1939. This distilling, unfortunate in view of later shortages, has been criticized as being an example of "dogmatic Malthusianism" resulting from the preoccupation, since 1931, with the concept of a plethoric market. Milhau, "L'Avenir de la viticulture française," *Revue économique,* IV (1953), 718.

Combes attributes this distilling to fright caused by a very temporary drop in wine prices due to lack of transport and the disorganization of the country. Combes, *Dix Ans d'histoire viticole,* p. 17.

28. Decree-law of July 23, 1940.

29. Law of August 22, 1940.

30. PAV, June 16, 1940, p. 473.

31. Law of August 22, 1940.

32. Douarche, *Le Vin et la vigne,* p. 76.

33. Ministerial order of August 31, 1943.

34. Ministerial order of February 9, 1943. These wines had been expressly left free of all the restrictions and controls of the *Statut.* They were not requisitioned during World War I. This was the first legislation that touched them, other than fiscal legislation and the long series

of laws which since the beginning of the century had attempted to delimit their region of origin and otherwise protect their name and quality from imitation.

35. Douarche, *Le Vin et la vigne,* p. 76.

36. Editorial in RV, November, 1946, p. 386.

37. PAV, December 10–31, 1944, p. 169.

38. *Ibid.,* p. 170.

39. *Ibid.,* January 7–28, 1945, p. 21.   This organization would seem to be the successor of the Confédération de Défense Viticole et de Propagande du Vin.   See pp. 99–100.

40. *Ordonnance* of June 14, 1945.

41. For the period 1930–39 the average annual yield per hectare in the four chief winegrowing departments of the Midi had been 50.8 hectolitres; for the rest of France, 32 hectolitres.

42. It will be remembered that this method of quoting wine prices was used in the Midi markets (100 francs the degree-hectolitre being equivalent to 1000 francs the hectolitre for a wine of 10° alcoholic content).   With the adoption of price fixing, and the revaluation of the currency, the use of this method became generalized.   Prices were fixed by regions with the lowest set in the Midi.   The average price of wine in 1946 was 1,380 francs the hectolitre.

43. Ministerial order of August 30, 1945.

44. Decree of September 4, 1945.

45. RV, November, 1945, p. 10.

46. ANCDOC, 1946, pp. 646–47 (Annex 673).

47. *Ibid.,* 1946, p. 696 (Annex 1005).   The abolishing of the "nest egg" appears to be another example of parliamentary bias in favor of the small grower.   The argument summarized above also took note of "great dissatisfaction" with the "nest egg" and a resolution passed against it by the local congress of the Confédération Générale des Agriculteurs de France in Hérault.   But as far as I have been able to determine the C.G.V. and the F.A.V. did not adopt a similar stand.

48. *Ordonnance* of August 15, 1945.

49. PAV, October 20–27, 1946, p. 254.

50. Ministerial order of September 9, 1947.

51. Law of August 13, 1947.

52. Ministerial order of September 25, 1947.

53. Ministerial order of February 4, 1947.

54. This price was proposed for Midi wines and was based on the production costs of a 9° wine coming from a property producing 50 hectolitres the hectare.   Other prices quoted subsequently in the text were based on the same considerations.

The Midi was considered the "pivot zone" of price fixing.   Thus another factor for determining prices, besides yield and alcoholic content, was the division of France into different viticultural zones, taking into account regional variations in production methods, the cost of which was reflected in the higher prices set for non-Midi wines. Algerian wines were, of course, priced lower than Midi wines, but their prices were set separately by decree of the governor-general of Algeria.

55. Ministerial order of September 10, 1946.

56. Combes, *Dix Ans d'histoire viticole,* p. 70.

57. *Ibid.,* p. 72.   58. *Ibid.,* p. 74.

59. ANDOC, 1949, pp. 1571–90 (Annex 4485). It is impossible to either overemphasize or evaluate the dimensions of the black market. RV (June, 1947, p. 180), mentions 5 million hectolitres of wine out of about 20 million hectolitres assigned to the Ministry of Food Supply in 1947 as being "unaccounted for." The parliamentary report does not give an over-all estimate. But in twenty closely printed pages it reveals a sorry story of large and illegal shipments of wine to Belgium and Switzerland, and of shipments from Algeria for the Ministry of Food Supply which simply vanished from the docks at Sète.

The findings of the committee which had been set up at the instigation of Yves Farge, the energetic Minister of Food Supply, implicated members of the Premier's (Felix Gouin) family and staff. No legal action was taken, but the inquiry is said to have cost Gouin his presidential aspirations. A sordid tale of influence peddling in the Ministry of Food Supply is told by Jean Galtier-Boissière, "L'Affaire du vin," *Crapouillot,* "Les Scandales de la IVᵉ," Tome II (Special number), no date, pp. 23–32.

Farge wrote a book about his experiences in the ministry called *Le Pain de la corruption.* It brought him a libel suit, from which he was successfully acquitted. He was dropped from the ministry after five months for having, as Alexander Werth puts it, "trodden on too many toes." Werth, *France, 1940–55,* p. 319.

60. PAV, February 16–23, 1947, p. 143.

61. Combes, *Dix Ans d'histoire viticole,* p. 74.

62. Ministerial order of September 4, 1947.

63. Quoted in Combes, *Dix Ans d'histoire viticole,* p. 76. This was a rhetorical and despairing statement. M. Philip was an avowed *dirigiste,* but the argument that decontrol was the only way to stamp out the black market had carried the day. Rationing of bread had been abandoned at the beginning of the year.

64. *Ibid.,* p. 79.

65. Ministerial order of October 30, 1948.

66. Ministerial order of November 18, 1945.

67. Combes, *Dix Ans d'histoire viticole,* p. 79.

68. Reported in *Agriculture pratique,* April, 1949, p. 164.

69. *Viticulture-Arboriculture,* February, 1949, p. 92.

70. Reported in PAV, March 20–27, 1949, pp. 166–67.

71. Combes, *Dix Ans d'histoire viticole,* p. 80.

72. PAV, September 4–11, 1949, p. 145.

73. *Agriculture pratique,* April, 1949, p. 164.

74. Combes, *Dix Ans d'histoire viticole,* p. 112.

75. *Ibid.,* p. 80.   76. Decree of July 21, 1949.

77. Decree of January 20, 1950.

78. The markets were those of Nimes, Montpellier, Béziers, Narbonne, or Perpignan. The price was for 10° red *vin ordinaire* or, as the decree phrased it, *vin de consommation courante.*

79. PAV, 1950, 1951.

80. Quoted *ibid.,* April 15–22, 1951, p. 215.

81. *Ibid.,* December 30, 1951, p. 377.

82. Ministerial order of February 21, 1951.

83. ANDEB, 1950, p. 8837.

84. Quoted in PAV, December 30, 1951, p. 377.

85. For a more detailed description of the alcohol situation, see pp. 206–13.

86. A decree of March 5, 1952, exempted those growers whose quota of alcohol came to less than 30 litres from delivering it. In 1951, 6,100,-000 hectolitres of wine were compulsorily distilled; in 1952, 5,900,000 hectolitres.

87. Ministerial order of September 8, 1951.

88. Decree of September 6, 1949. As an example of the confusion attendant on this matter it is interesting to note that a circular letter of the Contributions Indirectes dated September 2, 1947, reauthorized (or should it be said reminded) growers to make *piquettes.* This sent the C.G.V. into a rage and inspired it to launch a series of lawsuits against makers of *piquettes.* The Fédération des Caves Coöpératives also protested and enjoined its members not to make *piquettes.* The government backed down, and a second circular letter reduced the tolerance accorded in the first to, as the *Revue de viticulture* (November, 1947, p. 342) triumphantly put it, "practically nothing."

89. Combes, *Dix Ans d'histoire viticole,* p. 131.

90. Quoted in RV, April, 1947, p. 121.

91. Milhau tends to minimize illicit plantings although admitting that they undoubtedly augmented the limit of error in the official statistics of the vineyard area ("L'Avenir de la viticulture française," *Revue économique,* IV (1953), 720–21). Combes places more emphasis on them as a contributing factor in the viticultural crisis, but admits the impossibility of determining their true extent (*Dix Ans d'histoire viticole,* pp. 121–23).

92. Combes, *Dix Ans d'histoire viticole,* p. 133, points out that the

number of these agents assigned to the Service du Contrôle de la Viticulture had declined from 163 in 1938 to 129 in 1951, whereas their
number should have been doubled. The agents had no automobiles, and
in the interests of economy a number of them had been detached since
1947 to check tax returns. Combes has picturesquely described the fate
of the "survivors":
"The survivors inspire a sentiment half-way between admiration and
pity. Stripped of mimeograph machines, they beg the services of their
personal friends to save time in sending out their circulars to the tax
offices. Their desks are periodically installed in [former] dwelling
houses tottering under the weight of old records.
"The agents in the field are bewildered or else—in a milieu where indiscipline reigns—they hound the most available delinquent; or else
again they settle for a pittance such infractions whose enormity would
have fairly carried away their predecessors in a fit of anger.   .
"The enfeeblement of this administrative service, joined with the
lacunae in the legislation for the prevention and repression of fraud, is
the predominant cause of the indiscipline of viticultural production."
  93. Quoted in PAV, December 30, 1951, p. 379.
  94. Quoted *ibid.*, May 18–25, 1952, pp. 291–92.
  95. *Le Paysan du Midi*, May 5, 1952.
  96. ANDOC, 1952, pp. 954–58 (Annex 3261).
  97. The plantings were mostly small ones pursued in the interest of
wartime autarchy on the farm. Also, since they were not so likely to be
noticed as in viticultural regions, they offered an excellent opportunity
to take advantage of the black market. They undoubtedly contributed
to some extent to the decline in taxed consumption which was a feature
of the crisis of the 1950's. Thus Milhau (*Revue économique,* IV
[1953], 721), in a random sample, notes the following increases of the
vineyard area, given in hectares, in traditionally nonviticultural departments:

	1938	1951
Ardennes	14	22
Doubs	117	324
Vosges	500	596
Haute-Saône	445	945
Meurthe-et-Moselle	1173	1406

  During the same period, however, there was an increase of approximately 7,000 hectares in the department of Gironde, and in the Midi an
increase of nearly 1,000 hectares in the department of Gard. On the
other hand the concern of the Midi over plantings in nonviticultural regions is better understood when it is realized that the total Midi vineyard area had declined by about 13,000 hectares. Although the per-

centage of decrease in the latter region and the increase in area in the nonviticultural regions were relatively small, there was a great amount of controversy over the subject.

98. PAV, May 18–25, 1952, p. 284.

99. Quoted *ibid.*, p. 283.   100. Quoted *ibid.*

101. *Ibid.*, July 20–27, 1952, p. 30.

102. ANDEB, 1952, pp. 3569–70.

103. *Ibid.*, p. 5966.

104. Quoted in PAV, July 20–27, 1952, p. 32.

105. ANDEB, 1952, p. 3584.   106. *Ibid.*, pp. 3606–7.

107. This was obviously a sop for the Communists and would have involved sales to hospitals, the armed forces, and public-assistance agencies. The recommendation was not acted on, and it is doubtful that it had serious support.

108. By this and the preceding measure additional time would be gained to reduce the stock of wine, the amount of which influenced offering prices for the new harvest. Also, the amount of stocks in combination with the amount of the new harvest determined the percentages for blockage and distillation.

109. Bonvin, "S'Installer dans la crise," *Le Moniteur vinicole,* quoted in PAV, July 20–27, 1952, pp. 38–42. The author claims his estimate is not excessive. He would seem to be backed up by a survey of the Hérault vineyard which establishes a yield of 45 hectolitres the hectare as a break-even point. According to the survey, from 1930 to 1939, 30 percent of the total number of growers representing 10 percent of total production had an average yield of from 10 to 45 hectolitres the hectare or, as the survey puts it, a yield less or equal to the limit beyond which yields "do not have a calamitous character." Fifty percent of the growers representing 65 percent of total production had "acceptable" yields of 45 to 75 hectolitres the hectare. Twenty percent of the growers with yields of more than 75 hectolitres the hectare accounted for 25 percent of production under conditions which the survey describes as "excellent." "La Structure et les rendements du vignoble de l'Hérault," *Études et conjoncture, économie française*, pp. 16–17.

110. In France 2.2 percent of the winegrowers declaring their harvest in 1952 had a production of more than 200 hectolitres representing 37.2 percent of total production. Unfortunately there is no classification of this production according to yield per hectare. Percentages are based on figures supplied by the Ministry of Agriculture and published in PAV, February 15–22, 1953, p. 108.

111. *Ibid.*, November 30, 1952, p. 598. Loans were available to the winegrowers through the regular channels of agricultural credit and were based on the platform price of wine. In an uncertain market these would seem not to have been advantageous terms. Baron Le Roy, the

president of the F.A.V., called credit divorced from a guaranteed "social" price a "machine . . . for the creation of insolvent debtors." He particularly criticized the short term of the loans offered, which frequently caught the grower with not enough wine sold to meet payments. Baron Le Roy, "Il faut en finir," *La Journée vinicole,* July 8, 1954.

112. PAV, July 20–27, 1952, p. 41.

113. Decree of August 12, 1953.

114. Ministerial order of September 2, 1953.

115. Decree of September 18, 1953.

116. ANDOC, 1953, p. 980 (Annex 6399).

117. *Ibid.*   118. *Ibid.*

119. Reported in PAV, July 19–26, 1953, pp. 29–30.

120. ANDOC, 1953, p. 980 (Annex 6399).

121. PAV, July 19–26, 1953, p. 28.

122. Decree of March 20, 1953.

123. The *syndicats* were the local "cells" of the C.G.V. and the other confederations. They enjoyed a good deal of autonomy, however, and in the Midi a number of them supported the Comité de Salut Viticole.

124. Reported in *Le Figaro* (Paris), July 30, 1953.

125. Reported in *Le Figaro* (Paris), August 1, 1953. In the July 30 issue this newspaper commented on the lack of unity among the viticultural associations as to what immediate steps they wanted the government to take.

126. Decree of August 9, 1953. The same decree reestablished the *caisse annexe de la viticulture.* The latter was to be credited with the profits from the sale of quota wine alcohols. This may well have been a reason for reducing the purchase price of the latter. For a further discussion of this decree, see p. 211.

127. The right to increase the percentage, if conditions warranted it, for productions of more than 300 hectolitres was provided for. This right was exercised every succeeding year until 1957, and in 1955 a sliding scale was also introduced for blockage (decree of May 20). As these figures for 1956 show, the scales are much less complicated than the prewar ones. *Blockage:* 40 percent for a total production of less than 300 hectolitres; 50 percent for a total production of 300–1,000 hectolitres; and 60 percent for a total production of over 1,000 hectolitres. *Compulsory distilling:* 15 percent of blocked wines for part of harvest under 300 hectolitres; 30 percent of blocked wines for part of harvest between 300–1,000 hectolitres; 48 percent of blocked wines for part of harvest between 1,000–3,000 hectolitres; 60 percent of blocked wines for part of harvest between 3,000–5,000 hectolitres; 80 percent of blocked wines for part of harvest above 5,000 hectolitres.

128. Taxes on yields had remained at their prewar figures. The increases brought them in line with revaluations of the currency.

129. It will be remembered that *alcool vinique* was distilled from the residues left after pressing. Its distillation, therefore, did not cut down the quantity of wine legally produced. The purpose of the measure was to stamp out the making of "second" wines or *piquettes*. The measure, however, was criticized, coming as it did when the government was reducing the price and the amount of quota alcohols. A serious critic like Pierre Fromont predicted that while eliminating one abuse, it risked creating another—a significant rise in the production of alcohol. Fromont, "La Production agricole," *Revue d'économie politique*, LXV (1955), 649.

The winegrowers, especially the small ones, have found the distilling burdensome and expensive. Before both arguments the government appears to be backing down. A decree of September 14, 1954, has reduced the 12 percent figure to 10 percent, and to 8 percent for producers of less than 100 hectolitres. A decree of February 2, 1955, has exempted producers of less than 75 hectolitres and given the growers the option of destroying their residues.

130. PAV, March 1–8, 1953, p. 117.

131. *Ibid.,* November 1–8, 1953, p. 253.

132. Baron Le Roy was particularly critical of the return to definitive blockage. "The blocked quantities not destroyed weigh on the market as though they were present." Baron Le Roy, "Il faut en finir" (second installment), *La Journée vinicole,* July 7, 1954.

133. The government as much as admitted this in the *exposé des motifs* preceding the *Code.* JO, October 1, 1953.

134. These were the hybrids declared "undesirable" by the law of December 24, 1934, and the planting of which was forbidden. It should be pointed out that present legislation does not forbid the planting of all hybrids. Some of them give good wine.

135. Like previous legislation, the *Code* (with the exception of requisitions of *alcool vinique*) exempted *vins d'appellations d'origine contrôlées* from all restrictions and penalties. Since the right to make new plantings for the producing of these wines has always been implicit, its mention in the new *Code* must be considered in the nature of an encouragement. There has been a noticeable increase in production of *vins d'appellations* in recent years, but at most they do not account for more than 15 percent of total production, and in some years considerably less.

136. Of the ten members of the committee appointed in 1954, five were winegrowers, one was a winegrower and vine nurseryman, two were merchants and shippers, one was president of the *Chambre d'Agriculture de la Gironde,* and one was vice-president of the Union Nationale des Associations Familiales. The president of the committee was a member of the National Economic Council.

137. Quoted in PAV, November 1–8, 1953, p. 251.

138. Commissariat général du plan de modernisation et d'équipment, *Premier rapport de la Commission de modernisation de la production végétale,* p. 14.

139. ARCE, 1947, pp. 36–37.

140. Combes, *Dix Ans d'histoire viticole,* p. 120.

141. *Ibid.*

10. LATER DEVELOPMENTS AND THE FUTURE OF WINEGROWING
IN THE FRENCH ECONOMY

1. In a decree of October 19, 1953, the government established a minimum price of 290 francs the degree-hectolitre for Midi wines of the 1953 harvest. Since this sum had been the platform price of the year before, it was criticized as creating a bad psychological effect following the optimism inspired by the new *Code.* Worse, the decree was accused of driving prices down to the minimum level. The government has abandoned the minimum price, but there continues to be much agitation for a government-guaranteed "social" price. See PAV, November 15–22, 1953, p. 302. Baron Le Roy, "Il faut en finir" (fourth and last installment), *La Journée vinicole,* July 12, 1954.

2. *Le Monde* (Paris), October 11, 1957.

3. Institut national de la statistique et des études économiques, *Bulletin mensuel de statistique,* September, 1958, p. 26.

4. *Ibid.,* September, 1959, p. 27.

5. Browne and Buart, "Le Problème du vin," *La Documentation française—Problèmes économiques,* June 2, 1959, p. 9.

6. Some of the reasons given are (1) large imports due to the short harvest of 1957 which in the main came late on the market, just before the harvest of 1958; (2) a decline in wine consumption due to the heavy cider harvest of 1958 and new and relatively heavy taxes on wine; (3) the anti-alcohol campaign; (4) a decline in the purchasing power of many workers; (5) a decline in exports. Browne and Buart, "Le Problème du vin," *La Documentation française—Problèmes économiques,* June 2, 1959, pp. 9–11.

7. Quoted in Fromont, "La Production agricole," *Revue d'économie politique,* LXVII (1957), 623.

8. "Institut des Vins de Consommation Courante, Conseil Interprofessionel, séance 8 mars 1957—Exposé de M. Roland Maspetiol," *Revue de l'économie méridionale,* V (1957), 25.

9. Quoted in Fromont, "La Production agricole," *Revue d'économie politique,* LXVII (1957), 623.

10. *Ibid.*

11. Decrees of July 15, 1957; July 31, 1958; July 31, 1959.

12. See especially Fromont, "Les Problèmes de l'agriculture," *Revue d'économie politique,* LXVIII (1958), 194–95. On competition from Italian wines, see New York *Times,* March 6, 1959.

13. Ministère de la France d'outre-mer, *Annuaire statistique de l'Union Française outre-mer,* 1954, 1955.

14. The Convention of Saint-Germain-en-Laye, September 10, 1919, by which France bound herself not to permit the sale of alcoholic beverages containing more than 20 percent pure alcohol to the natives in all territories under her control except North Africa.

The following two tables give the dimensions of the increase in African wine imports and native consumption, and suggest some of the incidences of both wine and alcohol imports.

	French West Africa		Cameroons	
	1938	*1950*	*1938*	*1950*
Wine and wine *apéritif* imports (metric tons)	11,367	28,649	1,392	10,437
Native consumption of wine and wine *apéritifs* (metric tons)	6,867	18,369	1,312	8,277

Index of Increase, 1950, of Imports of Certain Goods and Foodstuffs
(*Base: 1938 = 100*)

	Wine	*Beverage Alcohols*	*Flour or Meal*	*Sugar*	*Cotton Goods*
French West Africa	257	3,632	339	175	130
Cameroons	2,654	1,688	1,450	382	274

Source: ARCE, 1952, pp. 99–101.

15. Browne and Buart, "Le Problème du vin," *La Documentation française-Problèmes économiques,* June 2, 1959, p. 9.

16. CDOC, 1930, p. 1355 (Annex 3765).

17. "From First to Second Monnet Plan," *The Economist,* November 21, 1953, p. 592.

18. *Ibid.,* p. 592.

19. Houiller, "Les Plans de modernisation de l'agriculture, 1946–1952," *Revue économique,* IV (1953), 662. This deficit breaks down to 231 billion francs for foreign countries and 244 billion francs for France overseas. The author concludes that the Monnet plan slogan, "*La France exportatrice agricole,*" is not even in process of realization.

20. Quoted in Maspetiol, "L'Intervention de l'État dans l'économie nationale," *Problèmes actuels de l'agriculture: Collection droit social, Fascicule XXVI,* p. 13.

21. Dumont is professor of comparative agriculture at the Institut Agronomique, and is also a professor at the Institut d'Etudes Politiques

de l'Université de Paris. His important works include *Le Problème agricole français* (1946); *Les Leçons de l'agriculture américaine* (1949); *Économie agricole dans le monde* (1954); and *Voyages en France d'un agronome* (2nd ed., 1956). He has been described sarcastically by the defenders of the *status quo* in agriculture as an "apostle of great mechanized farms" who would "Americanize" French agriculture and make the Midi into a second California. At the time of the presentation of his *Leçons de l'agriculture américaine* to the Academy of Agriculture, he was chided as being too severe on French agriculture. But in his masterful *Voyages,* he appears as a most sympathetic reformer.

22. Dumont, *Voyages,* pp. 385, 484. Dumont believes France could be an exporter of milk if pasturage and the growing of fodder could be expanded. Fodder is, of course, his first step in the proposed increase of milk and meat production. He is particularly distressed by the numerous survivals of regional autarchy which exist in France, such as the growing of wheat on Alpine pasture lands.

23. Both Dumont and Jules Milhau have suggested that any irrigation scheme for the Midi should include the pulling up of vines as a prerequisite to enjoying its benefits.

With the damming of the Rhône an irrigation canal is under construction that will run from Arles across the departments of Gard and Hérault and pour its overflow into the Aude River. The following predictions for the region covered have been made:

"Cereals, alfalfa, market gardening and fruitgrowing will prosper there, which, in combination with grazing and stock rearing, will with much less expense permit yields per hectare comparable in value to a yield of 130 hectolitres of wine whereas the present average is 60 to 100 hectolitres the hectare. And it will be a question of products for the larger part of which there is no risk of overproduction and certain of which even have to be imported." La Reconversion agricole de la région Bas-Rhône—Languedoc," *La Documentation française, Cahiers français d'information,* October 15, 1955, pp. 10–11.

24. Dumont, *Le Problème agricole,* pp. 102–03.

25. Dumont, *Voyages,* pp. 383–84.

26. Dumont, *Le Problème agricole,* p. 102.

27. Dumont, *Voyages,* pp. 383–83.

28. *Ibid.,* p. 376.

29. For Dumont's views on the problem of the inefficient and too-small farm, see his "Observations monographiques sur quelques fermes et communes de France," *Annales de l'Institut National Agronomique,* Tome XXXVI (1949), 6–131.

30. Dumont, *Le Problème agricole,* p. 105.

31. Dumont, *Voyages,* pp. 376, 386.   In this connection it is interesting to note that in France the price of grape juice is often higher than that of wine.

32. Laws of December 18, 1948, and May 24, 1951.

33. Law of July 20, 1940; of August 23, 1940; of September 24, 1941; of August 28, 1943; of October 4, 1943.

34. Laws of January 6, 1951, and May 24, 1951.

35. L. Dérobert, *L'Économie de l'alcoolisme,* "Monographie de l'Institut National d'Hygiène, No. 2" (Paris, Ministère de la Santé Publique, 1943).

36. Sully Ledermann, *Alcool, alcoolisme, alcoolisation,* Institut National d'Études Démographiques, Travaux et documents, Cahier n° 29 (Paris, Presse Universitaires de France, 1956).

37. Malignac, in collaboration with another member of the Sauvy team, has in the meantime written a very readable little book covering most aspects of the alcohol problem.   Georges Malignac and Robert Colin, *L'Alcoolisme* (Paris, Presses Universitaire de France, 1954).

38. J.-S. Brunaud, "Rapport sur le coût annuel et la prévention de l'alcoolisme," Comité central d'enquête sur le coût et le rendement des services publics (no date, mimeographed).

39. Decree of November 13, 1954, complemented by decree of May 22, 1955.

40. Appropriately, one of the first subsidies was to the long-established (and neglected) Comité Nationale de Défense contre l'Alcoolisme.

41. Rollet, "Le Haut Comité d'information et d'étude sur l'alcoolisme," *Le Documentation française—Cahiers français d'information,* December 15, 1955, p. 6.

42. *Ibid.*

43. Decree of November 13, 1954.

44. Decree of December 22, 1954.

45. Decree of November 13, 1954.

46. Decree of November 13, 1954.   There is no doubt Mendès-France would have liked to repeal the *privilège* of the *bouilleurs* as the Vichy government did, but this would have been one of the surest ways of alienating peasant support for his government.   Also, previous suspensions of the *privilège* have been difficult to enforce.   His decree, by outlawing movable stills and by other regulations, presumably makes supervision of the production of the *bouilleur* easier.   A large part of this production has been (and probably still is) in excess of the permitted amounts, especially in the Midi and the North.

47. Decree of October 1, 1954.

48. Decree of November 13, 1954.

49. Ledermann, *Alcool,* pp. 59, 62.

50. Quoted in Malignac and Colin, *L'Alcoolisme,* p. 19. The physiological and pathological effects of alcohol do, of course, vary with the individual. The Institut points out that its estimate of 100 c.c. is an attempt to determine a consumption norm in an empirical manner through a cross-sampling of subjects in good health. Actually various studies are in agreement that a man of average weight can completely oxidize about 250 c.c. of pure alcohol in his system over twenty-four hours. Such absorption, however, does not preclude immediate or long-range toxic effects. The problem is summarized by Malignac (*L'Alcoolisme,* pp. 18–19) as follows:

"The preceding observations on the course of alcohol in the system cannot suffice to determine the maximum physiological dosage, that is to say the quantity that an individual can absorb without any damage to his health. . . . Also the upper limits of consumption estimated according to the quantity of alcohol susceptible of being oxidized in the system do not offer a single guaranty from the pathological point of view. Physiological experiments in the laboratory are of hardly any help in revealing the whole problem of alcoholism. The difference between the domains of physiology and pathology has been distinctly underlined by M. Macabies. Experimenting with two subjects, one little accustomed to drink, the other regularly drinking one half to three quarters of a liter of wine per day, M. Macabies notes that a dose of one third of a liter of wine [3 c.c. of pure alcohol] always involved for the two subjects light [toxic effects]. . . .

"The toxic effect of wine is thus felt with a relatively feeble dose of one third of a liter and this with the subject accustomed to drink, even though M. Macabies has also demonstrated that physiologically the whole quantity ingested was oxidized by the system. . . ."

The report of the Institut National d'Hygiène by Doctors Laroche and Trésmolières can be found in the June 30, 1953, issue of the *Bulletin de l'Académie de Médecine.* For another discussion of the same problem see Howard W. Haggard and E. M. Jellinek, *Alcohol Explored* (New York, Doubleday Doran, 1943), pp. 77–108. Jellinek is a member of the Yale Alcohol Studies group.

51. Ledermann, "L'Alcoolisation excessive et la mortalité des français," *Concours médical,* April 18, 1952. Quoted in Malignac and Colin, *L'Alcoolisme,* p. 52.

52. Dérobert, *L'Économie de l'alcoolisme,* p. 168.

53. One litre equals 1.06 quarts.

54. Because of differences in the classification of diseases and formulation of statistics in the various countries, Ledermann (*Alcool,* p. 119) admits the difficulty of making international comparisons. Thus (p. 149) he suggests that the low English death rate from chronic or acute

alcoholism shown in Table 36 may be due to a lack of exact correspondence between what is understood by that classification in England and other countries.

The estimation of the percentage of deaths from alcoholic cirrhosis in relation to all forms of cirrhosis presents particular problems, since the former cannot be diagnosed unless there is a history of alcohol addiction. Jellinek has stated that alcoholic cirrhosis is "the most misunderstood issue in alcoholic research," and cites a dozen studies which place the percentage of deaths from the latter disease in relation to deaths from all forms of cirrhosis all the way from 86 percent to 27.5 percent. See E. M. Jellinek (ed.), *Alcohol Addiction and Chronic Alcoholism* (New Haven, Yale University Press, 1942), pp. 271–309. Ledermann's estimate of 84 percent for France is based on a statistical correlation of deaths from chronic or acute alcoholism and all forms of cirrhosis.

The figures in Tables 36 and 37 are based on reports by the public health authorities in the different countries. Those in Table 38 are based on a report of the Sub-Committee on Alcoholism of the World Health Organization based in turn on a formula worked out by Jellinek where N (number ill from alcohol) equals D (deaths from cirrhosis) times p (percentage of deaths from alcoholic cirrhosis) times 144. For France, Ledermann has brought some corrections to D because of the important number of deaths "not specified or not clearly defined." For an explanation of the corrections see Ledermann, "La Répartition des décès de cause indéterminée," *Revue de l'Institut international de statistique,* 1956, pp. 70–80. For the World Health Organization's report see *Rapports sur les 1re and 2e sessions du Sous-comité de l'alcoolisme,* December 11–16, 1950, and October 15–20, 1951 (Geneva, Office Mondiale du Santé).

55. Quoted in Malignac and Colin, *L'Alcoolisme,* p. 65.

56. *Ibid.,* pp. 65–66.

57. *Le Monde* (Paris), July 4, 1959.

58. In this connection it is interesting to note that current legislation is in many respects short of what would be considered acceptable in some other Western nations. One example suffices. The new legislation limiting sales of alcoholic beverages to minors prohibits the free distribution of "lightly alcoholized beverages" to children under twelve and the sale of hard liquor to minors under seventeen. French children of any age are still free to drink wine.

59. In his preface to Malignac and Colin, *L'Alcoolisme.*

60. In this connection it is interesting to note that since 1943 the activities of the Comité National de Propagande en Faveur du Vin have been limited to developing the export possibilities for French wines.

61. Jules Romain, *A Frenchman Examines His Conscience* (London, Andre Deutsch, 1955), p. 61.

62. Decree of September 25, 1942.

63. Decree of August 16, 1950.

64. Figures in this section, unless otherwise indicated, are from Taix "Étude des problèmes posés par les excédents d'alcool," ARCE, 1953, pp. 507–33.

65. These were extraordinary sales occasioned by defense requirements during the Korean war. They were made at a considerable loss in order to meet alcohol prices on the international market.

66. Commissariat général du plan de modernisation et d'équipement, *Premier rapport de la Commission de modernisation des carburants*, p. 133.

67. *Libération paysanne*, July 14, 1949, p. 6. See also PAV, June 2–9, 1946, p. 387.

68. ARCE, 1949, pp. 441–51; 1953, pp. 467–72, 512–15.

69. *Ibid.*, 1953, p.515.

70. Alcohol mixed this way has "anti-knock" properties. The outlet represented by *carburant ternaire* is limited, however, by supplies of benzol. Also, because of the price of benzol the state has had to sell alcohol for the ternary mixture at one franc per litre less than alcohol used in a binary (alcohol and gasoline) mixture.

71. Decree of August 16, 1950.

72. Ledermann, *Alcool*, pp. 56–57.

73. The following figures, given in francs the hectolitre, show this trend:

	Price for Beet Alcohol Paid by the State	Price of Gasoline, before Taxes, upon Leaving the Refinery
1926	260	194
1938	365	66
1949	7,500	960

Source: ARCE, 1949, p. 444.

74. ARCE, 1953, pp. 518–20.

75. *Ibid.*, p. 519.

76. These advances had escaped control of parliament and public notice by being included under the rubric of advances for the current operations of the Treasury. In 1950 the Treasury noted that reimbursement of these advances was not "anticipated" and that they were only carried as a "reminder" (ARCE, 1953, p. 519).

In 1950 a law was passed to permit parliament to vote a ceiling each year on nonreimbursable Treasury advances. The measure was strongly resisted by the alcohol lobby because of the publicity it gave to the hitherto unsuspected "subsidies" from the government to the Régie des Alcools. Since then amounts of nonreimbursable advances to the Régie show the following decline: 1950, 25 billion francs; 1951, 11 billion;

1952, 12 billion; 1953, 9 billion; 1954, 4 billion; 1955, 4 billion (Ledermann, *Alcool,* p. 58).

77. ARCE, 1953, p. 521.

78. To obtain equivalent productions of milk and meat Sauvy hypothesizes the replacement of an area devoted to beets by an equal area planted in fodder crops.

79. Sauvy says this figure has been deliberately calculated on the conservative side.

80. ARCE, 1953, p. 521.

81. *Ibid.,* p. 526.   82. *Ibid.,* p. 527.   83. *Ibid.,* pp. 528–33.

84. Although the Economic Council had no love for the quota system, it criticized this result as "illogical."   ARCE, 1953, p. 517.

85. Decree of November 13, 1954.

86. Decree of September 30, 1954.

87. Speech at Annecy, September 26, 1954.   Quoted in Mendès-France, *Sept Mois et dix-sept jours,* p. 242.

88. On this point see Werth, *France, 1940–55,* pp. 717–19.   According to Werth this was also true of Mendès-France's measures designed to reduce the consumption of beverage alcohols.

89. Ledermann, *Alcool,* pp. 57–58.

90. *Ibid.,* p. 57.   91. ARCE, 1953, p. 531.

92. Ledermann, *Alcool,* p. 21.

93. *Le Monde* (Paris), March 14, 1959.

94. Houiller, "Les Plans de modernisation de l'agriculture, 1946–1952," *Revue économique,* IV (1953), 661.

95. Klatzmann, "La Modernisation de l'agriculture," *Revue économique,* IV (1953), 654.

96. Klatzmann, *ibid.,* p. 656, estimates the cost for the "complete transformation" of French agriculture—"modernization of techniques as well as living conditions"—at 15,000 billion francs, or the national income for one and one half years.   He points out that at the present rate of agricultural investment, the transformation would take approximately two centuries.   One is tempted, however, to apply the cost of alcoholism and the alcohol regime against this figure.

It should be pointed out that Klatzmann's figure represents gross investment and thus includes such annual charges as fertilizers, etc., but he concludes that "the effort realized [for agriculture], meritorious as it is, represents only a minute part of what should have been done."

97. Editorial in *Agriculture pratique,* July, 1953, p. 326. For similar critical editorials, see *ibid.,* January, 1957, p. 5; April, 1952, p. 193; September, 1952, p. 429; December, 1953, p. 549.

This last argument calls for some comment. Sauvy's demonstration and other estimates by the Economic Council of the cost of the alcohol regime [see pp. 109–11] suggest that the protection and subsidies given beet and winegrowing are in fact a "unilateral increase" in the real incomes of agriculture through redistribution of the earnings of industry and commerce.

98. See the agrarian program of the Communist party adopted at their annual congress held at Gennevilliers (Seine), August 2–6, 1950. In view of the program and the stand taken by the party in the debate on the viticultural crisis in 1952 (see pp. 178–79), it is interesting that Communist representation in the Assembly from the four chief Midi winegrowing departments increased from 4 deputies out of a total of 18 in 1951 to 8 out of the same total in 1956. Significantly the greatest gains, from one out of 6 deputies in 1951 to 4 out of 6 in 1956, were registered in Hérault.

99. Maspetiol, "L'Intervention de l'État dans l'économie nationale," *Problèmes actuels de l'agriculture: Collection droit social, Fascicule XXVI,* p. 12.

100. *Agriculture pratique,* December, 1952, p. 606.

101. Quoted in *Le Figaro* (Paris), July 10, 1953.

102. "Bilan de l'ensemble du deuxième plan de modernisation et d'équipment," *La Documentation française—Problèmes économiques,* February 17, 1959, pp. 6–14.

103. Actually the 1957 harvest (32,125,000 hectolitres) falls far short of the planned target of 45,000,000 hectolitres for 1957. Previous wine harvests from 1954 on were, of course, considerably above it. And although the harvest of 1958 (47,012,000 hectolitres) is not seriously above it, it looks as though the 1959 harvest might be. In its report the Commissariat Général du Plan has obliquely criticized the subsidized overproduction of wine.

104. "Extraits du rapport annuel sur l'éxecution du plan de modernisation et d'équipment (1958)—Deuxième partie—Documents statistiques," *La Documentation française—Notes et études documentaires,* special number, April 25, 1959, p. 4.

105. David, "L'Évolution du remembrement rural en France," *La Documentation française—Les Cahiers français, documents d'actualité,* July, 1956, p. 43. See also *Annuaire statistique,* 1958, p. xi.

106. Ledermann (*Alcool,* p. 47), estimates that there is one *bouilleur* for every 4.3 male electors. In 23 departments the ratio is one to two; in 24, one to three.

107. For details of intimidation and coercion of newspapers by alcohol interests, see Malignac and Colin, *L'Alcoolisme,* pp. 82–83.

108. Law of April 3, 1955.

109. Werth, *France, 1940–55,* p. 719.

110. These charges are difficult to substantiate exactly, but Werth attaches significance to the fact that the investigation of the Dides affair (leakage of military secrets during the Indo-Chinese War), which was

intended to discredit the Mendès-France government, was launched by a M. Legendre, a deputy from the Oise and a "pillar" of the alcohol lobby (Werth, *France, 1940–55,* p. 719).

Malignac describes the lobby as an agent in the fall of the Pinay and René Mayer governments in 1952 and 1953. Malignac and Colin, *L'Alcoolisme,* pp. 90–91.

111. Mendès-France, *Sept Mois et dix-sept jours,* p. 240.

11. SUMMARY AND CONCLUSIONS

1. Of course restrictions schemes, by reducing supply, valorize the price of the product concerned, but I am here using "valorization" in its narrower meaning associated with the stabilizing of prices through "regulation of the flow of available supplies to the market over some period of time." See Rowe, *Markets and Men, A Study of Artificial Control Schemes in Some Primary Industries,* pp. 219–20.

2. See p. 255, note 107.

3. Milhau, *Traité d'économie rurale,* II, 345.

4. It will be recalled that the voluntary uprooting of vines on a permanent basis with payment of indemnities was also provided for, but that results were insignificant for lack of an aggressive policy in the matter.

5. See p. 270, note 129.

6. See Golob, *Méline Tariff,* p. 245.

7. See *ibid.,* p. 247.

BIBLIOGRAPHY

OFFICIAL PUBLICATIONS

Annales de la Chambre des Députés: Débats parlementaires, 1881–1909.
Annales de la Chambre des Députés: Documents parlementaires, 1883–1909.
Annales du Sénat: Débats parlementaires, 1881–1909.
Annales du Sénat: Documents parlementaires, 1883–1909.
Annales du Sénat et de la Chambre des Députés, 1871–80.
Annales du Sénat et de la Chambre des Députés: Documents parlementaires, 1881–82.
Commissariat général du plan de modernisation et d'équipment. Premier rapport de la commission de modernisation des carburants. Paris, 1946.
———— Premier rapport de la commission de modernisation de la production végétale. Paris, 1946.
Conseil National Économique. La Politique agricole de la France. Paris, Imprimerie Nationale, 1935.
———— La Politique agricole destinée à reduire le déficit de la balance commerciale et à coordonner les productions métropolitaines et coloniales. Melun, Imprimerie Administrative, 1939.
Gouvernement général de l'Algérie; Direction générale des finances, Service de la statistique générale. Annuaire statistique de l'Algérie. Blida, 1947–55.
Institut national de la statistique et des études économiques, *Bulletin mensuel de statistique,* 1958–59.
Journal officiel de la République Française. Assemblée Nationale: Débats parlementaires, compte rendu in extenso, 1947–56.
———— Assemblée Nationale: Documents parlementaires. Annexes aux procès verbaux des séances; projets et propositions de loi; exposé des motifs et rapports, 1947–56.

Journal officiel de la République Française (*Continued*)
────── Avis et rapports du Conseil Économique, 1944–53.
────── Chambre des Députés: Débats parlementaires, compte rendu in extenso, 1910–39.
────── Chambre des Députés: Documents parlementaires. Annexes aux procès verbaux des séances; projets et propositions de loi; exposé des motifs et rapports, 1910–39.
────── Documents de l'Assemblée Nationale Constituante. Annexes aux procès verbaux des séances; projets et propositions de loi; exposé des motifs et rapports, 1946.
────── Lois et décrets; arrêtés, circulaires, avis, communications, informations et annonces, 1871–1956.
────── Sénat: Débats parlementaires, compte rendu in extenso, 1910–39.
────── Sénat: Documents parlementaires. Annexes aux procès verbaux des séances; projets et propositions de loi, exposé des motifs et rapports, 1910–39.
Ministère de la France d'outre-mer; Service des statistiques. Annuaire statistique de l'Union Française outre-mer. Paris, 1950–55.
Ministère de l'agriculture; Office de renseignements. *Bulletin.* Paris, 1888–92.
────── La Petite Proprieté rurale en France: enquêtes monographiques (1908–1909). Paris, 1909.
────── "La Production viticole et son évolution," *Bulletin technique d'information* (Special number, 1951).
────── Statistique agricole annuelle. Paris, 1909, 1939–55.
────── Statistique agricole: Résultats généraux de l'enquête de 1929. Paris, 1930.
Ministère des finances. *Bulletin de statistique et de législation comparée.* Monthly. Paris, 1883–1940.
Ministère des finances; Direction générale des contributions indirectes. Évaluation des propriétés non bâties. 2 vols. Paris, 1913.
Ministère des finances; Direction générale des douanes. *Statistique mensuelle du commerce extérieur de la France.* Paris, 1925–31.
────── Tableau décennal du commerce de la France avec ses colonies et les puissances étrangères, 1877 à 1886. Paris, 1888.
────── Tableau générale du commerce (name varies), Paris, 1882–1907, 1910–14.
Ministère du commerce [name varies]; Statistique générale de la France. Annuaire statistique, Paris, 1878–1957. [Note: Title sometimes appears as Annuaire Statistique de la France. After 1945 the Annuaire is published under the direction of the Institut National de la statistique et des études économiques.]
Ministère du travail et de la prévoyance sociale. *Bulletin de l'Office du Travail.* Monthly. Paris, 1903–7.

OTHER PUBLISHED WORKS

Abric, L. Le Privilège des bouilleurs de cru. Montpellier, Imprimerie Firmin, 1909.

Antéric, Jean. De la répression des fraudes en matière de vins. Lyons, Bose Frères, 1935.

Atger, Frederic. La Protection légale de la viticulture et la crise viticole. Montpellier, Imprimerie A. Dupuy, 1907.

Auffray, Jacques. Étude de la législation relative aux fraudes et falsifications des vins. Paris, Librairie Sirey, 1911.

Augé-Laribé, Michel. L'Agriculture pendant la guerre. Paris, Presses Universitaires de France, 1925.

——— L'Évolution de la France agricole. Paris, Presses Universitaires de France, 1912.

——— La Politique agricole de la France de 1880 à 1940. Paris, Presses Universitaires de France, 1950.

——— Le Problème agraire du socialisme: La Viticulture industrielle du Midi de la France. Vol. VII of La Bibliothèque socialiste internationale. Edited by Alfred Bonett. Paris, Giard & Brière, 1907.

Aumage, Roger. Le Régime économique de l'alcool. Paris, Les Éditions Domat-Montchrestien, 1936.

Baudrillart, Henri. Les Populations agricoles de la France. 3 vols. Paris, Guillaumin & Cie, 1893. Vol. III.

Bergé, Pierre. Le Marché des vins du Midi. Paris, Presses Universitaires de France, 1927.

Bergon, François. La Législation française de l'alcool. Montpellier, Imprimerie Firmin et Montane, 1922.

Bonnard, Paul. "La Crise de la viticulture," *Journal des économistes,* XVI (July, 1907), 44–52.

Bonvin, François. "S'Installer dans la crise," *Progrès agricole et viticole,* July 20–27, 1952, pp. 38–42.

Brault, Pierre. Le Problème du vin. Paris, Imprimerie Guy Bigeon, 1932.

Browne, R., and C. Buart. "Le Problème du vin," *La Documentation française—Problèmes économiques,* June 2, 1959, pp. 9–11.

Brunaud, J.-S. Rapport sur le coût annuel et la prévention de l'alcoolisme. Comité central d'enquête sur le coût et le rendement des services publics, no date, mimeographed.

Caupert, Maurice. Essai sur la C.G.V. Montpellier, L'Économiste Méridionale, 1921.

Cauwès, Paul. Cours d'économie politique. 3rd ed. 4 vols. Paris, Larose, 1893.

Caziot, Pierre. "La Chute de la valeur de la terre." *Revue des agriculteurs de France* (March, 1935), pp. 67–68.

——— La Valeur de la terre en France. Paris, Baillière et Fils, 1914.

Cellier, André. La Viticulture française et les projets d'office national du vin. Montpellier, Mari-Lavit, 1938.

Chauvin, André. Répression de la fraude en matière de vins. Paris, Bonvalot-Jouve, 1908.

Clapham, J. H. The Economic Development of France and Germany, 1815–1914. 4th ed. Cambridge, Eng., University Press, 1951.

Clough, Shepard Bancroft. France: A History of National Economics, 1789–1939. New York, Charles Scribner's Sons, 1939.

Combes, Daniel. Dix Ans d'histoire viticole—1940–1950. Montpellier, S.E.A.M., 1952.

Courtin, René. "La Viticulture devant les pouvoirs publiques," *Revue politique et parlementaire,* CXLVII (June 10, 1931), 454–78.

David, Charles. "L'Évolution du remembrement rural en France," *La Documentation française—Les Cahiers français, documents d'actualité,* July, 1956.

Défossé, Gaston. La Place du consommateur dans l'économie dirigée. Paris, Presses Universitaires de France, 1941.

Degrully, Paul. Essai historique et économique sur la production et le marché des vins en France. Paris, Giard & Briere, 1910.

Dérobert, L. L'Économie de l'alcoolisme. No. 2 in Monographie de l'Institut National d'Hygiène. Paris, Ministère de la Santé Publique, 1953.

De Romeuf, Louis. "La Crise viticole du Midi." *Revue politique et parlementaire,* LX (May, 1909), 289–321.

Descamps, Paul. "Les Populations viticoles, l'évolution du type du vigneron et la crise actuelle." *Annales sciences sociales,* XXII (1907), Fasc. 37.

Didelon, V. Etude économique et législative sur les bouilleurs de cru. Nancy, Imprimerie Nancéienne, 1907.

Douarche, Léon. La Question du vin à la Conférence monétaire et économique de Londres. Paris, Librairie Alcan, 1933.

—— Le Vin et la vigne dans l'économie nationale française. Paris, Les Cahiers de la Réorganisation Économique, 1943.

Dumont, René. "Observations monographiques sur quelques fermes et communes de France," *Annales de l'Institut National Agronomique,* XXXVI (1949), 6–131.

—— Le Problème agricole français, esquisse d'un plan d'orientation et d'équipement. Paris, Les Éditions Nouvélles, 1946.

—— Voyages en France d'un agronome. New ed., revised and augmented. Paris, Librairie de Médicis, 1956.

Eysoldt, Grete. Der Zollkreig zwischen Frankreich und der Schweiz (1 Januar 1893 bis 19 August 1895). Stuttgart, Cotta, 1913.

Ferrouillet, M. "Prix de revient de l'hectolitre de vin dans un domaine moyen de l'Hérault." Comptes rendus des séances de l'Académie d'Agriculture de France, VII (1922), 631–35.

Fisher, William Edward Garett. "Phylloxera," in *Encylopedia Britannica*. 11th ed. 1910. Vol. XXI.

Flanzy, Michel. "Raisins hybrides et politique viticole," *Bulletin mensuel: Société Centrale d'Agriculture de l'Aude* (May, 1951), pp. 142–43.

Fleury, Gaston. "La Lutte pour la vigne." *La nouvelle revue*, XLVII (July, 1907), 46–50.

"From First to Second Monnet Plans," *The Economist* (November 21, 1953), pp. 592–93.

Fromont, Pierre. "La Production agricole," *Revue d'économie politique*, LXV (July–October, 1957), 631–62.

――― "La Production agricole," *Revue d'économie politique*, LXVII (July-October, 1957), 600–635.

――― Les Problèmes de l'agriculture," *Revue d'économie politique*, LXVIII (Jan.–Feb., 1958), 170–97.

――― "Splendeurs et misères de la vigne et du vin dans la France moderne," in *Le vin de France dans l'histoire* (*Conférences et documents*), special number of *Bulletin de l'Institut National des Appellations d'Origine des Vins et Eaux-de-Vie* (1953), pp. 25–46.

Galtier-Boissière, Jean. "L'Affaire du vin," in *Les scandales de la IVe*, special number of *Crapouillot,* vol. II (no date), pp. 23–32.

Gaston-Pastre, J. L. "Le Problème du vin," *Revue des deux mondes* (November 15, 1935), pp. 358–75.

Gayat de Wecker, Geneviève. La Limitation des plantations de la vigne. Paris, Recueil Sirey, 1934.

Genieys, Pierre. La Crise viticole méridionale. Toulouse, Librairie Privat, 1905.

Gervais, Prosper. "L'Exportation des vins." Extrait de l'enquête sur la production française et la concurrence étrangère. Paris, Association Nationale d'Expansion Économique, 1918.

Gide, Charles. "La Crise du vin dans le Midi de la France," *Revue d'économie politique,* XXI (July, 1907), 481–512.

――― "La Crise du vin en France et les Associations de vinification," *Revue d'économie politique,* XV (March, 1901), 218–35.

――― "La Question des vins au point de vue des traités de commerce," *Revue d'économie politique,* VII (July, 1892), 817–28.

Girou, Jean. Vie des personnages célèbres de l'Aude. Montpellier, Causse, Graille & Castelnau, 1940.

Golob, Eugene. The Méline Tariff: French Agriculture and Nationalist Economic Policy. New York, Columbia University Press, 1944.

Gourssies, Jean. Le Sucrage des vins. Paris, Imprimerie Henri-Jouve, 1904.

Grinberg, M. Ph. "Le Régime des alcools et les branches organisées de l'économie agricole française," *Revue d'économie politique,* LII (March–April, 1938), 404–29.

Haight, Frank Arnold. A History of French Commercial Policies. New York, The Macmillan Company, 1941.

Hamelle, Paul. "La Crise viticole," *Annales des sciences politiques,* XXIII (1908), 625–61.

Herubel, Marcel. "L'Exportation des vins-suite." Extrait de l'enquête sur la production française et la concurrence étrangère. Paris, Association Nationale d'Expansion Économique, 1918.

Hot, Alfred. Le Vin en France. Montpellier, Éditions de La Journée Vinicole, 1940.

Houiller, François. "Les Plans de modernisation de l'agriculture, 1946–1952," *Revue économique,* IV (September, 1953), 659–72.

"Indice des cours du vin à la production," *Revue de l'économie méridionale,* V (January–March, 1957), 27.

"Institut des Vins de Consommation Courante, Conseil Interprofessionel, séance 8 Mars, 1957—Exposé de M. Roland Maspetiol," *Revue de l'économie méridionale,* V (January–March, 1957), 25.

Isnard, Hildebert. "Vigne et colonisation en Algérie 1880–1947." *Annales—économies, sociétés, civilisations,* II (July–September, 1947), 288–300.

Klatzmann, Joseph. "La Modernisation de l'agriculture." *Revue économique,* IV (September, 1953), 643–88.

Lafforgue, Germain. Le Vignoble girondin. Paris, Louis Larmat, 1947.

Le Blond, Maurice. La Crise du Midi. Paris, Bibliothèque Charpentier, 1907.

Ledermann, Sully. Alcool, alcoolisme, alcoolisation (Cahier 29 of Institut National d'Études Démographiques, Travaux et documents). Paris, Presses Universitaires de France, 1956.

Le Roy, Baron. "Il faut en finir," *La Journée vinciole,* July 6, 7, 8, 11, 1954.

Leroy-Beaulieu, Paul. "La Situation du Midi et la crise viticole," *L'Économiste française,* May 25, 1907, pp. 761–63.

Levasseur, Émile. Histoire du commerce de la France. 2 vols. Paris, A. Rousseau, 1912.

Liesse, André. "Le 'Statut' du vin," *L'Économiste française,* June 27, 1931, pp. 801–3.

McConnell, D. W. "Liquor Traffic," in *Encyclopaedia of the Social Sciences.* 1933. Vol. IX.

Malignac, Georges, and Robert Colin. L'Alcoolisme. Paris, Presses Universitaires de France, 1954.

Marbeau, Pierre. Le Régime des alcools d'industrie et des alcools de bouche en France. Paris, Librairie Louis Arnette, 1932.

March, Lucien. Mouvement des prix et des salaires pendant la guerre. Paris, Presses Universitaires de France, 1925.

Marres, Paul. La Vigne et le vin en France. Paris, Librairie Armand Colin, 1950.

Marsais, Paul. "Comment se résoudra la crise viticole," *Revue des agriculteurs de France* (May, 1930), pp. 148–49.

Maspetiol, M. R. "L'Intervention de l'État dans l'économie nationale." Problèmes actuelles de l'agriculture. Fasc. XXVI, Collection droit social. Paris, Librairie Sociale et Économique.

Mendès-France, Pierre. Sept Mois et dix-sept jours. Paris, René Juillard, 1955.

Meyrueis, Roger. De la défense des intérêts de la viticulture méridionale par les syndicats viticoles. Paris, Rousseau & Cie, 1920.

Milhau, Jules. "L'Avenir de la viticulture française," *Revue économique,* IV (September, 1953), 700–738.

——— "Sur l'économétrie et ses applications," *Revue d'économie politique,* LII (January–February, 1938), 100–130.

——— Étude économetrique du prix du vin en France. Montpellier, Causse, Graille et Castelnau, 1935.

——— Traité d'économie rurale. 2 vols. Paris, Presses Universitaires de France, 1954.

Monvoisin, A. Alcool et distillerie. Paris, Octave Doin, 1910.

Morel, Léopold. L'Économie dirigée en viticulture. Paris, Librairie Sociale et Économique, 1939.

Muglioni, François. Les Accords commerciaux sur les vins. Paris, Picart, 1935.

Mugnier, Marcel. Essai sur l'exportation des vins fins de Bourgogne. Dijon, Imprimerie Barbier, 1909.

Nadel, August. "La Crise viticole dans le Midi de la France," *Revue générale,* LXXVI (July, 1907), 160–74.

Nogaro, B., and Lucien Weil. La Main-d'oeuvre étrangère et coloniale pendant la guerre. Paris, Presses Universitaires de France, 1926.

Numile, L.-G. "L'Alcool et l'essence français carburant national," *L'Économiste français* (August 31, 1935), pp. 260–61.

Olphe-Galliard, G. Histoire économique et financière de la guerre. Paris, Marcel Rivière, 1923.

Perrier, Louis. "La Crise viticole," *Revue politique et parlementaire,* LVIII (July, 1907), 53–72.

Peschaud, Marcel. Politique et fonctionnement des transports par chemin de fer pendant la guerre. Paris, Presses Universitaires de France, 1926.

Pinot, Pierre. Le Contrôle du ravitaillement de la population civile. Paris, Presses Universitaires de France, 1925.

Pirou, Gaëtan. La Valeur et les prix. Vol. VII of Traité d'économie politique. Paris, Recueil Sirey, 1951.

Planchon, J. E., and J. Lichtenstein. "De l'identité spécifique du phylloxera des feuilles et du phylloxera des racines de la vigne." *Comptes rendus des séances de l'Académie des Sciences,* LXXI (1870), 298–301.

Porcher, Pierre. "Le Marché des vins." *Problèmes actuelles de l'agriculture.* Fasc. XXVI, Collection droit social. Paris: Librairie Sociale et Économique, 1945.

Ray, Georges. Les Vins de France. Paris, Presses Universitaires de France, 1946.

Raynal, Paul. Le Vignoble français et l'Afrique du Nord. Paris, Emil Larose, 1917.

"Les Récoltes viticoles de 1939 à 1944." *Revue de viticulture* (November, 1945), pp. 6–8.

"La Reconversion agricole de la région Bas-Rhône- Languedoc," *La Documentation française—Cahiers français d'information* (October 15, 1955), pp. 10–11.

Ricard, J.-H. "La Vie paysanne d'août 1914 à octobre 1915," *Revue politique et parlementaire,* LXXV (December, 1915), 358–73.

Roger, Louis. "La Viticulture et ses destinées," *Revue des agriculteurs de France* (February, 1935), pp. 35–36.

Rollet, Jean. "Le Haut Comité d'information et d'étude sur l'alcoolisme," *La Documentation française—Cahiers français d'information* (December 15, 1955).

Rooy, Marcel. Le Carburant national. Paris, Presses Universitaires de France, 1925.

Rowe, J. W. F. Markets and Men: A Study of Artificial Control Schemes in Some Primary Industries. New York, The Macmillan Company, 1936.

Sabadie, Jean. "La Dernière Réunion du Comité Supérieur des Alcools," *Bulletin mensuel: Société Centrale de l'Agriculture de l'Aude* (January, 1938), pp. 43–58.

———— Le Nouveau Statut de la viticulture. Toulouse, Douladoure, 1932.

Sagnier, Henri. Le Crédit agricole en France. Paris, Librairie Agricole de la Maison Rustique, 1911.

Salavert, Jan. Le Commerce des vins de Bordeaux. Bordeaux, Imprimerie de l'Université, 1912.

Sée, Henri. Histoire économique de la France. 2 vols. Paris, Librairie Armand Colin, 1951. Vol. II.

Semaine Nationale du Vin. Compte rendu des travaux. Paris, Association Nationale d'Expansion Économique, 1922.

Siegfried, André. France: A Study in Nationality. New Haven, Yale University Press, 1930.

Sourdillat, J.-M. Géographie agricole de la France. Paris, Presses Universitaires de France, 1950.

"La Structure et les rendements du vignoble de l'Hérault," *Études et conjoncture, économie française.* Tirage à part extrait du n° 2 de Mars–Avril 1951, complété par une série de tableaux statistiques. Paris, Presses Universitaires de France, 1951.

Susplugas, Paul. La Répression des fraudes dans la production et le commerce des vins. Toulouse, Rivière, 1920.

Taïx, Gabriel. "Étude des problèmes posés par les excédents d'alcool," *Journal officiel: Avis et rapports du Conseil Économique* (1953), pp. 507–33.

Viala, Pierre. Les Maladies de la vigne. Montpellier, C. Coulet, 1893.

Volck, A. Le Problème viticole franco-algérien. Paris, Les Éditions Domat-Montchrestien, 1934.

Wagner, Philip M. A Wine-Grower's Guide. New York, Alfred A. Knopf, 1945.

Weill, Robert G. Le Monopole de l'alcool industriel. Paris, Recueil Sirey, 1932.

Werth, Alexander. France, 1940–55. New York, Henry Holt and Co., 1956.

NEWSPAPERS AND PERIODICALS

Annales des douanes, Paris, 1930–35.

Annuaire de législation française, edited by the Société de Législation Comparée, Paris, 1930–35.

Bulletin de la Chambre Syndicale des Distillateurs en gros de Paris et de la région parisienne, Paris, 1933–35.

Bulletin de la Société des Agriculteurs de France, Paris, 1922–25.

Bulletin d'information économique. Banque Nationale pour le Commerce et l'Industrie, Paris, 1936.

Bulletin international du vin, Rome, 1931.

Le Bulletin législatif Dalloz, Paris, 1930–39, 1945–55.

Bulletin mensuel: Société Centrale de l'Agriculture de l'Aude, Carcassonne, 1938.

Dalloz, *Recueil hebdomadaire de jurisprudence,* Paris, 1932 (in combination with the *Recueil périodique et critique* known as *Recueil Dalloz*).

Dalloz, *Recueil périodique et critique de jurisprudence, législation et doctrine,* Paris, 1920–35, 1945–53.

La Documentation française—Cahiers français d'information, Paris, 1955.

La Documentation française—Notes et études documentaires, Paris, 1959.

La Documentation française—Problèmes économiques, Paris, 1959.

The Economist, London, 1953.

L'Économiste français, Paris, 1878–79, 1900–1907, 1930–45.

Le Figaro, Paris, 1907, 1953.

Journal d'agriculture pratique, Paris, 1867, 1870–1935. Name changes to *Agriculture pratique,* 1947–53.

Journal des débats, Paris, 1907.

Journal des économistes, Paris, 1903, 1907.
La Journée vinicole, Montpellier, 1954.
Libération paysanne, Paris, 1949.
Le Matin, Paris, 1930.
Le Monde, Paris, 1957.
Le Paysan du Midi, Montpellier, 1952.
Le Petit Méridionale, Montpellier, 1926.
Progrès agricole et viticole, Montpellier, 1921–53.
Revue des agriculteurs de France, Paris, 1930–36.
Revue de viticulture, Paris, 1914–47.
Le Temps, Paris, 1903, 1915.
Le Travail national, Paris, 1901.
Viticulture-Arboriculture, Paris, 1949.

INDEX

Academy of Agriculture, 83, 192
Academy of Sciences, 6
Agriculture, place of winegrowing in French, 196–99, 210–11, 212, 214, 221; *see also specific products,* e.g., Beets; *see also* Viticulture
Agriculture, Ministry of: phylloxera epidemic and, 2–3, 4, 6, 9; crisis of 1900–1907 and, 25, 26, 44, 50; C.G.V. and, 46; crisis between the world wars and, 72, 73; investigation of hybrids, 78–79; parliamentary committee on wine industry, 93–98; Service for Repression of Fraud, 96, 113; obligatory uprootings and, 119; *carburants* and, 126, 127; Vichy regime, 159; "policy of quality," 174, 176–77, 179
Agriculture pratique (periodical), 214
Aimargues (Gard department), 22
Albert, Marcellin, 23, 27, 231(n. 43)
Alcohol: distilled from wine (1865–75), 33–34, 93; "war of the beet and the grape," 35–36, 115, 122, 128, 131, 132, 135, 150; production (1870–1907), 35 (*tab.*), 218; industrial, 68, 109, 123–25, 142–45, 239(n. 72); acceptable content in wine, 95, 263(n. 22); state monopoly of, 108–9, 114, 115, 121, 123–56, 212; *alcools de marc,* 115, 149, 161, 185, 254(n. 88); division of market, 123–25, 126–28, 133–40, 147; molasses, 132, 134–35; grain, 132–34, 138; sale for *vinage* and *mutage,* 138(*tab.*), 140, 142, 143, 146, 147; figs, carobs, and dates, 133; synthetic, 140; *vi-*

nique, 161, 185, 220, 270(n. 129); annual consumption per adult, 202(*tab.*); alcohol lobby, 215–16; rectification of, 257(n. 49); *see also* Alcoholism; Beets; *Carburant national;* Distillation; Régie Commerciale des Alcools (Service des Alcools); *Privilège des bouilleurs de cru*
Alcoholism: campaigns against, x, 67–69, 70, 157, 200–202, 215; rate of death from, in different countries (1950–54), 203(*tab.*); estimated rate of related diseases, in different countries, 204(*tab.*)
Algeria, viii, x, 15–16, 79–83; production in 1900, 17, 50; production and exports to France (1900–1907), 31 (*tab.*); production in 1922, 71; production in 1934, 73, 112; increasing importation from, 75, 99, 100, 218; yearly average of production (1900–1907, 1920–27, 1928–35), 80; C.G.V. and, 80, 81, 82, 99, 178, 244(n. 59); production in 1929, 101–2; *Statut du Vin* and, 106–7; production in 1931, 110; harvest of 1935, 115; harvest of 1938, 117; fruit alcohol distillation in, 133; "reorganization of offices" and, 151; production (1946–49), 163(*tab.*), 169; National Economic Council on, 189; production in 1954, 190; uprooting of vines in, 193; anti-alcohol campaign in, 200–201; *Code du Vin* and, 221; trade advantages of, 228(nn. 49–50), 243(n. 58)